THE MYSTERY OF WOMANHOOD

THE MYSTERY OF WOMANHOOD

Debra Evans

CROSSWAY BOOKS • WESTCHESTER, ILLINOIS
A DIVISION OF GOOD NEWS PUBLISHERS

The Mystery of Womanhood. Copyright © 1987 by Debra Evans.
Published by Crossway Books, a division of Good News Publishers, Westchester,
Illinois 60153.

Cover art: Mary Cassatt, *Little Ann Sucking Her Finger, Embraced by Her Mother,*
1897. Used by permission of the Cabinet Des Dessins, Orsay, and the Réunion des
Musées Nationaux, Paris.

Book and cover design by K. L. Mulder

First printing, 1987

Printed in the United States of America

Library of Congress Catalog Card Number 86-72262

ISBN 0-89107-426-0

The publisher would like to express appreciation for permission to use charts
from the following:

John J. Burt and Linda B. Meeks, *Education for Sexuality: Concepts and Programs
for Teaching* (New York: CBS College Publishing, 1985).

Cancer-related Checkups, brochure, American Cancer Society.

*NOTE: While the information contained in this volume is believed to be accurate
and reliable, the reader is advised that all health care decisions should be
made with the guidance and advice of a personal physician.*

To Dave,
who has become my best friend,
wise counselor, and lover for a lifetime.

Grow old with me!
The best is yet to be.
The last of life,
For which the first
was made.
Our times are in
His hand.
Robert Browning

Table of Contents

List of Figures

Acknowledgments

The only gift is a portion of thyself.
Ralph Waldo Emerson, *Gifts*

While writing this book, I often thought about the women in my life who have influenced the way I view myself and the world around me. My paternal grandmother, Marie MacMahon Munger, taught me the joy of cooking through her willingness to let me help her make pies when I was barely out of toddlerhood. My mom's mother, Helen Monroe Allen, shared her joy of new life, encouraging me by her example to have two of my children at home. Since Grandma had done the same thing and it had worked, I knew that it could work for me too.

Laura Marr patiently guided me through six years of piano lessons, during which I found the joy of music. The joy of writing arrived when I was a pupil in Nova Runyon's Honors English class in ninth grade. I learned the joy of dance through Rose Marie Floyd, an inspired ballet teacher whose love of creative movement was infectious. The joy of teaching was introduced to me through Peg Beals, a childbirth educator who knew how to combine gentleness with assertiveness and consumerism with compassion. Cheryl Bauman and Rea Siffring encouraged me by their example to nurse my children as they had nursed theirs, and it is to them that I give thanks for acquainting me with the joy of breast-feeding. Phyllis Gieleghem enabled me to embrace the joy of giving birth and supporting laboring women on several momentous occasions. Through Tryn Clark's open acceptance and unwavering friendship, I was shown the joy of *agapé* love.

Diane Vincent, Susan Beckwith, Theresa Dalton, Barb O'Malley, Linda Drinkard, Chris Easterle, Karen Dandurand, and Chris Graham surrounded me with the joy of sisterly affection during my earliest years as a Christian. My "real" sisters, Kerry and Nancy, have always been able to make me laugh, and through them I have received the joy of being an older sister.

My mother, Nancy Allen Munger, has taught me the joy of being able to appreciate the unspoken things in life and led the way to my accepting Jesus as my Savior through her many prayers and her own deep reliance upon God's strength. There is no greater gift a mother can give her daughter and I am thankful for having a mother who believes in the life-changing power of Christ's resurrection.

My first two children, Joanna Elizabeth and Katherine Laurel, initiated me into the joys of mothering. They are teaching me anew as they express their individuality (Joanna and a friend have just come in with green facial masque on while reading lyrics to a Second Chapter of Acts song about gossip) while discovering what it means to be young women. I cherish their presence in my life.

I thank God for the fullness of joy He has imparted to me through each of these women to whom I owe a debt of love and my sincere appreciation.

> No heaven can come to us unless our hearts
> find rest in it today.
> Take heaven.
>
> No peace lies in the future
> which is not hidden in this
> present instant.
> Take peace.
>
> The gloom of the world is but a shadow;
> behind it, yet within our reach, is joy.
> Take joy.
>
> *Fra Giovanni,* 1513 A.D.

Introduction

It's ten at night. You feel like it's your first chance to sit down
and relax all day. The dryer is still going, the oldest of your
three children is still squirming restlessly in bed, and your
husband has just arrived home from a men's fellowship
dinner. He looks refreshed, ready to talk; you are exhausted
and would prefer having just a few moments to yourself.
Thinking that all you've done is meet everyone's needs all
day, you wonder how you can find the energy to invest in the
next half-hour. What are your choices? As you mentally skim
your list, you think: I could act as if I've been sleeping . . .
but that's too dishonest. What about just telling him that I'd
prefer being alone for a while? No—he'd feel rejected. A
nice warm bath would be nice if I could convince him to
scrub my back while he talked about his evening, but I can't
picture him sitting on a stool next to the tub. Dream on . . .
Maybe if we just got into bed and hurried through some
lovemaking he'd be satisfied and I could finally get some
sleep . . .

Do you ever have moments when none of your choices are appealing?
When at the back of your mind you think of how you should be
responding to your husband but can't because your own needs are unmet?
Has your ability to be sexually available and responsive diminished as your
life has taken on greater responsibilities and more activity? Learning how
to balance a variety of roles with marital needs and expectations can be
confusing as well as challenging. As Christian women we receive multiple
messages from our churches and our culture, from ministers and the
media. We are influenced by the era that we are living in as well as by the
Biblical values we have accepted and adopted. Women have never had so
many choices, such diversity of information, and as great a selection of
role models to choose from. There are days when it seems possible to
accomplish everything God wants of us . . . but there are other days when
the tasks before us seem almost overwhelming.

Where do we find the balance? Who are we modeling our lives after? Which marriages will succeed? What do our husbands really want from us? What does the Lord expect of us? Pressures . . . expectations . . . roles. Where can we even find the *time* to sort out all of these things?

I believe that it is possible to find the answers to these questions and that walking with the Lord need not be burdensome. We are all inadequate in many respects and we won't always agree on things, but as we recognize the beauty of the Lord's design for our marriages and our sexuality, we can learn to laugh and sing for joy in the midst of our struggle for growth as women. Even on bad days, we can know that the Lord surrounds us with His love. His Word promises that He will complete the work He has begun in us. Like clay in the hands of a master potter, our Creator will mold and shape us until we are holy in *every* part. These days that we find ourselves walking through are bringing us closer to the day when we will see Jesus face to face. Now in the meantime . . .

Living with the daily realities of our sexuality brings up a need for understanding the diversity with which we were created. Because we have the capacity to nurture our children from conception and well into the early part of life through pregnancy and breast-feeding, female sexuality is more complex than that of males. We live with a cyclical nature that is much different in form and function from that of our husbands. In this book I have tried to combine practical information with a Biblical perspective of female sexuality. I hope that you will gain a greater appreciation for the body the Lord has given to you as you reflect upon the diversity of your design and the uniqueness of your ability to be the sexual partner of your husband.

In the abiding love of Christ,
Debra Evans

May God himself, the God of peace, sanctify you through and through. May your whole spirit, soul and body be kept blameless at the coming of our Lord Jesus Christ. The one who calls you is faithful and he will do it.
(1 Thessalonians 5:23)

What the Bible Says

*The male and the female know themselves only in relation to each
other because they are made for each other. This is the deep origin
of the powerful drive between the sexes to come together. It arises
from the body-life we share, with a difference. Male and female
are driven towards each other until they become "one flesh" in
intimate body-union. God did not wince when Adam, in seeing
Eve, was moved to get close to her. Male and female were created
sexual to be sexual together.[1]*

Lewis B. Smedes

The origin of human sexuality is recorded in elegantly simple language
in the second chapter of Genesis. For Christians today, the words can
either be a stumbling-block or a cause for joyous celebration. Regardless
of how the words are interpreted, the statements are there, having been
recorded by Moses thousands of years ago. These words have survived
into our age, beyond the downfall of civilizations and the passing of many
generations since that earliest time.

Moses transcribed the words of the living God, his personal Creator, as
he wrote these words about the first sexual relationship between a man
and a woman:

> The man said,
> "This is now bone of my bones,
> and flesh of my flesh;
> she shall be called 'woman,'
> for she was taken out of man."
> For this reason a man will leave his father and mother and
> will be united to his wife, and they will become one flesh.[2]

One flesh, one *bâsâr* in Hebrew, literally means one's entire body,
including our nakedness, our skin, and ourselves. These words were care-

fully recorded. We may try, but we cannot avoid them or explain them away. Embedded within the story of creation is the blossoming of a fruitful relationship that led to the population of our planet. As the words fit together into a meaningful description of God's plan for marriage, we can choose to read and believe them or to refute their authenticity; we can base our approach to sexuality within this framework or look in another direction. It seems that many who live in our culture today prefer to deny God's truth and look elsewhere. Many have "exchanged the glory of the immortal God" for worldly images of sexuality and in doing this have "exchanged the truth of God for a lie, and worshiped and served created things rather than the Creator."[3]

What has been happening to our outlook on sexuality as Christian women today? Why do feminists recoil at the sound of these verses? Where is the mocking coming from that accuses the "fable" of Adam's rib as being a source of oppression for women? How have these words in Genesis become an offense to so many? Has the meaning of creation changed or have we? Are we truly becoming all that we are meant to be as women who are dedicated to following Christ?

Only you can answer these questions in a way that will bring a life-changing awareness of God's truth into your marriage. Times have been altered dramatically since the beginning of the female sex. In the past twenty years alone we have witnessed tremendous shifts in attitudes, behaviors, lifestyles, and values concerning human sexuality. A revolution has taken place in our society, and we are now beginning to see its effects.

One thing that has not changed is the condition of the human heart. In spite of countless therapies and self-help movements, sin still exists. *Nothing* outside of God is pure. The first letter of John tells us that if we say sin does not exist in our lives, we are deceiving ourselves.[4] We have a tendency to look at *real* sinners as those who are thieves, murderers, and adulterers, or perhaps astrologers, spiritualists, or palm-readers. It is easy to forget that the truth of the matter has to do with living within the kingdom of God through confessing our sins and believing in the One He has sent to cleanse us from all unrighteousness, or choosing to remain in a kingdom of a different sort.

If we are seeking God's kingdom first, we can only be content there if we abide by the King's commandments. In basing our lives on the Word of God and embracing its truth obediently, passages like the one from Genesis will gradually, if not immediately, make sense to us. When we accept Christ as our Lord and Savior, we tend to appreciate some parts of the Bible more than others. As we continue reading, we are confronted with verses that we initially dismiss as being "less important" than what we view as the more "meaty" parts of Scripture, as if some parts of the truth are more true than other parts. There are portions that strike us as being cruel and unusual, or outdated and narrow, until we spend a significant

WHAT THE BIBLE SAYS

amount of time studying the things that bother us. We must dedicate ourselves to learning that the Bible means what it says, and we need to be taught by those who are gifted teachers of the Word. We can't reconcile what we feel to be the really irritating parts of Scripture with those that are more soothing until we do this.

One of the beautiful things about following Jesus is that He is gracious. He gently leads us into all truth through His Holy Spirit as we yield ourselves to Him. The Bible never becomes boring with the passing of time to those who are hungry for it. It either becomes increasingly clearer and more challenging, or more and more contradictory and less relevant.

Sin, therefore, is that state in which we find ourselves separated from God until we are redeemed through Christ, as well as an individual act of "missing the mark" of God's description *after* we have been justified by faith.

C. S. Lewis was fond of referring to human beings as "sons of Adam and daughters of Eve" to remind his readers of their origins. Through these two people we have inherited both the amazing fact of who God created us to be and how we became separated from our Creator. Our identity is as rooted in Genesis as it is in the finished work of the Cross.

Our sexuality is contained within our identity. We cannot distinguish our sexual selves from our spiritual selves or our intellectual selves, as if each part of us can be removed from all the other parts. How we express our sexuality is unique to each one of us. We are individuals, with different personalities, and each of us is loved by God; yet we share a common bond of identity and are governed by the same laws. Within creation and through the finished work of the Cross, we are linked together. As believers, we are the Body of Christ and we share the oneness of an identity that springs from the Word of God.

How we choose to express our sexuality will be affected by both our differences and our similarities and by our responses to what the Bible says about who we are as women. Are the first three chapters of Genesis allegorical? Is the account that was written by Moses hopelessly out of date? Does the Genesis account merely supply us with a general theory of the principles that we are to apply haphazardly as we see fit?

I think none of these things. I have found that I can't arbitrarily separate the first three chapters from the remaining forty-seven in Genesis. As I've grown in the Lord, I've tried to understand the Bible as comprehensively as possible while learning more about how to apply it to my life. You will be uncomfortable with this book if you replied yes to any of the questions in the paragraph above. I invite you to keep reading, because you will at the very least become more familiar with a point of view that isn't encountered in the media or through university classes much these days.

I have tried to the best of my ability to present a perspective of female sexuality that is based on a coherent interpretation of Scripture and upon the reality of the presence of Jesus Christ among us. I believe that when we leave the Word behind, denying who we are as women, we laugh in the face of a loving and holy Creator.

I have reconciled myself to my place in the universe, and I am learning to embrace the Lord's design for my life with joy and gladness. I have asked Him to break up the stoniness of my heart, and He has responded with tenacity. It hasn't been a comfortable process! But a wonderful thing has happened within me: I'm no longer ashamed of who the Bible says I am or to find the source of my being and the meaning of my life through a man. His name is Jesus, and He loves me with a love like no other man's (or woman's!).

I hope you will be encouraged and motivated by what I have written here to love more fully and freely the lover whom the Lord has given to you as your life's partner, to realize with greater clarity what it means to express that love through Christ in a world turned upside down by sin.

Common Errors

When we read the Genesis account of creation, we need to carefully avoid reading into the text things that are not there. This happens frequently, and there have been numerous misinterpretations related to women's roles as a result. Let's look at a few of the more common errors that have been made by those who accuse the Bible as one of the major sources of sexism.

Enslavement

Some women have interpreted the idea that the Lord "made a woman from the rib he had taken out of the man" as one that ensures that females will become the sexual property of their husbands at the time of marriage, denying that the woman's identity is as unique as the man's. The text says nothing about the woman's sexual position in relation to the man's except that they are to become one flesh.

Sexual enslavement debases the value of being made in the image of God. It undermines our personhood and the meaning of who we were created to be. Sexual bondage to one's mate is not the result of a loving union and does not fulfill the purpose for which the first woman was created.

The Lord chose to create a partner for the man who would *share a common identity* and yet be a *separate and unique individual*. There is no statement here to imply subjection, submission, or ownership. The Hebrew word for "help" used in this passage means "to surround, protect or aid":

16

And the man gave names to all the birds of the sky and all
the cattle, and to every beast of the field, but for Adam there
was not found a helper suitable for him. So the Lord caused
a deep sleep to fall upon the man, and he slept; then He took
one of his ribs, and closed up the flesh at that place. And the
Lord God fashioned into a woman the rib which He had
taken from the man, and brought her to the man.[5]

This event took place in response to the Lord's decision that it was
"not good for the man to be alone." In the first chapter of Genesis we are
given a summary of the events that took place as the Lord created the
world and everything in it. Of all that He created, this could be said of our
kind only:

So God created man in his own image,
in the image of God he created him;
male and female he created them.[6]

The Lord did not declare that all He had made was good until *after*
the woman was created. She was the counterpart of the man, different
from the rest of creation. The Lord had found that Adam's isolation from
the other living things was "not good." The woman was the Lord's idea of
how to complete His design; she was the missing piece of the interwoven
ecology that formed the basis of life on earth.

The union of the man and the woman resulted from the common
bond of their humanity as well as from the physical joining of their
separate, complementary identities as one flesh through sexual intercourse. Sexuality was the expression of the *reunion* through which the
man and the woman became joined together once again.

The Lord could have chosen to form the woman in the exact manner
that He had formed the man—by putting dust together and breathing His
life into it. That was not His choice, for these two "living beings" would
have remained isolated in their separateness. Any joining would have to
be *conceptual* rather than *actual*. What it means to "become one flesh"
would have been ideal rather than real.

Tragically, the man and the woman were moved away from their
original position through their disobedience to the Lord, and sin entered
the world. It was *after* the Fall that they covered their nakedness for the
first time. After the Fall, they hid themselves from their Creator for the
first time. The position of all human beings before God was altered.
Childbirth would become painful, and Eve would desire her husband in a
different way. Her husband became a partner to whom she would be
responsible, and he would find that the food he would supply for his
family would be obtained through laborious toil. Work became a daily

17

reality, and at the end of their lives they would experience death. We can be thankful indeed that Jesus Christ was sent to earth to be our reconciliation with God. Through Him, our situation in respect to the effects of the Fall, and how we cope with them, has improved considerably.

The idea that marriage equals a state of "mating in captivity," as a well-known feminist recently put it, is a clear demonstration of how separation from God spoils creation. Our view of God is warped, bent out of shape, distorted by sin. Until we are drawn back to our Father as He convicts us of sin, we are blinded by its effects on our outlook and to the truth of His love for us.

It is as if we had wandered a long way off in a stupor, only to awaken and find that we are far distant from home. We find that we must turn around and set foot in another direction, one step at a time, to return to where we belong. We begin the journey in a dense fog through which a glimmer of light shines through a break in the clouds. Even though there are many around us who encourage us to remain where we are, or to follow them in another direction, we find that we no longer fit in with them. It is as if we had become strangers in our own city. As we travel we meet other pilgrims along the way whom we identify with, and the fog around us slowly diminishes, eventually fading into a mist. The light before us becomes brighter and brighter. Since our eyes have grown accustomed to the dark, we have difficulty seeing things as they really are at first; we can't hear things very well either, because we had listened to the voices of so many different songs for so long. We are relieved when we finally realize that our vision is slowly clearing and our hearing is becoming better. We encounter so many things that are foreign to us along our way that we feel quite ill-at-ease for a while, even though more experienced travelers reassure us that we'll be able to relax and enjoy the trip more in a little while. Sometimes we are tempted to quit and give up the whole thing. Home seems so far away . . . but until we get there, we find that we'll never feel a part of the things that lie behind us in the same way again.

The idea of sexual enslavement within marriage comes from looking at the words of the Bible without being able to understand what they mean. It is an idea that was produced by a foggy mind far from home. The rightful place of sexual expression within marriage is part of what it means to be under the Lord's protection and covering as we travel heavenward. The idea that a husband's love enslaves his wife is based on a warped model of marriage, one that has been bent out-of-line and misshapen by sin. Just as Christ refuses to enslave us, so does the love of a truly Christian husband refuse to seek anything other than what the Lord would have for his wife's life. When any other attitude exists, it falls short of the kind of attitude that the Lord would have us use toward one another within marriage.

Sex As an Animal Act

There are many today who believe that the sex drive in humans has evolved from "lower primates" and is therefore instinctual, a type of built-in urge that is modified by cultural influences. This view produces two extremely different approaches to human sexuality, and a variety of beliefs arise out of a mixture of these opposing perspectives.

Some people look at our sexuality as being an irresistible force that is the primary motivating factor guiding human behavior: If we do not express our sexuality and give it a constructive outlet, it will become a destructive force internally within the individual or externally within society.

Hedonism is a way of looking at sexuality that incorporates this view. "If it feels good, do it," says the hedonist; "nothing matters beyond today." The hedonist denies that there is anything awaiting him in the hereafter, or else he thinks that an awesome white light is waiting to absorb him, a benign conclusion to a life spent in the pursuit of pleasure. "If it feels so right," he asks, "how can what I'm doing be wrong? I have a right to be myself." (Remember the song "Whether I'm wrong, or whether I'm right . . . I've gotta be me"?)

There are no moral absolutes to guide such a person; physical sensations reign in his life. The sensuality and the physical high of sexual experiences are all-important. The "day after" and long-term consequences are largely ignored. Chastity and celibacy are out of the question unless they are conscious choices made for a brief time. Women often end up the victims of hedonists, displayed in full color in the pages of men's magazines, kept in a penthouse to serve as an afternoon respite from a high pressure job, a third wife traded in for a fourth who is much younger and more impressionable. This view cannot serve the best interest of the family; and in the long run, society suffers as well. When sexual expression takes place outside of a loving relationship blessed by God, it can never be fruitful in a Biblical sense.

Does the Bible recommend chastity outside of marriage because God hates sex, as the hedonist claims? Or is it because the Lord's laws reflect His profound love for us? Ultimately, every time we sin we find ourselves farther and farther from home. If we act in a manner that cannot fulfill the needs we were created to have, we will feel hollow inside. This feeling may take years to surface, or it can drive a young person to commit suicide at a very early age. It is not a feeling that has been induced by "religion," but is instead a very real part of our inner nature.

When we act in ways that conflict with the Lord's commands, we are not behaving in accordance with the facts of our design. It is like pouring ice-cold water into a glass that has just been removed from a steaming hot dishwasher: the glass *must* crack if it encounters too rapid a decrease in its temperature. It cannot do anything else because of its molecular structure and how that structure must conform to the physical laws of nature.

Intimate sexual experiences expose the deepest part of ourselves to our partner. Two people become one flesh whether this occurs within a loving relationship or is simply the result of a one-night stand. That is the reality of how we are structured spiritually. When two partners who have been intimately joined together walk away from one another, their spirits are harmed; a kind of inner shattering takes place even if they deny the feeling exists. Some people become so splintered through repeated episodes of this nature that real loving becomes impossible: it hurts too much. In attempts to put the pieces together, they harden their hearts with self-made patches that become solid as cement. Instead of having hearts that are soft and pliable, tender and transparent, their hearts turn into stone. Only the powerful love of Christ can break hearts such as those, so that they are capable of truly loving another person and of loving God.

We can thank God that He is able to mend our broken hearts so they are better than new, that He can heal shattered lives and transform us with His incredible love. We must never forget who has called us home and that many of the voices we hear around us advocate lifestyles that will draw us away from where the Lord awaits us. We must learn to ignore the voices of those who have yet to surrender their stony hearts to Jesus.

Sex As a Dirty Deed

The other extreme view of sex sees sexuality as being part of a necessary act to perpetuate our species and to "consummate" marriage. Nakedness, freedom of expression, and full enjoyment of lovemaking are considered somewhat shameful, if not actually taboo. Sex is a necessary "fact of life" rather than a joyful, playful, or meaningful experience. The glory of what it means to become one flesh dissolves into being a dirty deed done in the dark, as if the Lord thinks sexual activity is disgusting. This view of sexuality within marriage denies the Lord the credit that is due Him for designing our bodies in the first place! This is a twisted perspective that can also lead to the destruction of families. Not surprisingly, the majority of sex offenders who have been arrested for crimes ranging from indecent exposure to rape have been found to have been raised by parents who gave them this impression about their sexuality. We cannot be the people we were created to be if we deny that our sexuality is a wonderfully satisfying way for a husband and wife to express their love to one another.

Think back for a moment and try to remember how you learned about how babies are conceived. Who told you? Did you feel surprised? Ashamed? Curious? Delighted? Horrified? How did you verify what you had heard? Did you talk to your mom about your reaction? Did she act embarrassed, or was she prepared to easily respond to your questions? Did she give you the impression that she was comfortable with her own sexuality or repelled by it? Was the atmosphere in your home conducive to talking about sexuality, or did you find that you had to rely on other sources to "fill in the blanks"? Were you expected to remain a virgin until after marriage without being told why sex outside of marriage is emotionally hurtful? Who became your authority on sexual values?

I have found that the majority of people my age were given a list of do's and don'ts regarding their sexuality without being given an adequate framework with which to interpret and make sense out of what their parents expected of them. Few were taught a thoroughly Biblical view that incorporated the tenderness of God's love for them in determining the values that should guide their behavior. Many of us found ourselves lost in the sexual wilderness created by the rebellious climate of the sixties and the "me-first" ethics of the seventies and early eighties, without understanding the beauty of sex within marriage or the long-term effects that can result from the emotional wounds suffered as a result of sexual promiscuity or divorce. For those who were virgins when they got married, few felt that they had made an excellent choice, and many doubted that sex could be as exciting with one's life partner as with a romantic lover.

Moving Toward a Biblical View

When the going gets tough within a marriage, sexuality can be turned into an ugly battleground. Feeling attractive and attracted to other men at any time in life can give one's ego a boost. Fantasizing about sexual relationships with fictional characters, or actual people, can make it easier to bear a disappointing marriage or a down time in life. Soap operas are filled to the brim with situations related to these things, as are many stories found in women's magazines and romance novels. Good sex is like a dream compared to the reality awaiting in the bedroom.

We are surrounded by messages that undermine our ability to understand who the Lord would have us be as His people. We have been torn in recent decades between a view of sexuality that urges fornication and one that suggests that we feel guilty if we get turned on by our mate. Is it any wonder so many of us are confused?

Sex isn't something that we talk to just anyone about. In order to find out if what we are experiencing is okay, we need factual information that is based on a Biblical view of sexuality. It is difficult to get such information, so most of us either listen to someone like Dr. Ruth (ugh!) or watch programs hosted by people like Phil Donahue (double ugh!) or avoid the topic of sex altogether (the worst!!). Sometimes we fluctuate between doing all of these things!

The American public is hungry to talk about sexuality, and advertisers

21

know that sex sells things well. I'll never forget going into the library downtown to do some research for the class I teach on sex education only to find that all the books on human sexuality had been checked out. I'm talking about three shelves' worth! Whenever I get to the library, I try to walk by that section and I've found that those shelves tend to be empty *most* of the time. I even checked with the librarian to see if the books had been stacked in a special area and was told that they were just *very popular* books! What an indictment of our culture this is.

We need to wise up. Men are not just animals with "uncontrollable urges" spurred on by high levels of the male hormone testosterone. Women are not obligated to "surrender themselves" to the sex drives of their husbands if they resent every minute of lovemaking. For both men and women to be fully sexual, they must be willing to be fully loving and *want* to live as the beings that God created them to be within His kingdom. To those who think that being a Christian wife means giving up one's sexuality or manipulating one's husband by it, I say: It is you who have been lied to and who has given up the true nature of your sexuality. You are the one who is being cheated by your lifestyle. It is only within marriage that sexuality gradually blooms into the beautiful flower it was created to be. Outside the marriage garden all the other flowers eventually wither, dry up, and die.

> Christ is the way out, and the way in: the way from slavery, conscious or unconscious, into liberty; the way from the unhomeliness of things to the home we desire but do not know; the way from the stormy skirts of the Father's garments to the peace of His bosom.[7]

Love Without Shame

*If human love does not carry a man beyond himself, it is not love.
If love is always discreet, always wise, always sensible and
calculating, never carried beyond itself, it is not love at all. It may
be affection, it may be warmth of feeling, but it has not the nature
of love in it. Have I ever been carried away to do something for
God, not because it was my duty, nor because it was useful, nor
because there was anything in it at all beyond the fact that I love
Him?[1]*

Oswald Chambers

When Adam awoke to view his partner for the first time, he must have beheld her with the kind of wonder that we feel when we view one of nature's grand spectacles: a shimmering waterfall cascading over pillars of rocks, an ancient range of mountains with glaciers gleaming in the sun, the turquoise depths of the sea rolling over a coral reef, the huge expanse of a midsummer sky late in the evening when the northern lights come out to play. It is with a mixture of awe and excitement that we behold the majesty of creation from our tiny reference points. We are moved and we are humbled by the power of our God as we view the products of His handiwork.

Eve was such a product! And when her husband looked at her he must have let out an audible shout of joy!

He probably noticed her humanness as well as her beauty, for it was so similar to his own. Creative intelligence, a hallmark of their Creator, sparkled in her eyes as she returned his gaze. Her smile radiated with a warmth that Adam had not seen in any of the other creatures, and her movements were so unlike those of the animals of the Garden. She stood tall and moved gracefully toward him with a gait that was nothing like the loping, lurching travel of the others. But when she touched him . . .

Adam must have acknowledged the wisdom of his God as he experienced the emotional, intellectual, and physical responses that he had toward his wife. She was the perfect partner. These two were unique in all creation. God blessed them and spoke freely with them. Their creation was conceived and carried out in love.

After declaring the woman's identity an integral part of his own—"bone of my bones and flesh of my flesh"—the first man (Hebrew, *Ish*), who had named all things, named the first woman (*Ishah*). He had been alone as a human being, but now there was another with whom he could share his mind, his body, and his spirit. He found his counterpart in this woman of his flesh and bones.

The maleness of the one and the femaleness of the other were combined to form the first human relationship. Their humanness was expressed in duality, not in singularity; in complementarity rather than in isolation. Self-knowledge became shared knowledge. Their bodies were the same yet different, designed to fit together and provide for the other what the self alone had lacked.

Completely naked in body, mind, and spirit before God, these two were naked before one another as well. Nothing stood between them. Shame and guilt were unknown. Before one another and before God, with their gazes unimpeded by clothing or deceit, every detail of their individual uniqueness stood revealed. Moses described it this way:

> The man and his wife were both
> naked, and they felt no shame.[2]

The significance of this is underscored by such a brief, concise statement. Our minds, however, find it difficult to comprehend such an intimate relationship, or to relate to those sinless moments when sexuality was experienced without any hint of lust or greed or envy. There were no other men for Adam to compete with for Eve's attention, and Eve had no other woman to compare herself to. Theirs truly was an exclusive, one-of-a-kind relationship, far removed from us in space and time.

We cannot return to the innocence of Eden, but we can appreciate the design of our bodies and the sexual use for which they were created: to end aloneness and to replenish the earth; to be joined in marriage and stand before the living God without shame.

If you are married, these words in Genesis can reassure you that your sexual relationship with your husband is something special and is nothing to be ashamed of when a loving union and open communication are your goals. As Christians, the grace of God abounds in our lives, grace that cancels sin and restores our fellowship with the One who has created us. The blood of Christ cleanses us from all unrighteousness as we walk in newness of life through the forgiveness that God extends to us through His Son, Jesus. Within our marriages, sexual expression can fill the sense of emptiness that we feel in our isolation from others. Husbands and wives are no longer separate from one another, but are joined together as one through lovemaking.

You are meant to be a blessing to your husband, as he is to be to you, as you learn to mesh your life with his as his counterpart and true partner. Your body has been designed to bless and complement his body—as his is yours—as you extend yourself freely and openly to become "one flesh." This isn't a neat package deal that takes place in a vacuum or on a television screen, but happens within the very context of your lives together on a daily basis.

The love that is born of the Holy Spirit in our lives as followers of Christ is a supernatural love, not a safe kind of love that refuses to take risks on our behalf. It is a radical love that sent Jesus to die for our sins. It is the kind of love that searches us out, knows us as we are, and accepts us. The love of Christ is not forceful or violent, rude or contentious: it is gentle and meek, kind and peaceful. At times the love of our Lord reaches out to us and seeks our loyalty as only a jealous lover might, wanting to save us for Himself alone.

Jesus enters our lives through the power of His Holy Spirit by invitation only. He stands at the door and knocks, never barging in to demand His rights and our compliance. Our submission to His love must spring from our own decision to respond to it and out of our desire to become united to our Lord. He has promised that where there is fertile ground that has been broken up to receive His truth, there will be much fruit. As we yield ourselves to Him, He keeps that promise by abiding in us and tending us like a shepherd. *He is love.*

This portrait of God's love for us is a far cry from the accusation that our Lord is a tyrant, screaming "Obey me!" while His subjects grovel on the ground and cower in fear before Him. Satan demands that kind of "adoration," *not* the God of Abraham, Isaac, and Jacob.

We need to keep remembering who it is that has called us to His banqueting table. Since many of us have been wounded by sexual sin, either as victims or as willing participants, it is natural for us to expect punishment and divine retribution. It has been estimated that sexual assault and abuse are part of the life experience of at least twenty-five percent of women living in the U.S. today. Divorce is an experience many women have struggled through. You would be quite an unusual woman indeed if you have never been touched in a sexual way by anyone except your husband or have never thought about other men in sexual terms. We no longer reside in the Garden.

You would also be in the minority if you said that your sex life is satisfying to you 100 percent of the time. If you've never felt guilty about your sexuality or endured a broken relationship, that would be pretty exceptional too! The point is: *we have all fallen short of the glory of God.* Some of us have felt as if we'll never be whole again or be able to give ourselves completely, without reservation, during lovemaking with our husbands *because there is still that nagging doubt that we aren't completely forgiven.*

Hurt, anger, fear, shame, and guilt are feelings that we associate with painful memories from our past and are part of the baggage that we carry away from sexual experiences and relationships that are not pleasing to God. These emotions put a stranglehold on our ability to become vulnerable during lovemaking. It is like glass that has been turned into concrete: *we want to protect ourselves from being hurt again.* But sexual sharing and making love were designed to take place *openly* . . . so we feel a deep dissatisfaction as we are torn between wanting to hide and needing to open up.

All too frequently, our own husbands are the source of our conflicting feelings because they can't love us perfectly, as Christ alone can, and they have dashed our expectations of them. Rather than patiently exploring our sexuality and that of our husbands, we attempt to neatly package our sexuality into manageable compartments and label each one to be used at the "appropriate time." Countless magazine articles have conditioned us to believe that we are only sexy when we are wearing the right clothing or aren't too tired or only when we have been wooed by our lover. We structure our sexual expression in ways that are predictable, to be run according to schedule. Then we wonder why we feel like we have fallen into some kind of a rut! Resentment, bitterness, and despair are the "little foxes" that can creep in and spoil the vine of marital sexuality, creating one more burden that must be borne rather than encountering freedom through Christ to experience sex as the gift of God that it really is.

If we shut the Lord out of this area of our lives, He cannot bring about our growth or deepen our level of satisfaction within our marriages. We lock *ourselves* into feeling condemned, cheated, and wronged; it isn't the Lord who does that! It is a vicious cycle that often ends up in an extramarital affair ("I was only looking for *real* love") or divorce ("If I just had another chance") or a marriage that is the equivalent of hell on earth ("I'm going to make him pay for this!").

The penalty of the law governing sexual sin in the Old Testament was death. Sexual sin, in any of its varied forms, is abhorrent to our holy and righteous Lord. Jesus offers forgiveness and the admonition that we "go and sin no more." He talked of what goes on in our hearts and minds as being just as important as our actual behavior. We may be fooling those around us as we harbor our hidden feelings, but the Bible tells us that God searches our hearts and knows our every thought. Thankfully, Jesus offers us forgiveness in return for the confession of our sins. He gives us the opportunity to be healed and reconciled to His Father through Him. It is almost unbelievable! To feel so dead or empty inside and be given a way out to where we can find life and fulfillment is like a dream come true.

26

It's so hard to believe! We expect to have to do more to find relief, but what He asks is that we forgive as He has forgiven us, to love as He has loved us. He promises that He will completely restore our minds and our hearts, not by some magical kind of hocus-pocus, but through His Holy Spirit working in our lives. All we need to do is cooperate and say, "Yes, Lord, I surrender my life to Your Lordship. I am Yours." We hear the words, we read His Word, yet we still can't really believe it.

Cleansed Through Christ

> If we confess our sins, he is faithful and just and will forgive
> us our sins and purify us from all unrighteousness.[3]

Praise God that His Word is true! We can read this promise again and again and still not understand the impact of it. It is like reaching out to grab hold of something that is covered with grease. It just keeps slipping out of our hands until we clean it off completely and make a determined effort to *hold on.* We don't have to approach the promises of God timidly. We don't have to hide anymore! Our Lord has promised that He will cleanse us and forgive us if we acknowledge our sin to Him. Through Jesus, we are redeemed from the heavy yoke of bondage that sin places as a burden on our hearts and minds. If we "walk in the light, as he is in the light,"[4] we are promised fellowship with the One who sits at the right hand of the Father. The blood of Jesus "purifies us from every sin"[5] and our lives become "hidden with Christ in God."[6]

If you are held captive by the weight of the sexual experiences, relationships, and/or fantasies that have kept you from being totally open with your husband sexually, you can be set free from that oppression in your life. You can ask the Lord to take away the hurt and the anguish that you have suffered as a result of broken or disappointing relationships, unmet expectations, clouded thinking, or being the victim of someone else's sexual darkness. You will also want to read Psalm 51, the Bible's most profound expression of what it means to cry out to God for help in dealing with sexual sins, written by David after he had committed adultery with Bathsheba.

Here is an example of the kind of prayer that you can use as you pray:

Dear Heavenly Father, I know that Your Word tells me that I am forgiven of sin if I confess it to You. Lord, I ask that You forgive me for ____(be specific here)____ and I also ask that You help me forgive ____(person's name)____ because it is Your will that I forgive others as You have forgiven me. I ask that You would change my mourning into dancing so that I might be able to be the partner for my husband that You would have me be. I thank You for the hope

27

that You have restored to me this day and for the freedom that You have granted me to love as You have loved me.

Please help me to love others as You love. Keep me from temptation so that I can serve You more fully. I praise You for the gift of my sexuality and for the sexuality of my husband. I ask that You would enable me to open myself up to him without shame, to Your glory. I pray this in the name of Your Son Jesus Christ. Amen.

Pressing On

The forgiveness that we obtain through Christ's sacrifice on Calvary is our *justification* for the remission of sin. It becomes a reality when we accept the finished work of the Cross as the means of our salvation. The living out of our belief in this reality, however, is an ongoing moment-to-moment process that continues throughout the remainder of our lives. This process as it is described in the Bible is called *sanctification* and is what Paul is referring to when he speaks of "pressing on":

> Not that I have already obtained all this, or have already
> been made perfect, but I press on to take hold of that for
> which Christ Jesus took hold of me. Brothers, I do not
> consider myself yet to have taken hold of it. But one thing I
> do: Forgetting what is behind and straining toward what is
> ahead, I press on toward the goal to win the prize for which
> God has called me heavenward in Christ Jesus. All of us who
> are mature should take such a view of things.[7]

It isn't always easy to keep "forgetting what is behind." We need to make a conscious effort to turn away from the memories that tie us to past events, threatening to pull us backwards away from "what is ahead." Paul tells us to *strain toward what we are called toward.* This is not an automatic process that suddenly overtakes us upon our conversion, but is the result of our walking away from the past.

If you find yourself becoming discouraged, there are several things you can do to make it easier to move on in the Lord:

Turn to the Bible for encouragement. There are numerous passages that can remind you of your heavenward call in Christ. Instead of doubting His ability to lead you home, build up your faith through disciplining yourself to read His Word, even when you would rather leave it on the shelf!

Share your concerns with the Lord. Don't be afraid to pour your heart out to God. We are reminded of Jesus in the garden of Gethsemane as He shared His inner turmoil about His betrayal, and what it would lead to, with His Father. We are given His promise in the Bible that He will draw near to us when we draw near to Him and that He will be near to us when we call upon Him with a sincere heart.

Talk to someone who is gifted in counseling. If you find that you have a lingering depression about your past, talk to someone referred to you by your pastor who will guard your privacy and will be able to give you sound advice and support. Be sure that you are very clear with your husband about what you are doing, and obtain his advice before you go to see someone outside your family.

Time is one of the greatest sources of healing. Every step that you take away from the source of your pain takes you that much farther away from it. Every time you turn around and embrace the past you create the feelings associated with it all over again. The passage of time makes it more difficult to remember the specific details of past events and reminds us that we are continually moving away from "what is behind."

Recalling the past is like a young child who has fallen down and skinned her kneecap: every time she scratches the scab off the wound, it reopens and begins to bleed again. Emotional wounds, especially deep ones, take time to heal and benefit from things that promote healing. They heal faster when they are given the right kind of care. Be patient as God tends the wounds of your past, always keeping in mind that the Lord desires to restore you. Trust Him to complete His perfect work in your life. Walk with boldness and confidence into the future, and don't think that it's strange when the Lord reminds you of what you need to work on along the way. Eventually your wounds will heal completely, although the scars will faintly remain until the day when you are completely restored in God's holy presence. The more willing you are to become the woman that He wants you to be, the more you will be able to receive what He has to give you, His very own precious child.

Solomon's Love Song!

> Listen! My lover
>   Look! Here he comes,
> leaping across the mountains,
>   bounding over the hills.
> My lover is like a gazelle or a young stag.
>   Look! There he stands behind our wall,
> gazing through the windows,
>   peering through the lattice.

My lover spoke and said to me,
  "Arise, my darling,
my beautiful one, and come with me.
See! The winter is past;
  the rains are over and gone.
Flowers appear on the earth;
  the season of singing has come,
the cooing of doves
  is heard in our land.
The fig tree forms its early fruit;
  the blossoming vines spread their fragrance.
Arise, come, my darling,
  my beautiful one, come with me."[8]

This song, written by King Solomon about his romance with a Shulammite woman, portrays the exuberant joy with which a lover and his beloved share their love and their physical bodies. In the verses above, the beloved calls to her lover in a celebration of her love for him. This book of the Bible stands out as a clear statement of the beauty of sexual expression in marriage. These are boisterous, wonderful chapters, examples to us of the honorable, freely yielded sharing that the Lord intends us to experience with our life's partner.

If we are embarrassed by this love song, it is because we haven't fully reconciled ourselves to the fact that our sexuality is *a gift of God*. This view of sexuality is unique to the Judeo-Christian tradition in that our sexuality is rooted in our physical creation and is an important aspect of marriage. It is a view that is under enemy attack and always has been since the serpent appeared to Eve in Eden. We can quickly lose sight of God's gift to us in a culture where pornography, homosexuality, teen pregnancies, incest, abortions, rape, and sexually transmitted diseases have all reached epidemic proportions. As Christians, we understand that sin has devastating effects on the human spirit. *Sexual sin* is merely a reflection of the *spiritual condition* of a human being.

That is why it is so difficult for us to understand *a healthy view of human sexuality*. We live in a sin-laden world! But praise God for the truth of His Word and the redemptive power of His grace. Paul wrote that "There is now no condemnation for those who are in Christ Jesus, because through Christ Jesus the law of the Spirit of life set me free from the law of sin and death."[9]

So let us leave this world behind as we ponder the magnificence of Solomon's poem. As wives, let us gather the words to our hearts as a fragrant bouquet and savor its sweet aroma. What is the woman's role in this courtship story? What are her desires like?

Let him kiss me with the
     kisses of his mouth—
   for your love is more delightful than wine . . .

My lover is to me a sachet of myrrh
     resting between my breasts. . . .

Like an apple tree among
     the trees of the forest
is my lover among
     the young men.
I delight to sit in his shade,
And his fruit is sweet
     to my taste.
He has taken me to the
     banquet hall,
and his banner over me is love . . .

My lover is mine and I
     am his . . .
All night long on my bed
I looked for the one
     my heart loves.[10]

These words of courtship may bring back memories of your own lovesick premarital days. Your thoughts were probably dominated by the feelings that you had toward your husband-to-be. We can relate to the words of how this woman felt, even though she lived thousands of years ago in Jerusalem. Sexual attraction is a potent force. When it is properly given and received, it takes us beyond ourselves and into the other person, merging two into one in an inexplicably powerful manner.

Belonging

I am my lover's and my lover is mine. . . .
Place me as a seal over your heart,
like a seal over your arm;
for love is as strong as death,
its jealousy unyielding as the grave.
It burns like blazing fire,
like a mighty flame.
Many waters cannot quench love;
rivers cannot wash it away. . . .[11]

Physical sharing through sexual intercourse creates a strong bond. The level of intimacy that is required for sexual sharing exposes the deepest part of ourselves to our partners. The bond that is created is strong even for those who are sexually active outside of marriage. People can deny this fact until they are blue in the face, but casual sex is not the "ultimate experience" that it is said to be. It may satisfy one's physical hunger temporarily, but it fails to nourish one's spirit in the same way that sexual expression within marriage over a long period of time can. The reality of the "morning-after blues" attests to the fact that sexual appetites can be filled in the evening only to be followed by an awkward morning of embarrassment and feelings of emptiness the next day.

We are warned to flee from sexual immorality[12] and commanded not to commit adultery.[13] Is this because our God is a terrible ogre ruling us from afar, seeking to deny us true sexual satisfaction? No, of course not! It's because statements such as these are made in the Bible *for our benefit*, showing us that our loving and holy Lord longs to convey to us that only He fully understands our physical, emotional, and spiritual needs. How can our Creator *not* know us? We are the result of His own design: "It is He who has made us, and not we ourselves," declares the psalmist, "for the Lord is good; His lovingkindness is everlasting, and His faithfulness is to all generations."[14]

Paul tells us that even the man "who unites himself [sexually] with a prostitute is one with her in body."[15] It is beyond our comprehension to be able to completely grasp the meaning of it all, yet this theme is expressed many times throughout the Bible: sexual intercourse is the joining of two people, a man and a woman, so that *they become one.* Paul summed it up well when he wrote:

> The wife's body does not belong to her alone but also to her
> husband. In the same way, the husband's body does not
> belong to him alone but also to his wife.[16]

In this passage, Paul tells us that our bodies are not to be merely self-oriented, but are to be joined together as *belonging* to one another. To be able to love our husbands freely, we must avoid reacting to these verses with thoughts like, "If it were up to *my* husband, he'd want to have sex all the time (or not at all or . . .). What about *my* needs? *My* rights?"

Paul didn't just pull these words out of a hat that happened to be sitting next to his desk as he wrote his letter to the Corinthians. Contrary to popular rumor, Paul did not hate women. He wasn't trying to pull one over on us as a male who was writing to a bunch of guys that wanted his approval to make love to their wives more often! This passage only makes sense when we integrate it with the rest of the Bible and the other things that Paul wrote about. It makes no sense at all if we think that women are supposed to blindly surrender their rights to their bodies as a purely sacrificial gesture. The results would not be a true joining of two into one, but a lop-sided type of bondage instead.

The belongingness that Paul speaks of here only fits within the context of marriage as it is defined in Genesis and from a viewpoint of understanding what *agapé* love is. Sexual expression involves passionate love (*eros*), the kind of love that fulfills our need to receive love; but it must have the protection that only *agapé* love can provide. *Agapé* love demands that we place the needs of another above our own needs. These two types of love need not be mutually exclusive, but should coexist within a marriage.

Agapé is that with which Christ loves the church and gives Himself to it. It is the type of love that Paul tells husbands they must express toward their wives.[17] *Agapé* love is the kind of love that can be expressed through our bodies as we share them as if they belonged to our husbands. This is a high view of the meaning of sexuality, not an uptight, prudish one. All other views pale in comparison! Paul is conveying that sexual sharing affirms who we are to be as wives in response to what our husbands are to be to us. We truly have been "made for each other"!

Our sexuality as women has been woven into the very fabric of our beings. We can't remove it and the more we resist loving expressively and creatively, the more fragmented we become. Sexual expression was designed to take us beyond ourselves, to end our sense of isolation. *Agapé* love is the Real Thing, not what we hear about in Top-40 songs or see in the latest made-for-TV romances. Everyone is grasping for the kind of love that *only the Lord can provide as we yield ourselves to Him, through the unique opportunity that He has provided for us within marriage* to be able to risk self-exposure, share ourselves without reservation, and give freely of ourselves to our husbands. Marriage is the sanctified means through which we become sexually liberated and fulfilled. Every other expression of sexuality is a poor imitation and is a rip-off of who we are.

We must change ourselves first if we are going to effectively model *agapé* love to a watching world. We need to demonstrate that we are unafraid to love and let others know that marital sexuality is a *positive choice* in today's world. We are going to need to be transformed from the inside-out, for external beauty says very little about who we really are.

> As for God, his way is perfect;
>   the word of the Lord is flawless.
> He is a shield
>   for all who take refuge in him.
> For who is God besides the Lord?
>   And who is the Rock except our God?
> It is God who arms me with strength
>   and makes my way perfect.[18]

Choices and
Challenges for
Christian Wives Today

*The important change [since feminism] is that she is no longer
permitted to accept her ancient role as keeper of the hearth, binder
of wounds, bearer and teacher and nurturer of the race. Instead
of being allowed to glory in this role, she is taught to despise it as
insufficient, as a biological aspect of her existence which interferes
with her destiny. Where once she found her pride and fulfillment,
now she finds only her chains. But if she sees them as such, what
she really begins to despise is the physical fact of being a woman.
Not all our no-iron apparel and instant food can change this
simple fact. And none of the technique we know can prevent
sexual failure in the woman who hates being a woman. Nowhere
is her rejection of her role more vivid than in her bedroom, for
nowhere does her success demand that she be more essentially
female.[1]*

Ronald M. Deutsch
The Key to Feminine Response

Our sexual identity is a part of our identity as a whole, influenced from
the time of our conception by our families, our bodies, our culture,
and our environment. The way each one of us expresses our sexuality will
be determined by the conclusions we have reached about who we are,
based on our values and beliefs about what it means to be a woman.
Sexual behavior is a reflection of our sexual identity. It is crucial that we
understand the significance of this.

When sexual behavior takes place that does not conform to the pattern the Lord created, our identity becomes eroded and confused. Allen
Wheelis made a profound statement when he wrote, "Values determine
goals, and goals define identity. The problem of identity, therefore, is

35

secondary to some basic trouble about value."[2] Knowing that we are created in the image of God and believing what His Word says about who we are enables us to resolve the questions we have about our identity by providing the values and goals that guide our lives.

As Christian wives living in today's society, we are called by God to base our identity upon the Bible, not on modern cultural interpretations of what it means to be a woman during our era. Our identity is to be an identity that is *derived* from what the Lord says about who we are rather than being an identity that we have woven for ourselves out of the fabric of our society. Paul made this crystal-clear when he wrote in his letter to the Romans, "Do not conform any longer to the pattern of this world, but be transformed by the renewing of your mind. *Then* you will be able to test and approve what God's will is—his good, pleasing and perfect will."[3] The Greek word that is used for "conform" in this verse means *to fashion ourselves according to the same pattern.* The pattern that we are to conform to is given to us in the Bible as our alternative to shaping ourselves according to a worldly pattern. Separating our identities from culturally normative patterns of female sexuality isn't easy when that pattern may have been all that we've been exposed to for most of our lives.

Becoming a "new creation" is like someone being told that they have a changed identity. If I had been raised as an English citizen named Claire Brett, I would have no reason to think that I was anyone but Claire Brett. But if I was approached by a policeman, a government official, an American ambassador, and an F.B.I. agent who informed me that I had been kidnapped as a young child, I would have to reconsider my position! The fact that I believe I am Claire Brett does not change the fact of *who I really am.* When I am informed of the crime, I am told that members of the English crime syndicate took me from my parents when I was two years old, that my name is Debra Evans, and that I am an American. How would I react to such news?

If I had been raised to believe that I am Claire Brett, the daughter of a powerful man who seemed able to control everything and everybody, I would feel shocked. My immediate reaction would be to deny what I was hearing. I would need some kind of reassurance, some actual proof that I am Debra Evans, an heiress to a large fortune and member of a socially prominent family in Chicago. In order to be able to change my identity to conform to the truth of my origins, I would have to see a birth certificate, my baby footprints, pictures of my real family . . . Without such things, the claim that I had been presented with wouldn't make any sense at all. After all, I would have been raised to be suspicious and secretive, always on the lookout for threatening situations. I might desperately hope that there was a means of escape from the life that I had been living; I might long to belong to a different family far across the ocean. But without proof, I would have a great deal of difficulty grasping the truth and would always wonder about who I *really* was. In order to *be* Debra Evans, I would need to believe that I *am* Debra Evans: otherwise I would feel like I was an actress playing a role in the theater. I would always be waiting for the curtain to fall, for the costume to be discarded, for the makeup to be taken off, so that I could eventually return to who I was in "real life." The process of being able to believe what I have heard about who I am would take some time because I have been told throughout my life that I was Claire Brett. My ability to conform to my true identity would not develop overnight. Day by day I would need to learn about my family, about the circumstances that surrounded my kidnapping, and about my heritage as a member of the Evans family. Everyone, including myself, would hope that my identity would be restored so that I would feel satisfied in my new life.

Returning to America would drastically alter the course of my life, changing the goals that I had set for myself and giving me a substantially different culture to adapt to. Many opportunities would be made available to me that had previously been denied to me. I would have to decide how to live my life in respect to my social position. The goals that I would make for myself, however, would be tied to the values and beliefs that I had been raised with. Since my outlook on life had been developed while I was living with my "adoptive" parents, it would be impossible for me to avoid being influenced by the corruption that had surrounded me during my upbringing. If I sincerely wanted to change my perspective and was welcomed by loving parents into a family that was willing to be patient with me as I underwent a transformation in my identity, then I might be able to eventually find comfort and meaning in being Debra Evans.

Our Identity in Christ

When we open our hearts to receive Christ, we obtain a new identity. Our former selves actually pass away and we become a "new creation." Just as in the story of Claire Brett, each of us needs to learn how to walk in our new identities and believe the truth of what the Bible tells us about our inheritance as coheirs with Christ. Here is Peter's proclamation to us concerning what we have obtained through our Lord and Savior:

> Praise be to the God and Father of our Lord Jesus Christ! In his great mercy he has given us new birth into a living hope through the resurrection of Jesus Christ from the dead, and into an inheritance that can never perish, spoil or fade—kept in heaven for you, who through faith are shielded by God's power until the coming of the salvation that is ready to be revealed in the last time. In this you greatly rejoice, though now for a little while you may have had to suffer grief in all kinds of trials.[4]

37

My heart leaps at these words, for in them I am told that I have been born into "a living hope" because of the death and resurrection of the Son of God. He was sent to earth to "give his life as a ransom for many" so that "we might become heirs having the hope of eternal life."[5] Each of us who believes in Christ will receive the inheritance that Peter and the apostles wrote about, and in this we are to greatly rejoice, in spite of what our earthly lives encounter. We are heading home. . . our inheritance is assured . . . and we are shielded by God's power as we await His coming! We have cause to celebrate! We can *know* who we are, in Christ, in spite of what our upbringing has taught us. We are *His*. God is our true Father, and our homeland is not of this world.

If we fail to grasp the amazing truth of what our redemption means in all of its fullness, we will feel torn between two worlds, two realities that are in opposition to one another. We either believe what God has accomplished on our behalf through his Son, Jesus Christ, or we doubt this truth. We can't both believe *and* doubt and still expect to feel restored in our relationship with our real Father. James referred to the person who does this as a "double-minded man, unstable in all he does."[6] Even worse is the condition in which a person pretends to believe, but chooses to live according to his flesh rather than according to the will of God. Such people are like actors in a play, like Claire Bretts who are always expecting the curtain to fall, instead of resting in the truth and the reality of their position in Christ.

Ridding Ourselves of Hypocrisy

> Therefore, rid yourselves of all malice and all deceit,
> hypocrisy, envy, and slander of every kind. Like newborn
> babies, crave pure spiritual milk, so that by it you may grow
> up in your salvation, now that you have tasted that the Lord
> is good.[7]

The Greek word for hypocrisy, *hupokrisis,* means to act under a feigned part or to pretend. A hypocrite is someone who decides, speaks, or acts under a false part.[8] This is a natural thing to do if we just "kind of" believe what the Scripture says about what we are to be as Christian wives while at the same time "kind of" believing what our culture, our adoptive family as it were, has told us about our sexuality and roles as females within our society. To be fully and completely *His,* we must derive our identity *from Him.* This is a very difficult and challenging thing to do at this time and place in history. We live in a culture that has come to value androgynous sexual roles rather than Biblical ones. It isn't easy to be a godly woman these days.

Androgyny is a botanical term referring to plants that have both anthers (pollen-producing organs) and ovaries (seed-producing organs). An androgynous person is one who has both male and female qualities, to the extent of seeming to be neither one or the other in a "traditional" sense. The fallacy that lies in the glamorization of androgynous sex roles is that human beings were not created to be asexual or bisexual or homosexual . . . we were created to be heterosexual! Every other expression of our sexuality is an aberration, a denial of our original design. The Lord created us to be male *or* female, to have testicles *or* ovaries, so that males and females would *complement* one another sexually, not become the *same* as one another. He did not create us to be part female/part male as he did certain varieties of plants and animals.

Within the last fifteen years there have been tremendous changes in sex roles in our culture. For those of us who have become Christians during this era, it is difficult to know how we are to live out the truth of our bodies' design. Feminism has had a far-reaching impact on the hearts and minds of women who were born after the Second World War. Traditional values that were based on the Bible are seen by many women today as being oppressive, outmoded, and archaic. Women's study courses at major universities invariably include such topics as abortion, lesbianism, rape, and sex stereotyping. Required reading is likely to include a very one-sided view of female sexuality. Articles are assigned that glorify the experience of self-stimulation (masturbation), the "sisterhood" fostered by sexual sharing between women, and the pervasiveness of "sexism" in our culture. Such courses encourage people to view God as whomever one visualizes him/her to be and ethical values as self-determined.

Paul warned us that in the end times there would be people who would "abandon the faith and follow deceiving spirits and things taught by demons. Such teachings come through hypocritical liars."[9] Such people, he wrote, would have consciences that have been "seared as with a hot iron" and would forbid people to marry. He told Timothy to "have nothing to do with godless myths" and to, instead, train himself to be godly.[10] James' brother Jude wrote that there are "godless men, who change the grace of God into a license for immorality and deny Jesus Christ our only Sovereign and Lord" who "pollute their own bodies, reject authority and slander celestial beings."[11] He cautioned that these people "speak abusively against whatever they do not understand; and what things they do understand [is] by instinct, like unreasoning animals . . ." and that they are destroyed by the very things they believe.[12] In summary, Jude described such people this way:

> They are clouds without rain, blown along by the wind;
> autumn trees, without fruit and uprooted—twice dead. They
> are wild waves of the sea, foaming up their shame; wandering
> stars. . . .[13]

What a desolate picture the Bible paints of those who turn their backs on the love of a living God who is holy, righteous, and just. We should mourn and weep over those who refuse to submit themselves to God; they are people who are lost in the fullest sense of the word. But we must turn our back on the seduction awaiting us if we join ourselves to their way of thinking. If we pray for wisdom, we must ask and not doubt, even when we have a hard time accepting what the Lord reveals to us. The wisdom of the Lord is pure, "peaceable, gentle and easy to be entreated; full of mercy and good fruits, without partiality and without *hypocrisy*."[14] We must rid ourselves of hypocrisy. We cannot pretend to be Christian women and yet base our lives on worldly value systems if we want to walk in the beauty and wonder of our sexuality. Our stability will come from knowing who we are as women in Christ; double-mindedness only produces confusion.

The Bible instructs us that "the way of the Lord is a refuge for the righteous."[15] We can choose to walk in that way as followers of Christ, or turn from Him and head in another direction. We can't walk along two paths, each aimed at different destinations, and expect to live out the fullness of our identity. Our identity will set our goals; our identity will determine which road we will decide to travel upon. Within our marriages, our sexuality will be appropriately expressed only when we are able to rest securely in the knowledge of who we are. Once we have discovered this, we will find it easier to walk in the way of the Lord.

The Way of the Lord

We can thank God that He has given His word to us as a timeless book to guide us throughout our lives. When we study the Scriptures, we find that even though the specifics might be different, little has changed. The New Testament contains enough information for us to discern what is going on around us within our culture. As the Church, or "called out ones," we are going to feel out of the mainstream if we are truly abiding in Christ.

When we are born again, the way we look at things changes. Paul wrote, "We have not received the spirit of the world but the Spirit who is from God, that we may understand what God has freely given us" and that "the man without the Spirit does not accept the things that come from the Spirit of God, for they are foolishness to him, and he cannot understand them, because they are spiritually discerned."[16] He went on to say:

> If any one of you thinks he is wise by the standards of this
> age, he should become a "fool" so that he may become wise.
> For the wisdom of this world is foolishness in God's sight. As
> it is written: "He catches the wise in their craftiness"; and

again, "The Lord knows that the thoughts of the wise are futile."[17]

We should take these words seriously. They apply to us today every bit as much as they fit the time that Paul was writing in. First John tells us that "the one who is in you is greater than the one who is in the world."[18] God alone is our safe fortress, our protective shield, and our mighty deliverer! He is able to protect, guide, and give us the things we need so that we will know how we are to live in this present age. We must pray for wisdom, which we need if we are to be able to see what is going on around us, and for the compassion that enables us to express Christ's redemptive love to those who are perishing. If we are to be the "salt of the earth," we should have a clear idea what the implications of our sexuality are and avoid sexual sin in any form.

What is at stake if we become obedient to God? Our pride? Our vanity? Our selfishness? Yes, and in exchange for surrendering our hearts to Jesus what has He promised to give us in return? Peace . . . joy . . . love . . . and everlasting life. We can't have it both ways; the way of the Lord demands that we turn away from the spirit of this world.

> Do not love the world or anything in the world. If anyone
> loves the world, the love of the Father is not in him. For
> everything in the world—the cravings of sinful man, the lust
> of his eyes and the boasting of what he has and does—comes
> not from the Father but from the world. The world and its
> desires will pass away, but the man who does the will of God
> lives forever.[19]

We can't love the Lord *and* love the world, even though we'd like to have it all: the fruit of the Spirit, eternal life, fellowship with Jesus *and* beauty, fame, and fortune. It just isn't Biblical. We can't rationalize our worldliness away either, by saying things like "The Lord has blessed me with a freedom to be all that I can be. I can have it all because I'm unattached to the things that He's blessed me with." The Bible is quite clear about where our treasure is to be: in heaven. "For where your treasure is, there your heart will be also," said Jesus as He taught the crowds from a Galilean mountainside.[20] Why should this be any less true for us today? It is a dangerous game to identify with the things of this world; like the man who doubts, we end up becoming double-minded and unstable in all our ways.

Walking in the Truth of Our Design

Learning to be comfortable with the bodies and roles God has given to us is a different process than exploring one's sexuality from a perspective of self-gratification. It means that we are to take a radical departure from the spirit of this age, delve into the Word of God, and be transformed by the renewing of our minds. It means that we are to tune out those voices and images of worldly sexuality that beckon to us to put ourselves first, choosing instead to consider sexual sharing within marriage to be the way God has ordained a man and a woman to share their bodies freely and openly with one another. It means that the "fruit of the womb" and the "blessings of the breast"[21] are to bring about real fulfillment as the Lord establishes our families and brings new life into His creation. It means being able to discern the will of God in our lives and being unashamed of proclaiming His truth to a dying world, not as arrogant know it alls, but as humble servants of the Lord Jesus Christ.

Within this framework, the Lord grants us flexibility to express who we are as individuals. Dick Keyes, the director of L'Abri Fellowship in the United States, put it this way:

> God's commitment to marriage extends beyond creating it. He has also given us a way of life within the institution he made. His form of marriage allows great freedom. Elaborate rules, roles and job descriptions for husband and wife are conspicuously absent from the New Testament itself. The Bible says nothing of who should earn the most money, cook the most meals, balance the checkbook, or change the most diapers. The form that God has given is flexible enough for Christians in many different times and cultures to be imaginative in the way they build relationships.[22]

What Keyes wrote is true, even though we each have our own opinion about the statement he is making! The most complete picture we have on women's roles in the Bible is found in Proverbs 31:10-31. These verses paint a picture of a woman who is resourceful, kind, diligent, trustworthy, fruitful, creative, loyal, and contented. She buys, sells, weaves, instructs, manages others, gives to the poor, sews, cooks, speaks wisely, bears children, and earns the respect of those around her.

I believe that the Lord desires us to follow the example of the virtuous woman. He gives gifts and talents to each one of us to use creatively and wisely during our lives. The principles that we have to guide how we express our individuality can be found in these Bible chapters: Ephesians 5, Colossians 3, 1 Timothy 2, 1 Peter 3 and 4, and Titus 2. Read each chapter several times, praying that the Lord will impress the wisdom contained in His Word upon your mind and heart. Take time to reflect on what you have read, then go back and read the chapters again. These are all chapters that describe what the Lord calls us to be as wives.

Many Bible translators place a subheading that says "Holy Living" above these chapters, a term that aptly describes the texts. We don't earn our salvation through living out the principles that are given here, but we do reap the rewards of what it means to be Christian women if we walk out the truth of these passages in our lives.

> See, I set before you today life and prosperity, death and destruction. For I command you today to love the Lord your God, to walk in his ways, and to keep his commands, decrees and laws; then you will live and increase, and the Lord your God will bless you in the land you are entering to possess . . . This day I call heaven and earth as witnesses against you that I have set before you life and death, blessings and curses. Now choose life, so that you and your children may live and that you may love the Lord your God, listen to his voice, and hold fast to him.[23]

Recognizing Your Assets

The woman was made of a rib out of the side of Adam; not made out of his head to rule over him, nor out of his feet to be trampled upon by him, but out of his side to be equal with him, under his arm to be protected, and near his heart to be beloved.[1]

Matthew Henry

If we are to be comfortable with our sexuality, we need to be on friendly terms with our bodies, knowing that there is nothing about our physical forms that should cause us to feel ashamed. Having a healthy attitude about one's body requires that a balance be achieved: We must neither worship our bodies nor degrade them; we must love them enough to care for them rather than abuse them. The Bible tells us that our bodies are actually temples of God[2]—the place where the Holy Spirit resides.[3] We are to use our bodies thoughtfully and considerately for the glory of God. This is a tremendous responsibility, isn't it?

Within marriage, both husbands and wives are to have their sexual needs met. "Do not deprive each other except by mutual consent," wrote the Apostle Paul.[4] Saying "No, not tonight" is not enough. We need to work at fostering an atmosphere in which we can talk openly with our husbands about our thoughts, feelings, and reactions to our sexuality. There is no replacement for the honest communication that must take place in our homes if we are to attain a mutual understanding of one another's sexual needs and thereby avoid misunderstandings, bitterness, and resentment. We can be thankful that the Lord calls us to maturity in our relationships with our husbands by emphasizing the importance of communication and the two-sidedness of sexual sharing within marriage.

God's Word makes it clear that we are not obligated to take part in any sexual activity that we are not comfortable with. It instructs us, however, to pay attention to the sexual aspect of our marriages, to focus upon meeting one another's needs, and to acknowledge the reality of our bodies' design. Ignoring our emotional and physical responses to our husbands' regular need for lovemaking and the realities related to our own cyclical nature is an unacceptable substitute for facing what is bothering us or preventing us from enjoying sex. Hurrying through lovemaking just to get it over with is avoidance behavior, a signal that we aren't able to say why we need a break from lovemaking and why we would rather be a passive bystander than an active participant in an area of our lives that the Lord tells us should be *mutually* satisfying. If we fail to see the complete picture of 1 Corinthians 3:16, we are in danger of performing as if sex were a *duty* instead of a *gift*. The Lord created women to express and experience their sexuality differently than men. Without communication, and a sincere willingness to meet one another's needs, husbands and wives cannot possibly enjoy sex the way their Creator seems to have intended them to experience it.

Flibs, Flab, and Flubs

Three common hindrances to creating an open atmosphere for discussing one's sexual needs and frustrations are what I call flibs, flab, and flubs. Flibs, flab, and flubs are self-defeating behaviors that prevent us from being transparent with our husbands. Each of us is born with the ability to hide from others as a part of our inner nature. Covering up our private thoughts and feelings comes easy for us. Even the youngest children among us can be the best of con artists as they attempt to manipulate their parents in one hilarious escapade after another, the humor of which is often lost on the youthful offenders. We all suffer the delusion of being able to get away with things, whether it be sneaking a cookie from the cookie jar or having an extramarital affair. Just as we wisely watch the mischievous capers of our children, the Lord beholds us. Flibs, flab, and flubs may fool others, but we can never trick our Maker.

A *flib* is a fib disguised as an excuse—that is, it isn't *really* a *lie* in our own eyes, but is a way of justifying our behavior to others. A flib might go something like this: "You know, dear, my back is bothering me tonight, and I'm afraid that lovemaking might really aggravate it." Instead of asking for a back rub or explaining why lovemaking doesn't interest her, a woman in this situation opts for using her back as an excuse for avoiding lovemaking. She does not feel comfortable enough with her husband to share what her needs really are. Perhaps this is because he has often ignored her needs or made fun of her back problem. When a woman cannot have her needs met one way, she will look to other sources to meet those needs. *Needs don't just disappear.*

46

Flibs block loving communication by enabling us to subtly manipulate others through hints, innuendo, and skirting around points of contention. *We must learn how to say what we mean and not be afraid to ask for what we need.* Asking is not the same as demanding. A gentle request, spoken because we value ourselves as well as our partners, fosters our husbands' ability to love us less selfishly. So the next time your back hurts or you are too exhausted to make love or for any of a multitude of reasons you feel unable to actively participate in lovemaking, try speaking the truth in love instead of hiding behind excuses. There is no substitute for the truth if we are to follow the Biblical principle of mutuality within marriage.

Flab results from overindulgence in the kind of stuff that is not nourishing to our spirits. Reading romance novels that glamorize extramarital sex, watching decadent soap operas, listening to captivating music about doomed love affairs, sharing the latest juicy gossip or glorifying sexual fantasy are examples of the kind of moral inertia that results from a lack of discernment about what to do in our spare time.

We hide our moral flabbiness from others because it is too embarrassing to expose. It is nurtured in secret away from the light of the Lord when we choose to "go with the flow" of our culture instead of looking to Jesus for the strength to stand in our present age. Flab turns up in our minds and hearts when we fail to exercise self-control and refuse to discipline our thought patterns. How very different our culture would be if the amount of time, energy, and money that is spent on getting rid of body flab was invested in ways that would encourage us to eliminate the moral flabbiness that prevails today!

The means that the Lord has given to us to combat our struggle with flab is clearly stated in His Word. *We are to confess our sins to one another and turn away from sin through repentance.* The fellowship that we have with other believers who are engaged in similar battles is meant to encourage us as we join hands to resist the temptations of this age together. We do not have to fight alone.

Flubs are what happen when we feel like we have done something stupid. The outcome of our mistakes is that we often engage in a running conversation with ourselves that lays an endless string of put-downs on our self-image. Flubs cause us to feel unlovable and unworthy whenever we seriously question how *anyone* could *possibly* love someone as clumsy or stupid or fat (or boring, inadequate, depressed, unattractive—you name it!) as we are.

Sometimes a flub is expressed as a put-down of another person: "You never seem to do anything right" . . . "I wish you were more caring, like my old boyfriend Chris" . . . "Can't you get it through that thick head of yours that you need to rinse the sink after you trim your beard?" Flubs are opinions, based on our inaccurate estimation of the worth of ourselves and the worth of others, that do not line up with what the Bible tells us about the dignity and respect we are to have for people. Flubs are devious little off-handed remarks and hurtful criticisms that eat away at our self-esteem to the point that real love of one's self, or anyone else, eventually becomes impossible.

We can diminish the impact of flibs, flab, and flubs in our lives if we follow the command to "put off all falsehood and speak truthfully" to ourselves and our husbands, realizing that we are each joined together as one flesh through marriage and as brothers and sisters in Christ.[5] Ridding ourselves of "all bitterness, rage and anger, brawling and slander, along with every form of malice"[6] is a call to be faithful to our Lord that cannot be ignored. In resolving to do and say only those things that are "helpful for building others up according to their needs,"[7] we prevent Satan from gaining a foothold in our marriages and acknowledge the transforming power that *agapē* love has upon our lives.

Open communication about our needs is the only way sexual sharing can be mutually satisfying. It allows us to heed the call to:

> Be kind and compassionate to one another, forgiving each
> other, just as in Christ God forgave you. Be imitators of God,
> therefore, as dearly loved children and live a life of love, just
> as Christ loved us and gave himself up for us as a fragrant
> offering and sacrifice to God.[8]

Can we do this perfectly 100 percent of the time? Of course not! But we can *aim* to be honest. We can avoid activities that produce a distance between ourselves and the Lord. We can rest in knowing that all of us who believe are his own "dearly loved children."

Turning away from the thoughts, behaviors, and attitudes that weigh us down enables us to break free from habits and perspectives that limit our ability to share who we are with our husbands. Take some time now to think of the flibs, flab, and flubs you have encountered in your own life recently and confess the things that have been pulling you away from your husband or from God. Know that you will be forgiven for falling short in your relationship when you in turn forgive your husband for things he has done to offend or hurt you. We *all* fall short. Thankfully, we are loved by a merciful God. The Lord loves us with an everlasting love. We can carry the love we receive through Christ into the hearts of our husbands as we refuse to play the kinds of games that prevent open sharing and as we put these words into practice:

> Love must be sincere. Hate what is evil; cling to what is
> good. Be devoted to one another. . . . Honor one another

above yourselves. . . . Live in harmony with one another. . . .
Do not be overcome with evil, but overcome evil with good.[9]

The Attraction of a Woman Who Loves

There is a story in the Old Testament that is a powerful example of communication based upon an attitude of humility, intelligence, and love. It is the account of Abigail, a wise and beautiful woman, and how she appealed to David to forgive her hard-hearted husband, Nabal, after he denied David's request for aid. First Samuel 25 recounts the way Abigail intervened on her husband's behalf, and in so doing, saved the lives of the men in her household. After the Lord struck Nabal down for his sin, David asked Abigail to become his wife. The humility of her response is impressive. It is a prime example of the way in which "a gift opens the way for the giver and ushers him into the presence of the great."[10] Read through this chapter and see how Abigail's life was changed through her willingness to act quickly in a godly way. What strikes you about this woman? Does her behavior appall or impress you? How did her words affect the situation she found herself faced with? How does the Lord influence her? What about her sense of timing throughout it all?

Here was a woman living in the middle of a desert, married to a drunkard and a scoundrel, who found out that her husband's wickedness was about to cost all the males at her compound their lives. She quickly organized a feast for David's men that consisted of two hundred loaves of bread, two wineskins, five dressed sheep, five bushels of roasted grain, one hundred cakes of raisins, and two hundred cakes of pressed figs. As she presented this incredible meal to David, she fell at his feet and asked that the blame rest upon herself alone. She blessed David's accomplishments in fighting on behalf of the Lord and implored him to remember her when the Lord brought him success in his endeavors.

Abigail's words as well as her gifts of food introduced her to one of the greatest men in history, delivering her from what would have surely been her ruin in the desert. In Abigail, we find a woman of strength, determination, grace, and understanding. These qualities, combined with her physical beauty, make Abigail one of the most striking Biblical examples of what it means to be submitted to doing the will of God. We can be inspired by her desire to be a peacemaker as she moved without hesitation into the midst of turmoil, most probably at the expense of her own pride.

Like Abigail, we too can approach difficult situations with humble hearts from a position of strength rather than weakness. For Christians, submission to doing the will of God is central to living out our calling as believers. The victory that is ours through Christ is won by lifting up the One who has made peace with the Father on our behalf instead of exalting ourselves. Jesus told us that "the least among you all—he is the greatest,"[11] and "the greatest among you will be your servant."[12] His Word informs us that those who exalt themselves will be humbled and those who humble themselves will be exalted.

We certainly have been sold a false bill of goods by our culture, haven't we? Jesus had a way of turning everything that was upside-down right-side-up. *His way of loving is costly,* but as we identify with our crucified Lord—apparently powerless as He poured Himself out as a servant for us all—we also experience the breaking forth of hope at His resurrection and taste the victory He obtained on our behalf.

It makes no sense from a world viewpoint to be humble. But from the perspective of the New Testament, it makes *complete* sense. In giving to others, we receive. As the Cross enters our marriages, we are broken of our pride and the need to be Number One; as the redemptive power of the resurrection breaks forth into our relationships, we are renewed and restored by God's love.

The attraction of a woman who seeks to love as Christ loves is part of a circular process that spirals heavenward as a "fragrant offering" to the Lord. When we love our husbands enough to serve and submit to them, our husbands' love for us expands and better enables them to love us in return. The progression of love's growth continues as our husbands' love draws us even closer to their hearts, influencing our responses. This process, as it goes back and forth, deepens the bond that we share with our husbands until it becomes a strong attachment that is expressed in many ways as our commitment is reinforced. The kind of mutual submission that the Bible teaches us to carry out is not a face-in-the-dust experience of humiliation, but is an act of the will as we conform to the example of our Lord and Savior.

There are many who ridicule women for following Christ's example, who caution us to assert ourselves against the "tyranny" of our husbands. There were also many who jeered at Christ for his apparent powerlessness on the Cross, history's most extreme symbol of love and submission. God is not a tyrant, and He does not call our husbands to be our enemies. We enter marriage free to be sexual and called to be open as we base our lives upon the enduring truth of Scripture and the transforming power of Christ's love for us.

Overcoming Fear and Ignorance

The New Testament is quite brief in its description of marital sexuality. The passages that refer to it are balanced by an emphasis on mutuality. We are told, for example, that "the husband should fulfill his duty to his wife, and likewise the wife to her husband."[13] There are no complicated instructions like the ones found in marriage manuals. *Only the principles that are to guide our behavior are given,* without any apparent concern for specific details.

No foolproof recipes exist that guarantee we can become better lovers if we follow Steps One, Two, and Three in the latest sex guide. Books such as *How to Make Love to a Man* by Alexandra Penney and *The Sensuous Woman* by "J" each sold a phenomenal number of copies. *The Joy of Sex,* by Alex Comfort, has become one of America's all-time best-sellers. People used to be embarrassed to talk about sex. Now it seems like everyone is talking about it—constantly!

Making love is not like baking a cake or putting together a complicated building project. Sex is not a mechanical act because we are human beings, not machines! There are many factors that influence how we experience the sensations produced within our bodies and the ways we express our sexuality (see Figure 4-1). Each one of us is a rather complex individual, with a unique set of physical, emotional, and intellectual capabilities and characteristics. Human sexual behavior is multifaceted rather than one-dimensional. We are "fearfully and wonderfully made," woven together by God, and watched over by Him every moment of our lives.[14]

How We Experience Our Sexuality

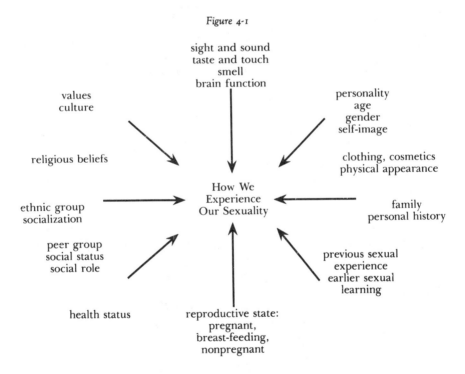

Figure 4-1

I have been professionally involved in teaching others about human sexuality because I have never been able to remain quiet about the amazement I feel about the design of the human body. I am absolutely fascinated by its intricacies, need for balance, and ability to carry out so many different functions efficiently.

A Summary of the
Reproductive Roles of Males and Females

Figure 4-2

Males:

> *Spermatogenesis*—the production of male sex cells, or sperm, within the testes.
> *Ejaculation*—the release of semen through the male reproductive tract which accompanies the orgasmic phase of sexual response. During intercourse, sperm are deposited at the base of the cervix within the vagina.

Females:

> *Ovulation*—the release of a female sex cell, or ovum, from an ovary.
> *Menstruation*—the monthly shedding of the superficial lining of the uterus.
> *Sexual response during intercourse*—the immersion of the cervix into the seminal pool which follows uterine contractions and facilitates conception after lovemaking.
> *Gestation*—an approximately 266-day period following the fertilization of an ovum during which an unborn child is nurtured within the uterus and develops the capabilities that are required for independent survival outside the mother's body.
> *Partuition*—the process of human labor and birth involving contractions of the uterus which move the baby through the mother's pelvis and out into the world.
> *Lactation*—the production of human milk by the mammary glands in response to the suckling of an infant at the breast.

A healthy female body is capable of performing six separate but interrelated reproductive functions (Figure 4-2). Have you ever stopped to ponder the ways in which the complexity and wisdom of God are reflected in the wonder of your design? Are you able to accept the beauty of your cyclical nature and praise God for the miracle that you are, head to toe, inside and outside, seen and unseen? You are precious indeed, one of a kind. There is no one exactly like you in the entire universe!

It is with joy that we can contemplate the meaning of our sexuality. We have cause to celebrate when we read:

> For you created my inmost being; you knit me together in my mother's womb. I praise you because I am fearfully and wonderfully made; your works are wonderful, I know that full well. My frame was not hidden from you when I was made in the secret place. When I was woven together in the depths of the earth, your eyes saw my unformed body. All the days ordained for me were written in your book before one of them came to be.[15]

These statements apply to *each* of us. We are walking testimonies to the handiwork of God.

When I watch a newly born child take her first breath of air, I can hardly believe that the baby I am beholding began just nine short months ago as two tiny cells. Each of us entered life in this way following the union of our mothers' and fathers' cells in the womb. Our growth and development has proceeded along a highly complicated, well-organized pathway since that time, resulting in our becoming who we are today.

When we take the time to learn how our bodies work and inform our husbands about our discoveries, we are able to put sensations and experiences into words. Through understanding what is happening to our bodies, communication with our spouses becomes easier because we can identify the things that please us, bother us, surprise, us, and excite us. Our husbands benefit from our ability to interpret our range of reproductive activities. Also, when we know more about our bodies, we tend to take better care of them and become better stewards of what the Lord has given to us.

Your Husband Married ALL of Your Body

You bring to your husband the ability to embrace him with the totality of your womanhood—with fertility as well as sexual fulfillment, breasts for nurturing an infant as well as for providing pleasure, cycles of peaceful inactivity as well as intense activity. These are assets that have been denigrated by our society through its "genital orientation" to human sexuality. Many men have been deluded by a Playboy mentality about female sexuality that emphasizes one aspect of our reproductive capabilities over all the others. Our assets as women have a far deeper impact upon family life than the space that is occupied by the marriage bed. Your husband married *all* of your body, with all of its capabilities, when he was wedded to you.

The qualities that enable women to be different from men are closely tied to the designs of our bodies. The ability to be nurturing, intuitive, sensitive, supportive, and receptive is bound up in our physical, emotional, and spiritual design. These qualities are assets that are to be appreciated and acknowledged because they enable us to be better wives and better mothers. I am well aware of what feminists would say about these statements: "Sexual stereotyping!" "Right-wing propaganda!" "Blatant sexism!" But I am not going to apologize or pretend any more. I know the qualities that make me strong! I love being a wife and a mother! I have a husband who depends on me as much as I depend on him! I'm tired of the worn-out accusations and the pressure to conform to a "nonsexist" lifestyle. It is only in being who I am, as God created me to be, that I have found real satisfaction.

What do you think? Is it possible to aim toward a genitally oriented sexuality and be fulfilled and satisfied as a woman? Do your assets reside in your bust, waist, and hip measurements rather than in the qualities that lie in deeper aspects of your sexuality? Is marriage simply a sanctified place for making love?

The assets that you bring into your marital relationship as a woman who has joined her life to that of her husband are precious, rich, fruitful, and diverse. It is only when we sweep the "flibs, flab and flubs" out of our lives and openly confront the truth of our sexual design as we learn about how the Lord created our bodies that we can encounter the fullness of our womanhood, not before. Let's not make the mistake of "starting from the outside in" like the sex guides and erotic magazines do. The strength of our femininity does not reside in the fact that we have breasts and genitals that are structured differently from males. They are structured differently for *a reason.* In an age of androgyny, breasts and genitals are thought to be the only things left that make the sexes different from one another— and even this isn't enough to prevent an increasingly larger number of people from ignoring the surface differences and being sexual toward members of their own sex. The Biblical basis of marriage is made null and void if we turn away from the differences that the Lord created us to have.

In summary, sexual openness and full sexual sharing can only take place when we are honest about who we are, rather than thinking that we will experience our sexuality in a similar manner to our husbands. Communication is to be based on love, promoting peace and harmony within our sexual relationships, so that our husbands can better understand and meet our sexual needs, and so we can better meet theirs. Knowledge fosters our ability to walk in the truth of our design and make decisions regarding our sexuality that are based on Biblical, rather than cultural, perspectives of who we are as women. When we avoid a genitally oriented mentality about our sexuality, we increase our understanding of the qualities that the Lord has given us to enhance and complement one another as husbands and wives. The Lord created us to have *real* differences, and those differences are to be *assets* rather than liabilities. Reducing ourselves to the level of playmates prevents us from being fulfilled as women and trivializes the institution of marriage.

From the first moment of our existence we were females, and turning away from the implications of that will only harm us. We can be truthful about our needs, open about our bodies, and expressive with the many facets of our sexuality that the Lord created us to have. Most importantly, as Christian wives we are to follow the example of Jesus and learn that we don't have to compete with our husbands or try to manipulate them with our sexuality: it is in our responsiveness and receptiveness that our best assets can be found.

> He who finds a wife finds what is good
> and receives favor from the Lord.[16]

Giving and Receiving the Gift of Our Sexuality

Love is the most intensive desire of the soul to enjoy beauty, and, where it is reciprocal, is the most entire and exact union of hearts.[1]

Algernon Sidney

Myths abound about female sexuality. There are some things to be learned from many current books and articles on this subject because it is interesting to find out how our bodies function! Factual information can be helpful, but learning to combine our reactions to sexual arousal with those of our husbands challenges us to let down our guards and recognize their needs and feelings as well as our own. As we open ourselves up to receive the gift of marital sexuality, we discover that we can be drawn exceptionally close to our husbands in a physical sense while at the same time not revealing our deepest emotions about lovemaking. Our heads may be packed full of information, and we may be going through the right motions, but all the facts in the world won't add up to much if we fail to recognize whether we are truly open to participating with our husbands in this area of our lives, with our hearts as well as our minds and bodies. The Lord gives us the gift of our sexuality to be *mutually* enjoyable and satisfying.

In earlier chapters, aspects of female sexuality were presented that have little to do with physical responses that take place during lovemaking—or so it seemed! In beginning from "the inside out," the information that has been brought up this far is closely related to being able to experience the joy and abandonment that bring sexual fulfillment: seeing the truth of God's Word as it applies to our marriages, accepting the forgiveness we receive from the Lord when we confess sexual sin, changing the attitudes of a stubborn heart, understanding the impact of our identity in Christ on our sexuality, and learning about the beauty of our cyclical nature. Too often, genital sexuality is paramount in sex manuals, detracting from our ability to discover the depth of our sexual identity as Christian wives. There is one more point I'd like to make in this chapter before we get down to the "nitty gritty" of female sexual response and the factual information that is an important part of understanding how our bodies work during lovemaking. It has to do with facing the emotions women have concerning their role in sexual arousal and their response to the act of making love.

Sexuality Is a Gift to Be Shared!

In our society, males used to grow up learning about female sexuality in terms of where various "bases" were located. This made complete sense in a culture that is fanatical about sports! High school locker room talk was likely to include the question "How far did you get last night?" on Monday mornings. The replies were diguised in baseball terms, but decoding their meanings was quite easy: "first base" meant that the guy was able to kiss the girl; "second base" is what happened when he managed to touch her breasts; "third base," petting below the waist; and a "home run" was the equivalent of "going all the way" to intercourse—which is when a guy could brag that he had "scored."

Unfortunately, this pattern of how to proceed over female "territory" found its way into the adult lives of men, becoming a type of coaches' guide on how to play the field of female sexuality. Without loving communication, this behavior—kiss, pet, fondle, and insert—becomes a standard way to approach sexual arousal with one's wife, over and over and over again. It is only when a wife feels free enough to discuss her sexual needs and responses with her husband that this type of scenario can be changed into a more creative situation! For now, I'd like to ask you to forget this pattern, or anything like it, as you take the time to think about your own sexuality and what matters to *you* in terms of sexual arousal and your responses to lovemaking. You may already feel very fulfilled in this area of your life. If so, this chapter will confirm the things that you already have discovered in your marriage. But if you feel somewhat confusd by the multiple messages you have received about your sexuality or have not found that this part of your life is as satisfying to you as you think it should be, I hope you will be encouraged by what I am about to share with you.

Your Body: A Masterpiece of God

The pattern of your body was shaped long ago by a Master Craftsman. He lovingly shaped every part of human anatomy to reflect His own character.

You are not the result of chance, for He skillfully designed one hundred trillion cells to function within His masterpiece, each with a power center and a nucleus containing directions to enable each cell to fulfill its specific mission.

Our Creator covered the bodies that He made with an elastic, living tissue that we call skin to provide a protective barrier against the elements. Another amazing feature of this covering was that He placed within it millions of nerve endings that had the capability of relaying information about the outside world to the very center of the nervous system within a split second of time whenever a change in the outside environment was sensed or felt. The brain was the seat of the body's ability to interpret and store information, as well as to analyze it. Within the brain the Lord placed many functions, including the capacity to reason, remember, feel, create, and control other functions in the bodies He designed.

Muscles were laid out under the skin, ligaments were put in place to support internal organs, and tendons were attached to bones. With a mere thought, an arm could be lifted, a finger curled, an eyebrow arched. Bones were fashioned to provide protection as well as support and movement: the skull to cover the brain, the rib cage to protect the heart and lungs, the pelvis to guard the reproductive and alimentary organs, the spine to encase the spinal cord. Each and every part of the bodies that our Creator made had a purpose and a function; all the various parts were put together in a way that would allow them to work in harmony with all the other parts. The Lord infused dignity, beauty, and joy into every aspect of His design, imparting the qualities that He Himself possessed into the beings that He declared were made in His image. When He was finished, He breathed His own life into the forms that He had fashioned, and upon their completion He proclaimed His creations to be "very good."

Just as He had designed each of the two bodies to function on their own, He planned and fashioned them in a way that they would function together. One would always be partially incomplete without the other. He created these two beings to belong to one another, to fill the void that they felt whenever they were apart. Self-sufficiency was not a part of the total picture of His design: each person would need the other to provide that which they were lacking alone.

The cornerstone of the joining together that the Lord seemed to intend to be both a symbolic and literal merging of "two into one flesh" was to be accomplished by their reproductive systems. Making love was *God's idea* of how men and women would dissolve their individuality into mutuality, their separateness into oneness. He created the sexuality of each to complement the sexuality of the other. This is the foundation of what the Bible tells us about the meaning of our sexuality and the difference of our identity as men and women.

Our part in this is that we can believe His Word yet today, in the closing years of the twentieth century. The Bible invites us to experience the same dignity, beauty, and joy that are evident in the account of the creation of humanity. The Master Craftsman who fashioned the first two people is the same One who fashioned us in our mothers' wombs. Our lives are derived from His even now. We exist because He exists.

The places that He designed to respond to the sexuality of our husbands are as dignified and beautiful as any other aspect of our bodies. Jesus asked us to "consider the lilies of the field" as a way to reflect on our worth to the Lord. In all of creation, *we* are the ones that are made in His image!

The Lord did not design our bodies to conceive with every act of intercourse the way He did other animals. *In addition to the reproductive role of our sexuality, our Father blessed our bodies with the ability to give and receive pleasure.* His stamp of approval rests on our physical form, including the areas that are private and to be shared in intimacy with our marital partners only.

The Contribution of Science

Scientists are only recently discovering the things that the Lord has known all along about our bodies. Bit by bit and piece by piece, researchers are attempting to unravel the complex mysteries of our design, often providing us with information that surprises us. Meanwhile, we can picture the Lord smiling as He agrees with Solomon that there is "nothing new under the sun." Our Creator is at home in the universe of His design and He is thoroughly acquainted with how it functions, down to the tiniest part of every atom, the smallest cell in every body.

When modern-day sex researchers clinically describe the phases of human sexual response, they are simply reporting their observations of the bodies that the Lord originally created, giving us information about how the bodies that the Lord has given to us work. When Doctors William Masters and Virginia Johnson investigated human sexual response patterns in the 1960s, they dispelled several myths about sexuality while at the same time confirming the fact that males and females share many similarities in their reactions to sexual arousal (see Figure 5-1). The four myths that they exploded were: sexual activity does not stop with aging; a man's sexual response is unrelated to the size of his penis; "vaginal" and "clitoral" orgasms are physiologically identical; and women do not necessarily experience rest following orgasm in the same way that men do. Masters and Johnson's research has had a profound impact on the treatment of sexual disorders and has contributed to an increased level of awareness about the sexual response cycle in our culture.

Men and women are greatly affected by the cultural attitudes that have developed since the time Masters and Johnson's book, *Human Sex-*

THE PHYSIOLOGY OF LOVEMAKING: CHARACTERISTICS OF BOTH SEXES

Figure 5-1

1. Muscular tension (myotonia)
2. Increased blood flow to breasts and genitals (vasocongestion)
3. Changes in pulse, blood pressure, and breathing rate
4. Release of secretions from the genitals
5. Muscular contractions accompanying orgasm
6. Analagous organs for receiving and transmitting sexual stimuli: the penis and the clitoris

ual Response, was published two decades ago. In addition, the emotional reactions that we have toward the information we receive directly affects the attitudes we form about our bodies and toward our husbands' sexuality. As Christians, our beliefs about our sexuality also arise out of our interpretations of Biblical references, teaching that we hear within our churches, what our parents taught us and how they expressed their sexuality, and how our peers view the role and purpose of sexual sharing. The beliefs that we hold have a tremendous impact on how we feel about the values and attitudes we have about our sexuality. Our emotions, in turn, directly affect our ability to give and receive sexual pleasure.

To demonstrate this more clearly, try to imagine what happens within your body when your husband gives you a tender kiss that has more than a hint of passion in it. Add to this the sensation of his hand stroking the back of your neck and his soft cheek brushing against yours as he whispers, "I love you, honey." In and of themselves, these combined actions can produce terrific sensations and act as a prelude to lovemaking. But, since the circumstances surrounding this behavior are not stated, how could we possibly tell where things might be headed? What if this happened just as you were about to hop out of the car on your way to a dentist appointment? How might your reaction differ if all of your children were watching from the table as you were getting ready to serve dinner? Or if you had just cuddled up together at a hotel on your weekend *away* from the kids? You see, the circumstances, and how you feel about them, make *all* the difference in the world.

It is through our emotions that we filter our physical responses to sexual sharing. Our minds hold the keys to how we perceive our body's ability to be sexually responsive. We need to keep in mind that sexual dysfunction is caused far more often by an unfavorable reaction to love-making than it is by a lack of hormonal stimulation, poorly developed genitalia, or disturbances of the nervous system.

Even though sexual response is affected by these, as well as many other factors, it is made up of a series of physiological events that are common to each one of us. The patterns of our responses can vary greatly; so each of us experiences our sexuality in ways that are as special and individually unique as we are. This makes it possible to learn about human sexuality with an open attitude since we know there are events that are common for all of us, and yet to retain our own ways of expressing this aspect of our lives within the privacy of our marriages.

It has been said that the most important part of human anatomy that affects sexuality is the brain, that the sexiest organ in the human body lies between our ears. This is true for a variety of reasons, not the least of which is that our minds help us to be creative and imaginative in the ways that we express our personalities. Our minds also empower our bodies to be sexually responsive through the way our nervous system functions. This is easy enough to prove. All someone has to do is *think* about something really sexy concerning one's wife or one's husband and the body kicks into gear—sometimes at the most unusual moments! Recent research even suggests that the grand finale of lovemaking—orgasm—takes place to a large degree in our minds rather than in our pelvis! This is why it's important to realize that how we *think* influences how we *respond* to lovemaking. Our minds have a tremendous impact on how we feel about sexual arousal.

This is true for both sexes. Because of the many similarities between the sexuality of our husbands and our own, it makes it easier to identify with what they experience. We can better understand our husband's body when we understand our own bodies. Our culture, however, has influenced the way that women view male sexuality, and we need to fill the gap that has been created so we can draw closer to our husbands and respond to their sexual makeup with sensitivity and honesty.

Your Husband Is a Work of Art, Too!

As women, we have not been raised to find the male body particularly attractive. We avert our eyes from Greek sculptures that encase the obvious difference between us and "them" in marble. But what about men? Males have been programmed by our culture to think of the female body as desirable and attractive. I'm not suggesting here that girls need more exposure to male nudity, only that it is a fact that many women are repulsed by their husbands' genitals initially (if not permanently) because of the differences in how our culture portrays the sexuality of females as opposed to males.

62

As Christian women, we can learn to view the intimate details of our husbands' bodies with as much pleasure as they do ours. They may get a "head start," but not all of their conditioning is positive! We can begin from a Biblical basis and allow the Lord to help us to receive the gift of our husbands' sexuality. This would be an important aspect of premarital counseling, wouldn't it?

The Bible encourages us to view our husbands' sexuality as if it were part of our own, because it is! They belong to us just as we belong to them. First Corinthians states:

> The wife's body does not belong to her alone but also to her
> husband. [Keep reading!] In the same way, the husband's
> body does not belong to him alone but also to his wife.[2]

In Song of Songs, the Shulammite woman expresses this another way when she says, "My lover is mine and I am his."[3] This is incredible! It means that we are to be as open and excited and happy about our husband's anatomy and sexual responses as they are with ours! It is to be a delight that is shared *together*. The needs of one are to be balanced with the needs of the other.

For many years, the reciprocal nature of marital sexuality has been underestimated. This is no less true today in many respects, even though we live in the postsexual revolution era. Christian wives are often so imbued with a spirit of service that they fail to recognize that *receiving* the gift of their husbands' sexuality is every bit as important as *giving* the gift of their own! This service-attitude reached its zenith during the Victorian era, when women were viewed as having a duty to be on the receiving end of their husbands' passions and for bearing the children that resulted afterwards. Women were discouraged from acting like they enjoyed sex, and a procedure known as a clitoredectomy was often performed on female infants. This consisted of the surgical removal of the clitoris, which is, as we know today, the only organ in either the male or female body that is designed for the *sole purpose* of receiving and transmitting sexual stimuli.

Thankfully that era is over. We can acknowledge that lovemaking is for the purpose of receiving, as well as giving, pleasure. In fact, the best part of making love for many husbands is knowing that their wives enjoy being sexually aroused as they touch them in pleasing and satisfying ways. Sexual ecstasy is not nearly as fun when experienced by one alone! It is safe to assume that the majority of men are greatly stimulated if they are married to women who react to their masculinity and expertise at lovemaking with obvious delight.

Allowing ourselves to *receive* sexual pleasure becomes one of the best ways to *give* sexual pleasure to our husbands for this reason. Mutuality in lovemaking means that there is an open interchange that takes place, back and forth, as two bodies are joined as one; that what happens sexually is done or felt by each toward the other. The sexuality between a husband and wife is held in common and shared by both when each considers the other's body to be their own. Isn't it amazing to think that the Lord built this concept of mutuality right into our minds and bodies? It is what He created us to desire and to be fulfilled by in our marital relationships. When I reflect on this, my reaction parallels David's as I read:

> Come, let us sing for joy to the Lord;
>> let us shout aloud to the Rock of our salvation.
> Let us come before him with thanksgiving
>> and extol him with music and song.
> For the Lord is the great God,
>> the great King above all gods.
> In his hand are the depths of the earth,
>> and the mountain peaks belong to him.
> The sea is his, for he made it,
>> and his hands formed the dry land.
> Come, let us bow down in worship,
>> let us kneel before the Lord our Maker;
> for he is our God
>> and we are the people of his pasture,
>> the flock under his care.[4]

Play Me a Love Song

Our bodies are like instruments that are tuned to play love songs to our husbands. The melodies that each of us has the ability to express lie within the depths of our sexuality, waiting to be released as we sing them as an offering of our love and commitment. Each of us has a melody that is as unique and different from all the rest as our faces and bodies are from all others. The love songs that our bodies long to sing can only be released fully when we feel protected and safe, unafraid and trusting. Marriage is the ideal place for the expression of these songs because we are only able to open ourselves up to the fullest capacity when we know that our songs will be heard and appreciated, when we know that our husbands are committed to us in return, before God. When we are assured of this, we can sing to our hearts' content! We can try variations of the melodies that we discover, and we find that our voices become more expressive as we use them for the glory of God.

Think for a moment about the hymns and songs that we sing to Jesus, the Bridegroom of the Church. Singing in worship is one of the most meaningful expressions of our love for Him. We sing as an offering of love, loyalty, thanksgiving, and joy. If we sing for the primary reason of performing for our Savior, we'll constantly be distracted from our task, wondering if we're on key and modulating correctly. But when we sing out, with the voice He has given us, not caring about anything at all other than singing *to Him only,* we are touched. As we minister to Him, He reaches forth and ministers to us. As the Body of Christ, we have learned that the offering of praise allows us to open our hearts before the living God as we worship Him "in spirit and truth."

Some of the most moving and beautiful music that has ever been written was composed so that it would bring glory to God, drawing listeners toward the Lamb who was slain so that sinners might live. Psalm 107 tells those whom the Lord has redeemed to offer, or give as a sacrifice, their thanks unto the Lord and "tell of his works with songs of joy."[5] The word *praise* can be found in 132 different verses in the *King James Version* of the Psalms, which Jewish people appropriately refer to as the Book of Praises! We are even told that the Lord *inhabits* the praises of His people.[6] In His promise of restoration to Israel, the Lord spoke through His prophet Jeremiah, saying, "There will be heard once more the sounds of joy and gladness, the voices of bride and bridegroom, and the voices of those who bring thank offerings to the house of the Lord."[7] The Lord *desires* our praises, for in them we yield ourselves to Him in song and thanksgiving.

One day during Sunday morning worship time I was struck by the similarity of what it means to open my heart up to the Lord in praise and what it means to open myself up to my husband during lovemaking. As I was singing, the words of an especially beautiful refrain were being lifted up as an offering to our Lord and Savior, and the impact of what I was doing dawned on me in a different way than it ever had before: the love that I was pouring out in song was very much like the love I pour out to my husband through my body during lovemaking! This isn't to say that Sunday worship is a sexual act! But I think the exchange of love that takes place, whether on a spiritual or a physical level, between Christ and His church, or between husband and wife, is a profound mystery and is beautiful beyond our expectations and abilities to realize it much of the time. The openness of our hearts is a key to being able to receive all that the Lord wants to bestow upon us.

Opening Up to One's Husband

It is a sacrifice to open up one's heart and body to one's husband. This is true for many reasons:

Sexual openness makes us vulnerable. When we share the most intimate places of our bodies with our husbands, we are inviting them to share those parts of ourselves that we have always kept guarded and hidden from others. The nature of female sexuality is different from that of men in that making love requires us to be entered into, with lovemaking taking place on the inside of us rather than just on the outside. This produces a feeling of vulnerability because we must share a part of ourselves that we associate with what we need to protect and guard; these feelings don't vanish overnight. It takes time to be able to feel safe and open during lovemaking.

Sexual openness reveals the depths of our femininity. We cannot escape the facts of our design when we make love! The same passageway that we menstruate and give birth through is that with which we caress the penis during lovemaking. If we are uncomfortable with other aspects of our womanhood, we will be unable to be fully responsive vaginally. It is only when we are at peace with the way God has designed our bodies that we can begin to explore the depths of our feminine nature.

Sexual openness reveals the depths of our husbands' masculinity. There is no getting around the reality of how the Lord designed the male body when the genitals are exposed during lovemaking! Being comfortable with the physical realities of one another's genitals, including the way they look, smell, and feel, is a necessary prerequisite for sexual openness between married lovers. Our husbands' bodies are likely to seem very foreign to us initially, causing us to look away or avoid intimately touching them. As we mature, we can explore the masculine features of our husbands' sexuality and learn to be as comfortable and familiar with their bodies as we are with our own.

Sexual openness reminds us of our creatureliness. When we open up sexually, our body chemistry changes in ways that can make us feel animal-like and instinctive rather than civilized and in control of what we do and say every moment. The physiology of lovemaking results in a feeling of abandonment and physical excitement that is unlike any other human experience. Our socialization has taught us to be in control of every situation that we find ourselves in rather than following the dictates of our bodies' desires. After all, if we had a banana split every time we wanted one, we'd really be in trouble! Self-control is a necessary part of our existence, evidence that we are able to resist sin and live in harmony with others. When it comes to lovemaking, however, it is beneficial to open up sexually to our life partners—and the expression of our sexuality is often full of surprises! The more we try to maintain control over how our bodies respond during sexual arousal, the less likely they are to be aroused at all.

Sexual openness is meant to be mutual, reciprocal, and complementary. Most women don't feel sexy 100 percent of the time. If we did, how would we ever manage to get anything done? Our days are filled with busyness. When the end of the day arrives, it's often easier to satisfy just our husbands' sexual needs rather than opening ourselves up to having our needs met as well. Many women would prefer a back rub or a nice long evening of hugs to passionate lovemaking after a long, busy day. There isn't anything wrong with this occasionally, but it can become habitual, a rut that gets more and more difficult to climb out of. Sexual pleasure is meant to be shared rather than seen as a gift or a need that was given to one sex alone. Sometimes it takes some pretty creative planning to be sexually active at the end of a tiring day.

Sexual openness often results in unpredictable outcomes. When we experience a state of sexual arousal, we are liable to say and do things that can seem somewhat embarrassing and ridiculous later! This is why privacy is *essential*. A good lock on the bedroom door and soft music playing in the background can offer a sense of security when there are others living in the house. We must be especially careful not to say things to our husbands later that will make fun of their sexual responses in a way that will embarrass or ridicule them. We should avoid sharing the intimate details of our sex lives with anyone except our husbands. These are a few examples of ways privacy and trust can be developed if lovemaking is to be fully expressive and playful as well as being an exclusive bond that is shared by a husband and wife outside the demands and stress of their everyday activities.

Sexual openness takes us beyond ourselves. Making love is an adventurous experience each time we participate in it. That is because it is full of risks! It takes us beyond ourselves and into the body and heart of our husbands. The Biblical reality of what it means to become "one flesh" is mysterious, and at times seems almost supernatural! It can be difficult to tell where the "I" ends and the "you" begins. Through lovemaking, two separate individuals are transformed into one, inexplicably, and the pleasure that we *receive* from this experience seems to be the same as the pleasure that we *give* when sexual expression is at its best. Love flows back and forth between a husband and wife during sexual sharing and lifts them beyond their separate selves and into a joint identity before God. We are told to honor God with our bodies;[8] within marriage, our sexuality finds its proper expression as we use it for the purpose for which it was created.

Femininity Is Multidimensional

Female sexuality, as we have seen, is not something that can be understood in mechanical terms. Sexual arousal is not brought about by pressing a set of buttons and getting the same reaction every time we want to turn the engine on! Many marriage manuals give step-by-step instructions for lovers to follow that remind me of a "how-to-use" manual. Any experienced woman knows that it is absurd to expect the same reactions every time, because femininity is multidimensional. Sexual responsiveness can vary with the time of day, the time of the month, the time of year, and the time of life. It is affected by our moods, hormones, physical condition, surrounding circumstances, and the situations that we have encountered in the last ten minutes or the past ten days. Sometimes arousal seems to take place almost automatically, initiated by the whisper of a meaningful word, the catching of a sideways glance, a whiff of after-shave. At times, even extended caressing and stroking produce . . . nothing! We really can't predict our responses any more than we can the weather.

This is why the whole idea of "bases" and a magical, foolproof kind of "foreplay" really misses the mark in terms of female sexuality. There just is no single "right way" to proceed every time we want to be sexually expressive. In order to relax and respond, the pressure to perform according to a mythical standard must be removed. Forever.

Each one of needs to determine what works best in our own relationships, within our own bodies, with our own husbands. This means everything from positions used for intercourse, to how best to reach an orgasm, to what clothes we think we should wear to bed—if any, what perfume to wear, when to refrain from lovemaking, and how frequently to engage in it. The Bible is completely *silent* on all of these things, other than the verses that have already been mentioned. We are not told what to touch and how to touch, how to kiss or where to kiss, or how to make love to a man. The Lord has given us the basics, which he fully expects us to abide by; beyond that, it is safe to assume that we are free to use our imaginations!

This is wonderful! There are so many books today that tell us in detail how to "do it," how many children to have, how to achieve the best orgasm, etc. There are articles on G-spots and how to reach one's "orgasmic potential" and how some orgasms are better than other orgasms. Some of the information can be educational, but it can also make us feel that somehow we just aren't measuring up to what we should be as women. For this reason, I want you to consider this book as a resource *only*. If it enables you to live life more joyously as a woman, great! But if you aren't in agreement with me or can't relate to what I'm saying, keep praying and don't stop here!

The person who ultimately has to decide what activities are pleasing to the Lord and right for your life is *you*, along with your husband. He must also be comfortable with how you approach the sexual aspect of your relationship, but don't forget that he doesn't live inside your body and he can't feel the way you do on the inside. *You are the best authority on what is sexually arousing to you and when you are most easily aroused.* As you share your reactions and perceptions with your husband, you enhance his ability to meet your sexual needs, and vice versa. Sexual openness is the result of gentle communication about one's likes and dislikes, shared with courtesy at the right place and the right time.

Be kind to yourself. The Lord loves you with an everlasting love that is exceedingly greater than you could possibly imagine. The body that He has given to you is not your enemy if you use it to honor your husband. Opening up to our sexuality is risky, but we cannot experience our femininity to its fullest if we hide or protect our bodies instead of yielding them with joy for the purpose for which they were intended within marriage.

> Like an apple tree among the trees of the forest
>   is my lover among the young men.
> I delight to sit in his shade,
>   and his fruit is sweet to my taste. . . .
> I am a wall,
>   and my breasts are like towers.
> Thus I have become in his eyes
>   like one bringing contentment.[9]

Welcoming
Your Husband

God designed the sexual union to be a truly intimate experience.
This is demonstrated by the primary word for sexual intercourse
used in the Old Testament, the Hebrew word yâdâh, "to know."
. . . Yâdâh speaks of an intimacy wherein two parties see each
other as they really are. The concept is not of some distant,
objective, or academic acquaintance but a personal, intimate and
experiential knowledge of another. Yâdâh is the same word that is
used of a believer's relationship with his God (e.g., Daniel 11:32).
To know one's marriage partner in the act of sex is analogous to
developing intimacy with God.[1]

Randy C. Alcorn,
Christians in the Wake of the Sexual Revolution

It seemed like she had waited for this night forever. As she slipped on her silky
nightgown, she dreamed of being held in her husband's arms and the intimate
ways that he would share his love for her. The picture in her mind was a
combination of scenes from the cinema and literature she had read with fascination
over the years. Songs from the wedding drifted through her mind while she dabbed
her neck with perfume and brushed her long, lustrous hair. She imagined her
husband waiting in the room beyond—he was still a mystery to her even though she
felt closer to him than any other person she had ever known. Would he find her
body pleasing? What would it feel like to make love? How would their relationship
change over time? How could she possibly grow to love him more in the years
ahead if she felt so much love tonight? Two weeks alone on this beach on the
Carribean! She felt overwhelmed by happiness as she opened the door to walk into
this aspect of her life that she had been anticipating for so long . . .

As you pictured this scene of a young bride's wedding night, what did
you imagine would be awaiting her on her honeymoon and the years
ahead? It is only in the ideal realm of fantasy that such a scene would

satisfy the character's every hope, every desire, and every secret longing waiting to be fulfilled! In "real life," for most women, lovemaking is initially disappointing compared to the romantic ideas and portrayals of sexual sharing that abound in our culture.

The glorious abandonment that is associated with lovemaking in the minds of many young women just doesn't correspond with reality. Making love is an art that is learned gradually, over quite a long period of time, as one's body relaxes and becomes familiar with the body of one's partner and as two distinctly different personalities blend together and grow to complement one another. Instant happiness is a fictitious representation of sexual harmony within marriage. The type of sexual fulfillment that satisfies our deepest longings is costly. Pretending that it isn't merely perpetuates a mythical ideal that has made many women feel inadequate because they have found it difficult to live out the dream of what lovemaking *should* be like, but often isn't.

In this chapter I'll be focusing on how women can learn to enjoy lovemaking more fully by avoiding myths, accepting the way the Lord has designed their bodies and responses to sexual arousal, and moving away from a goal-oriented "performance" model of sexual sharing.

The true goal of sexual sharing as the Lord created us is *to know our husbands,* as the Hebrew word *yâdâh* implies, so that a man and a woman may become *as one.* A Biblical approach to lovemaking emphasizes this goal rather than the worldly perspective that stresses sexual pleasure alone. Sexual pleasure in and of itself is only superficially gratifying, leaving our deepest needs for intimacy and safety unfulfilled. If we are to give and receive the gift of our sexuality as the God-created aspect of our lives that it is, we must recognize that our culture's current emphasis on "me-ness" rather than oneness is in opposition to the Biblical norms that have been presented in earlier chapters, while at the same time acknowledging how important it is to gain a personal appreciation of our own uniqueness. In other words, we must try to find a balance between complete self-absorption and total selflessness. Both extremes warp the theme of marital sexuality and turn sexual sharing into a dissatisfying, empty experience.

Avoiding Myths and Confusing Folklore

There are a number of myths and "old wives' tales" that are responsible for creating inhibitions that prevent women from being free to explore marital sexuality or experience sexual intimacy with their husbands. Let's take a look at the most prevalent misconceptions and what we can do to refute them:

1. *Lovemaking is always more enjoyable for men than it is for women.*
    It is true that lovemaking is often initially uncomfortable for most

women as the hymen that partially covers the entrance to the vagina is gradually stretched to accommodate a man's penis. Since anxiety is often present, the muscles of the pelvic floor may be quite tense until a woman learns how to creatively use these muscles during intercourse. New sensations that are experienced can be confusing and even alarming at first as a woman learns to open a very private place to receive her husband. Many women are surprised to discover that the vagina is a tender and sensitive organ that is not necessarily as responsive to stimulation as the clitoris is. The muscles that surround the vagina, termed the pubococcygeus or P.C. group, are believed to be more sensitive to pressure in their ability to convey pleasurable sensations during lovemaking. The responsiveness of the P.C. group is directly related to their strength and flexibility. The strength of the P.C. group can be promoted by doing exercises (see Chapter 13), and their ability to stretch is learned during exercises that teach women how to relax as well as tense these muscles.

Some women find that a particular area of the vagina is capable of producing pleasing sensations when pressure is applied to it during lovemaking or when their husbands touch them there. This area lies just behind the urethra on the front wall of the vagina and feels like a sponge that is about the size of a dime. When stimulated, it enlarges and grows to be the size of a nickel or a quarter. Women who have strong P.C. muscles bring this area into better contact with the penis by tensing their pelvic floor during lovemaking. Since this "urethral sponge" responds best to deep pressure, there are some positions that can be used during lovemaking that enable the penis to apply greater pressure to this area: rear entry, woman above, and man above, with woman's knees brought toward her chest or a pillow used under her hips.

It takes time for a woman to learn how to complement, rather than match, her husband's sexuality. In discovering how her body responds to her husband's body, a woman can find an almost endless variety of ways to make love creatively and pleasurably. Lovemaking is just like any other skill: it is learned and developed instead of inherited or acquired through instinct. A man and wife actually *teach each other* how to respond to one another's bodies and how to make their sexual relationship mutually satisfying.

Women have been created with the ability to enjoy lovemaking every bit as much as men do, but there is a difference. Lovemaking for men is almost automatically enjoyable; women must be willing to share their bodies openly with their husbands and communicate their responses to their spouses. Time, energy, and motivation are required to learn the womanly art of sexual responsiveness. As with any other skill, patient practice is essential. Unlike many other talents a woman might have, the art of lovemaking takes place in the privacy of marriage and is developed as a gift for one's husband alone. It is a skill that unfolds over the years as a

THE MAP OF SEXUAL RESPONSE

Figure 6-1

Feminine Response

EXCITEMENT/ arousal	PLATEAU/ pleasuring	ORGASM/ release	RESOLUTION/ recovery
EXTERNAL SIGNS:			
- clitoris becomes longer - outer lips open, flatten - inner lips swell, darken - nipples become erect - breasts become larger	- clitoris withdraws under its hood - inner lips turn red, enlarging about one minute prior to orgasm - pelvis moves rhythmically - muscles become tense	- no noticeable change in external genitals - facial muscles become tense - gasping may occur	- external genitals return to normal size and color - skin may perspire - body relaxes - breasts and nipples return to normal state
INNER SIGNS:			
- uterus rises in pelvis - vaginal lining lubricates	- Pulse, breathing rate, and blood pressure become elevated - inner ⅔ of vagina widens - outer ⅓ of vagina swells and tightens, forming the orgasmic platform - uterus rises higher	- pelvic floor contracts 3-12 times - uterus contracts rhythmically - heart and breathing rates rise more - woman feels her entire body respond with pleasure	- vagina relaxes, thins out - uterus drops back into its normal position overlying the bladder - cervix drops into seminal pool to encourage conception

woman grows closer to her husband. Perfection isn't the goal for which this art is nurtured, because being the "best" is not what a woman is aiming for in this area of her life. Love, the kind that flows from a heart that has received much from God, is the purpose and the end to which we are called within marriage. Sexual expression that is rooted and grounded in love is fulfilling, even when lovemaking is awkward, humorous, or initially embarrassing. Each encounter can be a new revelation rather than an end in itself, a fresh look into the husband with whom you have made a covenant to share life's journey.

2. *"Vaginal" orgasm is more fulfilling, more complete, more feminine, or more mature than "clitoral" orgasm.*

This belief can be traced to Sigmund Freud, the father of psychoanal-

THE MAP OF SEXUAL RESPONSE

Masculine Response

EXTERNAL SIGNS:

- penis becomes erect as it fills with blood - scrotum rises, thickens	- penis becomes darker in color, swells more - scrotum becomes thicker - muscles tense, pelvis moves rhythmically - pre-ejaculatory fluid drips from penis	- penis contracts rhythmically, expels semen - facial muscles tense, gasping occurs	- erection subsides - scrotum thins out, droops - body muscles relax - skin may perspire

INTERNAL SIGNS:

- no significant changes	- testes become larger - pulse, breathing, and blood pressure become elevated - prostate and seminal vesicles contract just prior to ejaculation	- entire seminal duct system contracts - pelvic floor tightens - pulse, breathing, and blood pressure rise more - man feels pleasure concentrated in his genital area	- testes return to normal size, drop - relief is felt as blood leaves genital area

ysis. He believed that any orgasm resulting from directly touching the clitoris was "childish" due to its association with genital exploration during infancy and later in masturbation. He stated that it is only when a woman "grows up" and graduates from her earlier levels of sexual experience that she would become capable of achieving a "mature" kind of orgasm that Freud associated with sexual intercourse.

There are several problems with Freud's theory. In studying human sexuality, Masters and Johnson defined four identifiable phases of sexual response. They defined these as: the excitement phase, characterized by arousal; the plateau phase (pleasuring); orgasm (release); and the resolution phase (recovery). Figure 6-1 outlines these phases and the physical events that are associated with them. Notice the differences and the similarities between the sexual responses of males and females and how the Lord has designed our bodies to correspond with our husbands. You can also see that the characteristics of a female's orgasm consist of a combination of physical activities that are fairly predictable. These activities take place with varying intensity from woman to woman and within the same woman at different times.

While some women may never have an orgasm and feel quite satisfied in their sexual relationships, other have found that the experience of having an orgasm is one of the most physically rewarding aspects of their sexuality. Whether a woman has an orgasm through vaginal or clitoral stimulation is beside the point: sexual sharing is to be mutually pleasing and beneficial between husband and wife, and the Bible isn't terribly explicit about the specifics! We aren't meant to compare ourselves against a "standard model" of how to achieve an orgasm, and the Lord has clearly given most women the ability to experience this phase of sexual response. This is a matter for couples to discuss so they can develop an awareness of one another's preferences and needs.

There is no discernible difference between an orgasm that is produced by stimulating the vagina and one that results from clitoral stimulation. Most women have a preference of one over the other, but this seems to be purely a matter of personal preference. The differences are subjective, a matter of opinion, and quite frankly, nobody else's business!

What a relief it is that the Lord has created women with the ability to enjoy their sexuality as well as be a source of pleasure for their husbands. Since Freud held many beliefs that contradict Biblical teachings, why are Christians often using a Freudian model to interpret their sexuality?

3. *Having an orgasm at the same time as one's husband during love-making is the best way to achieve an orgasm during intercourse.*

Herbert Miles in his excellent book, *Sexual Happiness in Marriage,* states that in his surveys of sexual behavior, only 13.7 percent of the couples that he studied reported that they regularly experienced having an orgasm at the same time. The vast majority of couples seem to prefer experiencing this phase of sexual response at different times. This is likely to be due to the fact that having an orgasm is an intensely personal experience, and it is hard to focus on one's partner during the brief time that an orgasm takes place. Also, keeping track of one's "timing" can be terribly distracting, with each partner thinking "Is it happening yet?" instead of abandoning himself or herself to the joys of lovemaking.

A sense of oneness during lovemaking is not merely the result of performing sexual acrobatics. It is produced by an intense desire to please one's partner and by an attitude of mutual submission. Once again, it is self-defeating to try to live up to someone else's ideas of what "good sex" is because we fail to discover our own uniquely personal ways of expressing our sexuality with our husbands. What is meaningful and special to one woman might seem boring or shocking to another. Having an orgasm, or "coming," at the same time is not the "best" way of achieving an orgasm for all couples. For the 13.7 percent of the couples who said it was in Miles' study, this indeed was an enjoyable aspect of lovemaking; but we should avoid the perspective that what makes *us* feel best will also be what's "best" for others.

4. *Lovemaking should last for as long as possible if intercourse is to be truly fulfilling.*

This belief is probably related to the idea that it is best for a woman to have an orgasm during intercourse or for a couple to experience orgasm at the same time. Since many women require fairly direct stimulation of the clitoris in order to have an orgasm, lovemaking must take place over an extended period to sufficiently excite the nervous tissue of the clitoris. When a couple is focused on this "goal" to the exclusion of genuine enjoyment during lovemaking, the experience can become one of *work* rather than *play*.

The "average" male reaches the point of ejaculation within the first two to four minutes of lovemaking. For a man to partake in extended lovemaking, he must often avoid an extended amount of pleasuring beforehand. When he does make love, if he is emotionally as well as physically aroused he usually must think of something else (other than his wife or the pleasure that he feels) in order to avoid having an orgasm. How strange it is that lovemaking is often turned into an athletic event to determine if a man can "go the distance" while performing like a super-lover and at the same time keeping his mind *off* his wife! It's his wife that he should be thinking about, not playing a mind game that transports him away from a sense of oneness with his partner. When a man has an ejaculation the instant he starts making love, some training is in order. But for the man who wants to make love freely, why should he have to live up to some sort of image that forces him to distance himself from his wife during lovemaking?

The majority of time that most couples spend in sexual sharing takes place throughout the pleasuring, or plateau, phase of sexual response rather than during intercourse. Characterized by caressing, kissing, rubbing, squeezing, and stroking, this phase creates an emotional openness and often results in a couple moving ahead to intercourse. It is as if the Lord designed us with a built-in need as women that would require us to have a time of physical closeness and skin-to-skin contact with our husbands prior to being able to experience sexual release through orgasm.

The extensive amount of touching and fondling that takes place during pleasuring promotes bonding, or feelings of attachment, between a wife and her husband. It is during this phase of sexual expression that a woman becomes increasingly more able to open her body up to her husband and "let down her guard." (See Figure 6-2.) Also, stroking of the skin enhances the autonomic nervous system's ability to relax the body

THE MYSTERY OF WOMANHOOD

and thereby allow blood to flow into the genitals. When the plateau phase produces an atmosphere of intimacy as well as heightening sexual arousal, intercourse becomes the natural extension of lovemaking rather than an end in itself. When the "act" of intercourse becomes the goal of all sexual sharing and every sexual encounter between a husband and wife, it is possible for a couple to miss out on the joys that accompany this phase and the emotional satisfaction that it produces. When the pressure to perform according to a mythical standard is removed, a couple is free to become more creative, expressive, and adventuresome in respect to the sexual aspects of their relationship.

THE PATTERN OF SEXUAL RESPONSE

Figure 6-2

EXCITEMENT PHASE	PLATEAU PHASE	ORGASMIC PHASE	RESOLUTION PHASE
Main Characteristic: Arousal	Main Characteristic: Pleasuring	Main Characteristic: Orgasm	Main Characteristic: Recovery
Sign in Male: erection	Intercourse may proceed at any time	Sign in Male: ejaculation	This phase is reversible for many women
Sign in Female: lubrication	This phase usually makes up the majority of lovemaking time	Sign in Female: contractions of the pelvic floor muscles	Most men experience a period that does not allow them to become erect, called the refractory period
		orgasmic contractions	
	Arousal in the male is approaching "the point of no return"		
Husband has been thinking about making love all evening			
		Male reaches the point of "ejaculatory inevitability"	
	Wife is just beginning to think about making love		. . . . . . : female ———— : male

This diagram represents a typical sexual response pattern for men and women. Of course, many variations in the length and intensity of each phase are possible. The important thing is to learn to please one another through sexual expression that is mutually satisfying.

Adapted from Masters, W. and Johnson, V.: *Human Sexual Response* (1966)

5. *Deep thrusting of the penis is an important aspect of intercourse.*

This isn't necessarily true! Since many women find that the most responsive parts of their anatomy are the clitoris, the external portion of the vagina (approximately the first two inches), the P.C. muscles, and the breasts, how could this belief possibly mesh with reality? Obviously, it doesn't in all cases.

When a woman becomes sexually aroused, it is likely that the outer third of her vagina will swell, causing it to become "tighter" and more restricted in diameter. This creates what is known as an *orgasmic platform*. (See Figure 6-3.) There is a dual purpose behind this physiological event: the tightening that takes place allows a woman to grip the penis more firmly while experiencing greater pleasure during lovemaking, and a seal is formed so that when semen is deposited in the vagina there will be a better chance of it remaining there as a means of promoting conception.

ORGASMIC PLATFORM, SEMINAL POOL

Figure 6-3

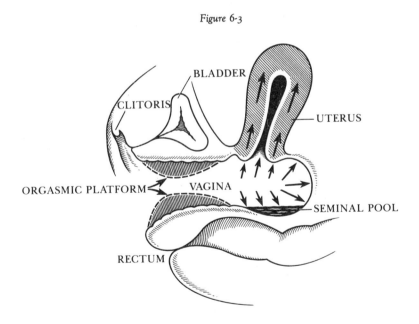

When the penis is forcefully thrust deeply into the vagina without a woman's guidance, there may be very little satisfaction in lovemaking; when movements of the penis are directed toward stimulating areas that are more sexually responsive, there is greater friction exerted against the orgasmic platform and the urethral sponge. Another advantage to a woman providing feedback for her husband during lovemaking is that she can obtain better contact with the clitoris if she finds that this area is more sexually responsive than vaginal stimulation alone. By using a variety of positions, pelvic movements, and rhythms, a woman may find herself surprised by the degree of responsiveness she is capable of!

The rhythm of lovemaking, the depth of penetration, and the length of time spent making love with one's husband will vary with a woman's mood, level of sexual desire, the setting, the time of the month, the amount of energy she has, and the ability she has to communicate her needs to her husband. Lovemaking need not always be cautious, slow, or concentrated on stimulating specific areas. In fact, there are times when it's terrific to get totally carried away! Since we have been created with the ability to experience such variety in this area of our lives, why settle for an oil-rig approach to lovemaking when it can be more like an intimate conversation?

6. *Men have a greater "sex drive" than women.*

Notice the period that lies at the end of that sentence. That little bit of punctuation is what makes it a myth! It isn't true that men have a greater "sex drive" than women, *period*. Men's and women's bodies have been designed to be affected by thoughts and feelings, culture and environment, values and beliefs, lifestyles and attitudes. While it is often true that men have a greater desire for expressing their sexuality through sexual intercourse than women do, it is conversely true that women often have a greater need for expressing their sexuality through caressing and nongenital forms of sexual sharing.

It is easy to adapt an outlook that views only intercourse as the end-all and be-all of sexual interaction—after all, that is what our culture has taught us to believe. But we cannot dismiss the fact that the Lord has created our bodies with a fabric of skin that responds favorably (and sexually) to touch. When we place the focus of sexual sharing on orgasm or intercourse, we can miss out on the marvelous ways our Creator has established for us to express our love through touch and nongenital expressions of our sexuality. *This aspect of sexuality is experienced by many women as a physical need that is just as deep as a male's need for intercourse.* Does this mean that women are less sexual than men, or is it that we're actually made to complement one another in these areas?

This myth can also be disputed when we consider that sexual desire fluctuates during the life cycle. There may be times when women experience a more intense desire to make love than their husbands. Most males reach a peak of feeling the need for sexual release when they are in their late teens to midtwenties, whereas females are often "late bloomers," resulting in a greater desire for sexual interaction in their thirties and forties. While these patterns vary from person to person, we can be encouraged by the fact that sexual desire isn't static, but changes with the seasons of our lives. When we consider that marriage is intended to last for life, it's reassuring to know that men and women can enhance one another's sexuality by "peaking" at different times. Just as a husband's interest might be waning, the female's body may kick into gear and renew the relationship!

It is unfair to compare male and female sexuality in terms of which gender has the greatest sex drive when the Lord created us to express our sexuality differently from one another, with a man and woman each contributing their own unique blend of feelings and abilities to the marital relationship. Whoever said "Variety is the spice of life" really knew how to cook!

7. *The thing that men like best about sex is intercourse itself.*

This commonly held belief doesn't fit the Christian model of sexual expression within marriage. For the hedonist, penile stimulation may be the pinnacle of sexual experience; but for a Christian husband, the sexual responsiveness of his wife brings him greater joy and satisfaction than do mere physical sensations alone. Women often wrongly assume that their husbands are more interested in their own bodies than in the bodies of their wives. What a surprise it is when a woman discovers that the source of her husband's sexual fulfillment springs from *her* openness and excitement!

There is a tendency to view male sexuality as being selfish and female sexuality as being sacrificial. Song of Songs refutes this line of thinking. It is Solomon's *reaction* to his wife that seems to give him the greatest pleasure—the more she responds to him, the more joy he seems to experience. He barely speaks of his own reactions, but refers over and over again to how delightful his wife is![2] When he finally does speak of himself, it is in reaction to the Shulammite's openness with her body.[3] The belief that men "will take whatever they can get sexually" is harmful and not based on a Scriptural perspective of sexuality. The Lord created men and women with the capability of finding their source of sexual fulfillment in each other rather than alone.

Because of the way our culture portrays male sexuality, men are expected to want to have sex with the greatest variety of partners possible in order to prove their masculinity. We need to be careful that we see our husbands as God created them to be—with the ability to express their love through the physical design of their bodies toward their wives—instead of assuming that all men are sex-starved and always "on the prowl." The desire that a man expresses towards his wife is not the same as lust: it is a natural desire that God created men to have for the purpose of enhancing marriage. Yet how many times do we react to our husbands by thinking,

81

"He only wants my body" or "He isn't interested in what I've gone through today—all he wants is sex"? How many times have Christian wives rebuffed their husbands when a hand has reached out to touch a breast or lips have yearned to be kissed? *God made our husbands to respond to us that way!* We can rejoice that He did, for the physical bond that is created through sexual sharing is a strong one.

Unfortunately, many wives declare that the "honeymoon is over" when they realize just how often and how intensely their husbands desire to be physically close to them. It may be okay *initially,* but somewhere along the line women begin to wonder when things will "settle down." May our prayer be that things will never cool off instead!

Even Shulamith struggled with her husband's continuous desire for her.[4] Her relationship to Solomon deepened when she realized that she *needed* her husband as much as he *wanted* her. Their relationship matured after she dreamed that she had rejected him, and it was after this that she spoke lovingly of his body for the first time (5:10-16) in a manner similar to how her husband had spoken of hers (4:1-15).

Think for a moment about what you like the most about your husband's sexuality, his body, and his lovemaking. Have you reached a place in your relationship where you can see your husband's body as a gift to you? Do you feel free to stroke and touch him intimately and respond to his eagerness? God has created your husband to be your counterpart in every respect. Are you drawn to his differences, or do they confuse or repel you? Does his desire for you make you love him all the more or make you want to run? Sexual sharing that is open and fulfilling requires that a woman be comfortable with the maleness of her husband, and the way she views his sexuality will either enhance or detract from her willingness to be sexually and emotionally available to him.

· May our prayer be as Shulamith's as we seek to respond to our husbands in ways that are pleasing and satisfying. As you read the following verses, consider Shulamith's attitude toward her body's ability to attract her husband and his overwhelmingly joyous response. What is he responding to? His union with his wife! What a picture this is of a satisfied husband! Most importantly, the Lord's benediction reassures us that He blesses this scene and invites them to fully enjoy their sexuality.

> [The Bride to Solomon:]
> Awake, north wind;
> And come, south wind!
> Blow on my garden that its fragrance
> may spread abroad.
> Let my beloved come into his garden
> And taste its choice fruits.

[Solomon to his bride:]
   I have come into my garden, my sister, my bride;
   I have gathered my myrrh with my spice.
   I have eaten my honeycomb and my honey;
   I have drunk my wine and my milk.

[The Lord:]
   Eat, O friends, and drink;
   drink your fill, O lovers.[5]

Acknowledging Your Delights

"Breasts like clusters of fruit" . . . "your mouth like the best wine" . . . "beds of spices" . . . "How beautiful you are and how pleasing, O love, with your delights!"[6] Solomon realized that his wife's natural attributes were a bountiful, aromatic treasure. Clean skin, radiant eyes, freshly washed hair, and the natural fragrance of a recently bathed body are much more appealing to embrace than heavily perfumed skin, eyes plastered with makeup, stiffly sprayed hair, and a body hidden from view in an old nightgown. Some women make themselves sexually unapproachable through their overuse of cosmetics, beauticians, and sleepwear. Rather than accept the natural beauty they were created with, they think they can improve on God's design, as if *external things* are what sexual attraction is all about. When we get right down to it, the fact of the matter is that few men probably care what makeup or lingerie their wives have on once the fun begins!

   The point of what we wear and put on is often to make *ourselves* feel more attractive because we're insecure about our faces and our bodies. What woman wouldn't feel this way in a culture that highly values perfect complexions, expensive clothing, youthfulness, and bodies with less than 12 percent body fat? Few women are 100 percent satisfied with the way they look. Cosmetics companies and clothing manufacturers have made fortunes by taking advantage of this fact. But let's consider what we are underneath it all *without* their assistance.

   In an intimate situation with one's husband, the natural odors and lubricants of a woman's body are more sensual than the most expensive products. When a woman becomes sexually aroused, the Lord has designed her body to prepare for lovemaking by making the vagina more slippery as it is moistened by a fluid secreted by the Bartholin's glands. This is a sure sign that a woman's body is responding to her husband and lets him know when his wife is sexually aroused.

   As women, we have been socialized to find this kind of thing embarrassing instead of stimulating, however! We need to remind ourselves that this natural reaction to lovemaking was designed into our bodies for the purpose of making sex more comfortable and pleasurable. Lubrication is intended to be a signal that we are relaxed and responsive rather than a warning to head for the nearest washcloth! Like Shulamith, perhaps it would be better to think of this unique fluid as a kind of spice that enlivens sexual sharing, not a nuisance that we have to put up with in order to participate in lovemaking.

Vaginal odors are another aspect of female sexuality that can make a woman feel self-conscious about her genitals. Daily bathing of this area is a sufficient means of getting rid of the bacteria that exaggerate the odor of vaginal secretions. Regular douching is not recommended as a means of cleansing the vagina because it alters the acid-base balance of the vaginal lining. When the pH of the vagina is thrown off by douching, "good bacteria" are destroyed. Harmful bacteria and other potentially troublesome organisms can thrive in the absence of bacteria that keep the vaginal tract healthy by consuming foreign germs. A condition known as vaginitis results. Vaginitis is the term that is used to describe irritation and inflammation of the vagina. (See Chapter 13 for further information.)

Oils, bubble bath detergents, and deodorant soaps should be avoided in women who have recurring bladder or vaginal infections. Simply cleansing the genitals with water is normally sufficient. In addition to a daily shower or bath, getting up and using the toilet after lovemaking is an easy way to promote a feeling of cleanliness. Toilet tissue or a washcloth that has been moistened with warm water can be used to quickly wipe away secretions that are left over after lovemaking. Urinating after intercourse rinses out the lower portion of the urethra, discouraging the growth of bacteria that may have been introduced into this area during lovemaking. Any woman who has struggled with recurrent bladder infections already knows how important this is!

Vaginal health is also promoted by avoiding tight, restrictive clothing, wearing cotton underwear, using panty hose with a cotton panel between the legs, and sleeping without underwear at night. The circulation of air discourages bacterial growth and prevents the accumulation of excess moisture in the vaginal area. As long as vaginal discharge is not foul-smelling or producing itching or redness, it is considered to be perfectly harmless.

I recently read a book that was published in the 1930s that gave advice on how to achieve sexual happiness within marriage. It was a darling little book filled with many practical ideas and was obviously from a different era because it approached its subject so sweetly. The authors, a married couple, wrote about the importance of bathing before going to bed together. The even recommended changing one's daily bathing routine so that it would take place at the end of the day as a kind of "fresh start" that recognizes the value of structuring one's day around *lovemaking* instead of *work*. What a marvelous idea this is! Why not take an additional bath or shower late in the day even if you can't give up your early morning shower habit? There is nothing like getting into bed with clean skin. Showering or bathing together on occasion is a fantastic prelude to lovemaking. Who knows what might happen while you're scrubbing one another? It's a great way to save on your electric and water bills at the same time!

There's Nothing Like the Real Thing

One of the nicest things about sexual sharing within marriage is that it allows us to do away with pretenses. By this I mean that as a couple grows to be increasingly more intimate with one another, they stop trying to impress one another and can just "be themselves." Once a woman knows that her husband cares for her, she no longer has to go to extremes to make herself attractive to him.

Consider the following example: A young woman has been asked to go out on a date by a young man that she has had her eye on for quite a while. She spends hours daydreaming about him, taking days to decide what she'll wear, how she'll fix her hair, and what she'll say to him. She can't help wondering whether the upcoming date will lead to a deeper relationship. How she'd love to know what's going on in *his* head!

It's easy to imagine the kinds of things that this young woman thinks about throughout her evening out because we were once in her position. Because she sincerely wants to get to know her friend better, she is on her best behavior and tries her utmost to be congenial, attractive and, well, impressive. The young man is smitten, so he is also doing his best to display his strengths and hide his weaknesses. As their feelings for one another deepen over the months that follow, they allow themselves to become more transparent, taking greater risks in conversation as they talk about private things and share previously undisclosed hopes and dreams. They begin to think less about themselves and more about one another. Consequently, the young woman spends less and less time in front of the mirror before she sees her boyfriend and no longer worries about whether he'll see her in her old clothes or without her makeup. She wants him to know her real, true self—not a manufactured identity—for it is only when she knows that she has been accepted for who she really is that she will be able to feel that their relationship is built upon the truth of who she is.

Knowing that we are loved enables us to more closely identify ourselves with another. After all, if I haven't let you see me as I am, how will I know that you won't reject me once you see the *real* me—minus my makeup, my color-coordinated outfits, and my polite conversation?

Adam and Eve were naked before one another in body, mind, and spirit, without walls, without cover-ups, without pretense. We need not fear our natural design or the reality of being naked before our husbands when we know that we are loved and when we have dedicated our lives to Christ. Between the sheets, there isn't room for our transparent selves to share our beds with a superficial, manufactured type of sexuality. The female body as the Lord created it is *more* than capable of satisfying our partners!

There is just one small catch to all of this: there is a difference between a woman being natural and going out of her way to *avoid* looking nice. Poor hygiene, overeating or self-starvation, lack of exercise, disinterest in wearing clean, pressed clothes, and neglecting one's health are all symptoms of going too far in another direction. A healthy woman has a glow about her that is unmistakable; a woman who is depressed, bitter, resentful, or hurting deeply sometimes wears her condition in an external fashion as a signal to others that she feels victimized by her life. Thankfully, the Lord sent His precious Son to transform us, take away our sins, and set us free. We can be relieved of our burdens as we give them to the Lord. It is *costly* to be well, to become whole, to be restored to what it means to have been created in God's image: Jesus asks us to carry our share of the responsibility as we lay down our anger, our resentments, and our attitudes of self-pity and condemnation. If you feel like a failure, Jesus can make you whole again! He asks us to lay things aside, which isn't always easy, but He is tender and gentle with us as we seek to be the kind of wives that He wants us to be. He *wants* us to experience the wholesome joy of our sexuality and carries our marriages close to His heart. Each and every one of us, each and every marriage, is special to our Lord and Savior.

Finding the balance between accepting our natural, God-created beauty and doing what we can to be healthy results from earnestly desiring to portray Christ to the world through our womanhood and through our marriages. Discovering our husbands' preferences enables us to be comfortable as we live out this truth within the context of our own relationships. If your husband could care less if you wear fingernail polish, high-heels, or ruffled shirts, why wear these things? What *does* your husband prefer you to wear (or not wear!)? Does his opinion matter to you more than the latest fashion magazine's? Do you take the time to talk about your wardrobe with him? Your plans for a change in hairstyle? Or does he prefer to be kept in suspense and be surprised? Even though you don't *need* his approval as an adult woman, isn't it nice to consider his opinion? Knowing what your husband thinks can make a real difference in your ability to feel that you are desirable and attractive to him.

Relax and Enjoy

Have you ever been surprised by the strength and magnitude of your body's reactions to your husband's touches? I hope so! For it was with amazing tenderness that the Lord must have created our bodies—as well as with an incredible sense of humor!

Women don't seem to be nearly as automatic as men in terms of their sexual responsiveness. One moment a woman might be totally disinterested in sexual sharing, and then, suddenly, she can be transported to the brink of ecstasy. I don't think anyone will ever be able to completely figure this phenomenon out; so we may as well relax and enjoy the element of surprise that the Lord has blessed our lives with! Perhaps we were made this way to make life more interesting, less boring, or just plain fun at times. At any rate, a loving husband will recognize the lack of predictability that exists in his wife when it comes to sexual responsiveness and will plan accordingly.

A wise husband will know that sometimes his wife's lack of interest in sex is genuine. At other times, he'll figure out that he really has been a grump or a baby all day, so he'll apologize and say a few words to set things straight. He'll even come up with some pretty remarkable ways to convince her that she'll really be missing out if she turns down yet another wonderful opportunity to have some fun. Who said that women are more cunning than men!

When a woman is emotionally open to sharing sexually with her husband, she will become aware of sensations that will let her know that her body is becoming sexually aroused. The feelings that accompany sexual excitement are meant to be pleasant as a means of encouraging us to want to be physically close to our husbands as we draw nearer to them in intimate ways. In addition to vaginal lubrication, the signals of sexual arousal in women include swelling of the lips around the vagina and a feeling of warmth as blood rushes into the pelvic area; a tightening sensation in the breasts as the nipples and areola (the pigmented ring around the nipples) become erect and the breasts increase in size; an increase in the heart and breathing rates; and swelling of the clitoris, which is probably the most noticeable sensation of all for many women. It is as if the body is awakening from its quiet state and discovering its sexual abilities all over again.

If a woman has had premarital sexual experiences, it isn't unusual for her to associate feelings of sexual arousal with fear or guilt. Once married, memories of previous sexual encounters may cause her to emotionally withdraw from the strength of her physical reactions to sexual arousal and interfere with her ability to fully relax and enjoy the sensations that she is experiencing with her husband. Within marriage, if a woman's husband has ever had sex with her without an invitation, her reactions to sexual responsiveness might be associated with pain or sadness. If you have found yourself having difficulty in either of these areas, reread Chapter Two and pray that the Lord will help you respond to your husband without such feelings. If you find that you can't relax even after seeking the Lord, you might find it helpful to see a Christian counselor, preferably a woman, who would be able to help you resolve your feelings about your body's reactions to sexual arousal. You aren't alone—I am sure that literally thousands of women have struggled with the same feelings. Be confident in the Lord's ability to *cleanse, heal,* and *restore* you as you are conformed to His image and accept His design for your sexuality. There are no "hopeless" cases in God's kingdom! His Word is *true.* We don't have to walk in darkness once we have made the decision to accept Jesus as our Lord and Savior.

The Power of Sexual Love

Sex is powerful. That is because our sexual nature is interwoven with the most intimate, private parts of ourselves. Sex was designed by God to meet the need of Adam to be joined to another human being. It is easy to use sex to manipulate, denigrate, or fascinate another human being. But the purpose of our sexuality is to promote unity, or oneness, within marriage. A husband who is living out his Christian beliefs has no need to "conquer" his wife because a loving wife *humbles* him! A wife who is seeking to do the Lord's will in her life has no need to seduce her husband because her love for him is without guile. Love that is pure is like crystal-clear water that one can drink without fear of contamination; a polluted stream defiles anything that dares to partake of it. The power of sex, when infused with the Holy Spirit, becomes mysteriously and profoundly beautiful instead of being inherently twisted and corrupted by the carnal mind.

Our hope as Christian wives can be that we express our sexuality in pleasing ways as we seek to welcome our husbands to share our bodies through lovemaking. We can acknowledge the beauty of God's design for sexuality within marriage and the way He created our bodies to respond to the sexuality of our husbands. Good sex is *real* sex: unpretentious, freely shared, exuberantly enjoyed. Sex is a gift of God, and we know that "every good and perfect gift is from above, coming down from the Father of lights, who does not change like shifting shadows."[7] Let us receive the good gift that He has given to us as we welcome our husbands in joy and gladness!

> I will listen to what God the Lord will say;
> he promises peace to is people, his saints—
> but let them not return to folly.
> Surely his salvation is near those who fear him,
> that his glory may dwell in our land.[8]

7

Speaking
Without Words

Your hands lie open in the long fresh grass,
The finger points look through like rosy blooms:
Your eyes smile peace. The pasture gleams and glooms
'Neath billowing skies that scatter and amass.
All round our nest, far as the eye can pass,
Are golden kingcup-fields with silver edge
Where the cow-parsley skirts the hawthorn-hedge.
'Tis visible silence, still as the hour-glass.
Deep in the sun-searched growths the dragon-fly
Hangs like a blue thread loosened from the sky:
So this winged hour is dropped to us from above.
Oh! clasp we to our hearts, for deathless dower,
This close-companioned inarticulate hour
When twofold silence was the song of love.

Dante Gabriel Rossetti,
"Your Hands Lie Open"

"This close-companioned inarticulate hour when twofold silence was the song of love." What a beautiful way to describe the language that a man and woman speak with their bodies when they make love. Speaking without words through the sexual design of our bodies is what becoming lovers is all about. Becoming fluent in the language of lovemaking takes time and patience as one tries out new sounds and expressions. Each of us will sound awkward at first as we say something we have never said before or try a different way of saying the same old thing. The love songs that our bodies create during lovemaking have words that vary with each melody we share with our husbands. Each song has a rhythm and a tempo of its own; each episode of lovemaking has a character and a harmony unlike any other.

Every time a kiss is shared or two bodies are joined in lovemaking, a conversation is taking place between a wife and her husband that tells them about their love for one another. It is God who has given the gifts we share with our husbands within the shelter of marriage. When a woman looks into the eyes of the man she has vowed to spend her life with and responds to him with her body, she tells her lover a great many things about what she thinks and how she feels about him. This profoundly simple language is the way love is communicated through our sexuality. All we need to do is let our bodies do the talking!

Since every healthy male and female is born with the capacity for sexual response, the language of sexual love can be discovered with joy when feelings of fear, shame, and guilt are out of the picture. The natural, inborn responses that we are capable of do not require us to spend years of study in developing a satisfying love language. If we learn to listen and respond to the messages our bodies send to us, we will find that we do not have to work to acquire an entirely new skill because we are *already* capable of speaking in rich and meaningful ways. Our Creator has given us the ability to be sexually expressive and fully responsive with our bodies when we feel loved and accepted by our husbands.

When a woman feels silly or embarrassed about speaking with her body, she will receive little satisfaction if her side of the conversation is stilted and artificial. On the other hand, if her husband's body does most of the talking, the one way conversation that results will fall incredibly short of the dialogue that God has given them the ability to share together. Because our sexuality is so much more than our physical actions, the "speech" that we use during lovemaking is to be an expression of the totality of who we are to our husbands. Lovemaking is the experience of our bodies, our minds, and our spirits as two are blended into one flesh. If we are to bring ourselves completely into the experience of lovemaking, it cannot be done out of a sense of duty or responsibility alone. Sexual fulfillment, therefore, results from letting go as we open up our bodies to *enjoy* the way God has designed them—with hilarity at times, with passionate exultation at others. Our sexuality is a dynamic force that, when unleashed, makes time seem to stop and causes us to forget everything else that is happening in the world around us for a few moments.

The need to always be in control of the conversation during lovemaking prevents creative dialogue. A woman's past experiences, a lack of trust in her husband, or the belief that she has no right to experience or express sexual pleasure all interfere with the capacity that every woman has been given to take a full and active part in sexual sharing within marriage. We each need to give ourselves permission to release the fear we hold in our hearts that can block our ability to be sexually loving and lovable. We have been given the freedom in God's Word to say yes to the gift of our sexuality within the holy bond of marriage. It is for *this* reason, the Bible tells us, that a man is to leave his father and mother and be united to his wife.[1] We are able to make the decision to speak articulately with our bodies, to talk freely without reservation, because we know that our Heavenly Father has bestowed the gift of sexuality upon us. Accepting the ways our bodies behave and sound during lovemaking is not only possible, but is preferable to holding back the wonderful things He has created us to experience.

As your heartbeat quickens and your breathing becomes louder, relax and let it happen. If you feel like moving your pelvis with pushing or thrusting motions, go right ahead if this pleases your husband. The words of the English language (or any other for that matter) cannot fully describe the joy or the ecstasy that can take place during lovemaking that is fully relaxed and mutually satisfying. The capacity of a woman's body for responsiveness is at its absolute best when she learns to enjoy the language her body was designed to express. When we stop trying to be what we're not and accept our own styles of responsiveness, we begin to understand the tremendous range of expression we are capable of: shouting, whispering, chatting, enunciating, crying out . . . the female body speaks in all these different ways.

Personal Impressions

Our speech tends to be sloppy when we are careless, distracted, fatigued, or uneducated. The effects of stress upon sexual expression are presented in the next chapter, which presents ways to improve sexual conversation through recreation and relaxation. But what about the results of ignorance on speech patterns? Just as with verbal expression, the physical expressions of our sexuality benefit from our being able to understand the phrases, patterns, and words we are using.

In this analogy, your body is equivalent to the medium of spoken language. Like words, it is the tool that conveys a vocabulary of love to your husband. It is the means through which you send messages about how you think and feel about yourself, as well as how you communicate what you think and feel about your husband. If you take the time to understand what your feelings are about your husband's body, as well as your own, you will be able to improve your sexual relationship by facing areas that keep you from expressing yourself eloquently.

The next time you take a shower or bath—whichever is the most relaxing for you—spend some time deciphering the way you talk about your body to yourself. As you lather your skin, look at it. What are your personal impressions of this magnificent covering that God has given to you for protection and sensation? If there are folds of fat, do you view them as smooth and feminine or lumpy and ugly? Do you often think about how unattractive you are and how you wish you could look, "if only?" Do you ever think, "If only my breasts were bigger" (or smaller or fuller or firmer) or "If only my buttocks and hips weren't so wide" (or so flabby or muscular or bony)? Do you find yourself ever enjoying your body and appreciating it for all it's worth? Try that now, as your washcloth glides over the amazing fabric that covers the entire surface of your body. How does the soap feel, and what sensations does the water produce? Do you take delight in the fact that the body God has given you is able to provide you with pleasurable sensations as you bathe? In *everything* we can give thanks to God and praise Him for the loving-kindness He bestows upon us.

Have you ever witnessed the vitality and exuberance of a toddler in the bathtub? (Or had to mop the floor up after the adventure was over?!) Splashing, soaking, swishing, blowing, reveling in the wetness of it all, a young child springs with enthusiasm from one bubbly escapade to the next with apparent disregard for how loud, how messy, or how crazy it all is. Caught up in the moment, a child at this age is a bundle of spontaneous energy ready to explore the world with each new opportunity.

Is there a childlike curiosity in you that invites you to splash? To revel in the wetness of the water around you? Go ahead and blow at the bubbles and see what new shapes you can make. Growing up doesn't have to mean that simple pleasures in life such as bathing become dull or tedious. As the water wakes up your skin, sing . . . laugh . . . turn your head toward the shower spray and gargle. It is great to be alive, isn't it?

As you step out of the tub, look into the mirror and say the words that come to mind right out loud. Verbalize the first things you think of—don't filter out words that are unkind or sound stupid. After you are finished, think about what you have expressed about yourself. These words form the basis of your opinion of yourself and have a very real impact upon your ability to be sexually responsive. Do you realize how significant and valuable you *really* are?

During our vacation last summer we had the chance to return to our native state and spend some time on the shore of Lake Michigan. How I love the air there, so cool and fresh as it blows over the water and creates waves that move back and forth over the rocks and shells. The constant friction of the water over the surface of the stones lying along the shore rubs away all their rough edges. Over hundreds of years these rocks become so smooth that they look as if a sculptor has worked diligently to create them.

I walked along the shore and picked up one stone after another and marveled at how beautiful each one was and at the amazing process that went into making them. Each one appeared to be a work of art, but had no monetary worth, no price tag to signify its value. So unappreciated, and yet so significant, it survived year after year of hardening, shaping, and smoothing. The rocks in the sand were warm as I picked them up. I brushed one against my cheek and kept turning it over and over in my hand. As I looked out over the vastness of the water, I thought about a postcard I had just bought describing Michigan's state rock, called a Petoskey stone.

When we returned to our cottage, I picked up the Petoskey we had found at a sand hill the day before. I read the card once more. It told me that what I held in my hand was petrified coral, an ancient slice of history about three hundred million years old using current dating methods. I will never forget that moment, and the Petoskey stone I held that day will always be one of my prized possessions. Why? Because God used that small gray rock to teach me an important lesson about Himself. However old that rock was, it was beyond my ability to even comprehend it. Someday my life would be *older*. I realized in a new way that God, who had created this rock so long ago, loves me with an *everlasting* love. Eternity became much more real to me that day. Can you too appreciate how wonderful and mysterious it is to be loved by such a God . . . to be significant to the Creator of the universe . . . to have been given the gift of *life?* Our God is a living God who speaks to us today through His Word and through His creation:

> Love and faithfulness meet together;
> righteousness and peace kiss each other.
> Faithfulness springs forth from the earth,
> and righteousness looks down from heaven.
> The Lord ndeed will give what is good,
> and our land will yield its harvest.[2]

How Does Your Body Speak?

As you speak to yourself about the areas of your body that were specifically created for expressing sexual love, do you feel comfortable about these places? Do you enjoy sharing these areas of your body with your husband? Are you familiar enough with your body to use it to speak the language of love?

Solomon extolled the joys of female sexuality as he gave advice on the importance of being sexually faithful to one's wife:

> Let your fountain, the wife of your youth,
> be blessed, rejoice in her,
> a lovely doe, a graceful hind, let her be your companion;
> you will at all times be bathed in her love,
> and her love will continually wrap you round.
> Wherever you turn, she will guide you;
> when you lie in bed, she will watch over you,
> and when you wake she will talk to you.[3]

Another version reads, "May her breasts satisfy you always, may you ever be captivated by her love." Bathing your husband in your love . . . letting

93

THE FEMALE REPRODUCTIVE SYSTEM

Figure 7-1

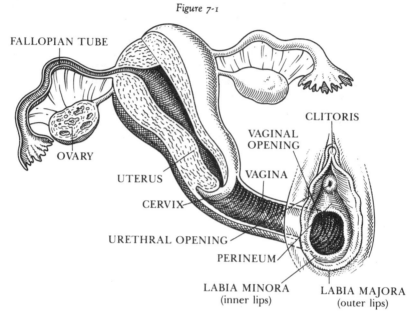

your love continually wrap him around. This is the essence of female sexuality as it is expressed through sexual sharing.

The next time you are with your husband, notice how your body responds and communicates to him. Look at your breasts. Did you know that most women have breasts that are not an identical pair? When your husband touches your nipples, how do they respond? In both men and women, there are muscle fibers that lie beneath the nipples to cause them to become erect when they are stimulated. This makes the nipples easier to grasp and is a way of telling your husband that you are responsive to his touches.

Have you found pleasure in sharing your breasts with your husband? Are you able to let him know what pleases you? Stroking, rubbing, and squeezing the nipples with the lips, tongue, fingers, or hands can produce a variety of sensations that heighten sexual arousal. If you have not explored how different types of touch feel, and how you respond to each one, perhaps you could guide your husband in stimulating you. Teach him what feels most pleasurable to you and encourage him to touch you in ways that satisfy you.

If you are unfamiliar or uncomfortable with your genitals, you will benefit from becoming more familiar with this area of your body as well. As women, our genitals are discreetly concealed between our legs and therefore are difficult to see; but our husbands have seen and touched their genitals for as long as they can remember. Because we urinate sitting down and use toilet paper afterwards, we are likely to have a minimal amount of contact with this area of our bodies compared to our husbands.

Your genitals may not seem like a very real part of you if you have never seen them or were taught that this area was "dirty" when you were a little girl. Using the diagram in this book, ask your husband to help you to identify each structure. If you wish, you may use a mirror.

You will see a fold of skin lying over the clitoris, which helps to protect the glans of the clitoris from excessive stimulation during lovemaking. The clitoris itself is a loose fold of skin with many nerve endings that extend deep beneath its surface. This delicate structure is designed to bloom like the soft petals of a flower as it swells with blood during sexual arousal. The number of nerve endings in the clitoris vary greatly from woman to woman, accounting for some of the differences that exist in the responsiveness of this organ among women. Some women require very direct stimulation of the clitoris to reach orgasm, while others merely press their thighs together or receive indirect stimulation during lovemaking in sufficient amounts to reach this response.

Your husband will enjoy learning more about your body as you are able to be more open with him. It will also be helpful for you to become intimately familiar with your husband's body. Ask him to show you how he

FEMALE EXTERNAL GENITALIA

Figure 7-2

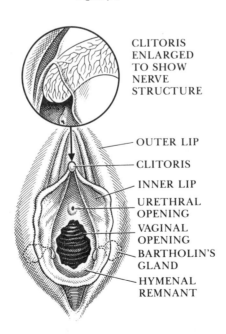

CLITORIS
ENLARGED
TO SHOW
NERVE
STRUCTURE

OUTER LIP
CLITORIS
INNER LIP
URETHRAL
OPENING
VAGINAL
OPENING
BARTHOLIN'S
GLAND
HYMENAL
REMNANT

NERVE ENDINGS SENSITIVE
TO SEXUAL STIMULATION

Figure 7-3

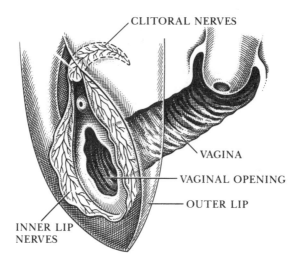

CLITORAL NERVES

VAGINA

VAGINAL OPENING

OUTER LIP

INNER LIP
NERVES

likes to be stroked and kissed. What areas does he say are the most sensitive? What types of stimulation give him the most pleasure?

Notice the texture of skin on the different areas of his body. As you consider the ways that his body complements yours, what impresses you most about your differences? Your similarities? What are the positive things that you feel about your husband's body? Is there anything about his physical form that embarrasses you?

Think about how perfectly suited his genitals are to yours. As his body responds to yours, and yours to his, express your delight in ways that will encourage him to feel accepted by you. The harmony of your interaction is what "making beautiful music together" is all about! It is your loving Creator who has given each of you this ability. Are you able to joyfully acknowledge His gift to you with thanksgiving?

There are so many ways for you to touch your husband. Encourage him to tell you what he finds enjoyable, and be creative. Surprise him with the pleasure that *you* receive from touching *him*. Listen to what your body is "saying" as it seeks to lovingly respond to the exciting ways your husband's body expresses his love for you. Who would have thought that two people could converse so silently, with a love language that is theirs alone?

Teaching each other about the sexually responsive areas of your bodies will help to dispel the fears and ignorance that you may have concerning one another's differences. Each of us have different tastes and our own

MALE REPRODUCTIVE SYSTEM
(SIDE VIEW)

Figure 7-4

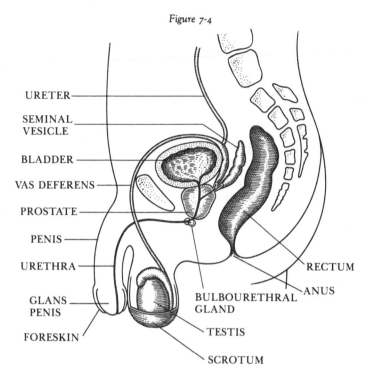

URETER

SEMINAL VESICLE

BLADDER

VAS DEFERENS

PROSTATE

PENIS

URETHRA

GLANS PENIS

FORESKIN

RECTUM

ANUS

BULBOURETHRAL GLAND

TESTIS

SCROTUM

unique set of responses to lovemaking. It is not unlike the differences that exist between people in their tastes for different foods. What if you were to cook the same meal twice every month that your husband totally disliked but was too embarrassed to tell you about? Wouldn't you much rather know his opinion instead of continuing to fix him food that he could not stand to eat? The only way for you to discover what his preferences are would be for him to communicate that to you.

Learning to be sexually intimate with one another as husband and wife is no different. You each have the right and the responsibility to inform one another of your preferences before engaging in any sexual activity that might cause one of you to feel uncomfortable or embarrassed. In this way, the two of you will come up with many successfully combined recipes for lovemaking!

If you have been unfulfilled by the way your husband touches you or responds to you, it may be because you have yet to explore the types of touch that feel best to you or to learn which areas are the most responsive during lovemaking. Either you or your husband can try using different types of touch to discover what areas of your genitals are most responsive.

97

In many women, the clitoris is by far the most sensitive area, but there is no one "right" way to touch it.

The glans of the clitoris is almost unbearably sensitive during the peak of sexual arousal in much the same way that the penis is. Stroking, rubbing, or pressing along the sides, the base, or the top of the clitoris all create different sensations. Together, you and your husband will discover what will feel best as you relax and enjoy the pleasurable sensations that this part of your body was designed to produce.

During clitoral stimulation, you may also wish to explore what effects vaginal stimulation produces by having your husband touch this area at the same time, or you may want to have him stimulate this area all by itself. You will discover that the walls of your vagina are able to stretch open or close tightly through your use of the pelvic floor muscles that surround it. This area is capable of birthing a baby with a head size of up to fifteen inches in diameter! This is due to the pleats, or rugae, that allow this muscular membrane to stretch so well.

The muscle group that makes up the pelvic floor is actually what is stimulated through the vaginal wall during lovemaking, producing sensations that are pleasurable to both the wife and her husband (see Figure 7-5). These muscles are what contract during orgasm and grip the penis during intercourse. Can you tighten these muscles around your husband's fingers or penis when he touches you there? Just squeeze them as if you were closing the openings to your bowels and bladder *very* tightly. He will feel a ring of muscles tighten about one and a half to two and a half inches

VAGINAL MUSCLES

Figure 7-5

CONTRACTION MUSCLE

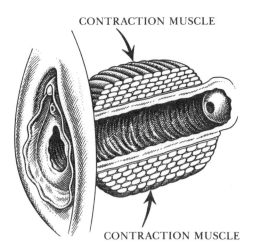

CONTRACTION MUSCLE

up within your vagina. Ask him to press the top, sides, and bottom of the ridge that he feels and let him know what sensations this produces. Have him try stroking the tightened area along the rear wall of the vagina (toward your rectum) and along the front (underneath your bladder). Then he may go deeper beyond the muscular area to see how your vagina widens and expands. What areas are most sensitive? Let him know if any of the sensations are especially arousing or uncomfortable. Compare light touch to firm pressure, and share what feels best. Take your time. There is no need to hurry, and you need not be embarrassed to guide your husband's hands as you teach him how to satisfy you.

What Can You Say with Your Body?

Now that you are more familiar with the places within your body that provide you with the greatest pleasure, you will be able to speak elegantly with those private, special words that your body has been created to say. There are an endless number of ways to say, "I love you" through intimate sexual contact with your husband. Boredom in the bedroom can be like boredom in any conversation. What if you had exactly the same dialogue with someone every time you were with that person? You probably would stop listening to what that person was saying after a while and focus your attention on something more interesting. The Lord seems to have made us with a need for diversity as well as stability. In lovemaking, it is no different.

Varying positions, as well as settings, can allow you to say new things with your body when you make love. When a couple naturally arrives at a new idea together and isn't afraid to experiment, memorable interludes result. Varying the time of day, when possible, will allow you to see how changes in your energy level affect your responsiveness. Music, candlelight, clothing, and accouterments such as feathers or wool may all be used to enliven lovemaking. Powders and perfume, or aromatic candles, can make a woman feel more sensuous as well. If women put as much thought and planning into sexual sharing as they do into a sewing project or the evening meal, their latest work assignment or newest volunteer effort, there would be many more happy marriages. Creativity, as well as spontaneity, is what makes sex so fun. Showering together, being playful with one another, and sending out the signal that you are interested in making love ("Now? Here?") are just a few of the ways to add spice to your marriage.

By varying the positions you make love in, you will find that different angles produce different sensations and allow for a different range of movement. In a face-to-face position with the husband above, an intimacy is shared that makes a woman feel protected. This positon, however, is restrictive to movement at times. The wife can put her legs nearly together, on the inside of her husband's thighs with his legs on the outside, to allow him greater freedom of movement and to decrease the depth of penetration. Another variation would be for the wife to elevate her hips by putting a pillow underneath herself, which would allow for deeper penetration. If a woman raises her knees up toward her chest, or even puts her legs up toward her husband's shoulders, this also enables him to move more freely. Each of these positions allows for different sensations and a different tempo.

When the wife is in the above position for lovemaking, her husband can view her body even after intercourse begins. She may choose to sit or squat, kneel or lie down. Because a woman's body is usually smaller than her husband's, a woman has a wide range of possible movements as she finds the rhythm of lovemaking conversation that fits her mood. Manual stimulation of the clitoris is generally easier in this position as well. If your husband enjoys looking at your body and seeing how you respond to him during lovemaking, this position is an excellent way of meeting his needs. You can also face away from him if you are on top by turning toward his feet. But watch out—things can get quite carried away if you make love this way!

Other variations can involve whether you are sitting down or standing up. A woman can sit on a chair, edge of the bed, or other supportive surface and have her husband kneel or stand in front of her during lovemaking. This is an especially useful position during late pregnancy when pressure on the abdomen is uncomfortable. Where she places her legs or knees will vary the angle and depth of lovemaking.

Lying side by side during lovemaking produces greater friction within the vagina because of the pressure exerted there by the thighs. If a woman turns around so that her back is facing toward her husband, they may lie in an X-shape or "spoons together" position. Other variations of the husband-behind position can be accomplished in a standing or kneeling position as well. The main disadvantage to this posture is that eye contact between the couple is lost, but the pleasure that is gained through the angle of lovemaking can increase sexual enjoyment for both partners. The closer a woman's chest is to her knees while kneeling, the deeper the penetration will be. In these positions the husband has a greater range of control over the depth and rhythm of lovemaking as he responds to his wife's behavior and expressions.

Marriage is to last a lifetime. There is no reason to hurry and try to achieve some sort of world's record for the number of positions tried in a single week or month or year. There are many intimate conversations that will take place over your years together, and some years will bring more satisfaction than others. There will be plenty of chances to try new and exciting things during your relationship. You are able to say so many things with your body! At times you will talk slowly and marvel at the ability of your body to make love-talk throughout an entire evening with your husband. There will be many moments when all you will have time for is a five-minute explosion of joy. As you learn to listen to your body and hear what your husband's body is saying in response to yours, you will know when and how to vary your movements, how long you both will want lovemaking to last, and what you are interested in trying at a given time. No two conversations will ever be exactly the same.

Because women were created to be both givers and receivers of the gift of their sexuality, it is truly fascinating to discover the strength and beauty of your sexual responsiveness. The intensity of feeling that a woman is capable of can be just as surprising at sixty-two as it is at twenty-two.

Alternate Expressions

There are times during a woman's life cycle when she may be unable to actively participate in lovemaking or days when the pressures of daily living drain her level of sexual desire. For these reasons, it is important to examine the role that pleasurable touch plays in satisfying a couple's sexual needs. The Bible clearly mandates the value of sexual release within marriage without pauses, except for the purpose of spending time in prayer and fasting by mutual consent.

Loving caresses and stimulation of the genitals leading to sexual release involve sexual behavior that is not specifically addressed in the Bible. "Do not deprive each other," states Paul.[4] But what is a couple to do when a woman takes months to recover after giving birth? Or during lactation when a mother's estrogen levels fall and her sex drive plummets too? Or following a disabling accident . . . or after surgery that temporarily requires her to cooperate with the healing process as she recuperates?

Clearly, our bodies were designed to be able to achieve sexual release without penetration, as were our husbands'. If sexual expression within marriage is to be consistent and mutually satisfying, each couple must consider the needs of both partners when intercourse itself is undesirable or not feasible. A husband and wife should avoid neglecting this vital part of their relationship even during times of stress, illness, recuperation, and childbearing.

The hormonal differences that exist between men and women account for a certain amount of the contrast in their sex drives as well. Presumably, most men will have consistently higher expectations for the frequency of sexual sharing, partly because their bodies produce high levels of testosterone, which is the hormone that is closely linked to producing the desire for sexual release. Because of this and other factors that can influence a man's sex drive, it is safe to assume that the majority of healthy men greatly benefit from having *daily* sexual interaction with their wives.

In looking at a woman's ovulatory cycle, her hormone levels vary significantly from one time of the month to another. Peaks in sexual interest reportedly correspond to the timing of ovulation and the days that immediately precede menstruation, with many women preferring not to make love during their periods. So where does this leave our husbands, whose bodies are geared for a high level of interest in sex at almost any time of the month?

As with other areas of our lives, a balance is necessary. Individual couples find that time spent together meeting one another's sexual needs draws them closer together and nourishes the bond that they share. How these needs are met vary between couples and with the same couple at different times. Life is not static. When a couple is able to openly discuss their sexuality within the context of their daily lives together, their need to be flexible and understanding toward one another becomes evident. In developing a love life that is mutually satisfying, a husband and wife grow to complement one another physically as well as emotionally and spiritually. Their creative use of loving touch expands over the years to include embraces that fulfill their need for sexual release whenever there is a need for sexual activity for one partner and a need for rest from sexual release on the part of the other.

Speaking without words in the sexual dimension of our lives must take into account that some conversations allow for one partner to listen while the other is speaking. There is freedom to meet one another's sexual needs when one partner is unable to play an active role in the conversation. To be locked into a mentality that views intercourse as the end-all and be-all of sexual interaction is to condemn a great many couples to either periodic or permanent abstinence. This view is without Scriptural basis. Unfortunately, many books fail to address this issue, and the statistics of extramarital sex during times when a woman is unable to make love, such as during the time surrounding childbirth, prove that many couples believe that avoiding intercourse means avoiding sexual expression altogether.

This can serve to remind us once again of the Lord's love for us in speaking through Paul's letter to the Corinthians. Our God created males and females to be sexual together within marriage and gives us permission to meet one another's sexual needs with joy. The need that a husband has for regular release from sexual tension calls for a loving response on his wife's part as she balances her needs with his. A woman does not ever have to resentfully engage in intercourse when alternative expressions can provide the release that her husband desires, and a husband does not need to resent his wife for being unable to make love.

Breathe a sigh of relief as you reflect upon what this means to you and what effect frequent sexual sharing will have on your husband as you aim to spend time together on a daily basis. As you discuss what you have learned, explore ways you will each be comfortable with as you provide the opportunity for sexual expression to one another even when one of you will assume a less active role during your time together. This may end up being one of the most significant talks that you will ever have about your sexuality if you are honest about your own feelings concerning how frequently you desire intercourse, your need for loving touch, and an outlook on sexual sharing that avoids abstinence without demanding penetration. If you are unsure about my interpretation of Scripture, check it thoroughly for yourselves so that you feel confident in developing your own approach to meeting one another's sexual needs.

The Etiquette of Lovemaking

The art of sexual responsiveness requires us to accept rules of etiquette similar to those that govern any polite conversation. These rules are:

1. *Do not interrupt once the fun begins.* You will have time to talk about it later! Speaking without words is just that—words spoken about an important piece of news have nothing to do with the matter at hand. Bringing up something you forgot to tell him earlier will distract both of you from what your bodies are trying to say to each other. To begin to talk about something unrelated to lovemaking in the middle of a caress is a declaration that you are not "all there." Avoid interrupting the flow of love-talk and tune into the expressions of your husband's desire for you.

2. *Do remember to say please and thank you.* Courtesy between lovers is a sure sign of their respect for one another. Expressions of appreciation are always welcome, and neither partner *ever* has the right to demand something without asking! Forceful activity that takes place without one's consent is unkind, unloving, and illegal. There are many nice ways to ask and just as many ways to say thanks as you show your love to one another: flowers, special dates, a surprise note tucked into a sack lunch . . .

3. *Do not make fun of one another.* Each of us feels vulnerable about our bodies. When we jest one another about an area that we are already sensitive about, we feel a sense of exposure that causes us to become defensive and protective. Even casual remarks made in passing can hurt our feelings and close us off from being sexually open. Be careful about the words you use about your husband's body. Being blatantly honest about his "spare tire" or latest pimple will not help either of you to be more open with one another!

4. *Do give compliments and affirmations freely.* Lovers never get tired of hearing the words "I love you." Neither do they refuse to accept genuine compliments, no matter how frequently they are given. Affirmations are positive verbal strokes that people give to one another to validate someone else's special qualities and lovableness. They do not have to be earned! An affirmation boosts our self-esteem in healthy ways and better

103

enables us to appreciate the unique things about ourselves that the Lord has given to us: our bodies, our minds, our talents, our abilities, and our histories. Affirmations invite us to grow. Solomon's book, the Song of Songs, is chock-full of affirmations between himself and his lover as they share their appreciation and love for each other. What deep physical love they had for one another! Here are a few examples of the kinds of affirmations you can use during lovemaking:

> "I really like to hold you."
> "You look great tonight!"
> "I am so thankful for you."
> "Your body feels good to me."
> "I like the way you do that."
> "You are the perfect lover for me."
> "I am so glad I am here with you."
> "You don't have to rush . . . I enjoy that!"
> "I love touching you there."

5. *Do say "excuse me" when it's appropriate to do so.* No matter how long a couple has been married, it is polite to say "excuse me" when digestive upset causes gas and burps or when one of you needs to make a trip to the bathroom in the middle of all the excitement. Showing this small courtesy is so simple to do that it need never be dropped as a habit.

6. *Do respect one another's need for privacy.* This can be difficult if you have only one toilet in your house or apartment! Barging in on one another during moments that are meant to be private goes beyond the boundaries of marital intimacy. We all need at least a *few* moments to ourselves every day.

7. *Do not laugh at the wrong times.* During lovemaking, humorous events can and do happen. Laughing right out loud is an appropriate expression *some* of the time. Be sensitive about not using laughter at times when it will be interpreted as making fun of something that your husband actually feels quite badly about.

8. *Do come dressed for the occasion . . .* or undressed, if you prefer! Become familiar with what kinds of clothing your husband likes seeing you in and don't be afraid to experiment. Clothing says a lot about who we are, and bedclothes aren't any different! Sexy things to wear include everything from men's T-shirts to silk teddies. Put as much thought in dressing for your husband's eyes alone as you do for going to work, going to church, or going out for dinner.

9. *Do make the atmosphere conducive to lovemaking.* Having a toddler snuggled up to you when your husband comes to bed or trying to get together in the middle of a messy bedroom are two examples of creating the *wrong* type of environment for lovemaking. Fresh flowers, sheets dried out on a sunny day on the clothesline, a cool fan, a blazing fire

in the fireplace . . . these kinds of things add real comfort to sexual sharing. Invest in a tape player for your bedroom, and play instrumental music such as that recorded for the purpose of promoting relaxation. Some couples prefer Bach while others enjoy listening to the jazzy guitar of someone like Larry Carlton. One couple wrote in their book that they light a candle as a signal that they want to make love. What are your unique signals? What things can you do to make your love nest secure and attractive?

10. *Do pay attention.* Attentiveness is always appreciated by those who are engaged in a dialogue. If you have to work at paying attention, you should view that as a sign that you are having trouble becoming aroused. Rather than frustrate your husband with your lack of attentiveness, take time out for a moment to talk about where you are at and whether or not you feel up to actively participating in lovemaking. You may have other needs that haven't been met (food, rest, touch, affection) that are preventing you from opening up sexually. Remember—ignoring your needs won't make them go away. Your love life will be much more satisfying once you realize the importance of this and are able to share your feelings honestly with your mate.

There they are: the top ten rules for courteous lovers! Some couples never lose their ability to be polite to one another, witnessed by the fact that some men still open the car door for their wives (seen any lately?) and women may be found who wait up at night for their husbands (read Edith Schaeffer's *Common Sense Christian Living*). Developing our own sense of style in courteous ways of expressing our love to our husbands is up to each of us as individuals. We must never take this area of our lives for granted. It is far too precious and central to our marriages for that!

After the Conversation Has Ended

The sense of satisfaction and the fullness of heart that accompanies love-making is especially felt during the resolution phase of the sexual response cycle. Basking in the afterglow that sexual release brings provides couples with a unique opportunity for bonding.

The term *bonding* refers to the process of attachment that is fostered between two human beings as they are involved in reciprocal interactions through the experiences of touch, sight, sound, and speech. You may be familiar with this word in the context of the bonding that occurs between parents and their infants, but bonding takes place between husbands and wives also. It is part of the glue that cements two people together in such a way that even the stresses and strains of daily life can't pull them apart. The special bond that results from lovemaking is particularly evident in the moments that follow intercourse or orgasm.

God has created us to be emotionally and spiritually vulnerable to one another during sexual expression. When the physical intensity of lovemaking has subsided, it is as if we lie naked before our lover in more than just an actual sense. When we are willing to be mutually transparent along with our husbands, our hearts are joined to theirs in a remarkable way as we reflect upon the closeness that results when two are joined as one. Relaxing in the afterglow of lovemaking while being held in one's husband's arms is one of life's most sublime experiences.

The next time you drift off to sleep as you snuggle against your husband, praise God for the beautiful gift that He has given to you to enjoy as a married woman: the incredible feeling of tranquillity that follows the end of your silent conversation of love. What a blessing it is to drift along quietly in the moments that follow lovemaking, without guilt or fear. The tenderness and warmth of these times in our lives are a welcome shelter from the stormy world outside.

Stumbling-blocks to Communication

Not all conversations flow smoothly. Sometimes it is even difficult to whisper, let alone talk. The ability to speak with one's body requires a willingness to be not only informed *about* it but to be informative *with* it. One of the great myths about sexuality is that men are *always* willing if they are able and that women are to be passive followers rather than active initiators. Men are affected by the stressors in their lives, too. To expect your husband to be the one to initiate lovemaking every time you interact sexually is unrealistic. On the other hand, your husband might be misunderstanding *your* needs.

Imagine the following scene: A woman has been thinking about lovemaking off and on all day in anticipation of what will happen after a candlelight dinner she and her husband plan to have that evening. She rushes home to get the groceries into the refrigerator, feed the kids, and whisk them off for an overnight at Grandma's. While she is gone, her husband arrives and discovers that his favorite symphony is being performed downtown that evening. (This could just as well be his favorite sports team, musical group, or evangelist.) Wanting to surprise his wife, he leaves to get the tickets. When he arrives back home, dinner is waiting for him and his wife greets him with a lingering kiss in the front hall. As she begins undressing him, she feels his body tense up and asks him what's wrong. The tickets he picked up are handed to his wife like a bouquet of flowers, but when she sees that the concert starts in just an hour, she is not impressed. Frustrated and confused would be a better way to describe her reaction!

What would you do? Have you ever been in this situation? Is your husband so preoccupied with his own plans that he forgets to ask you about yours? There are some who would say that a wife must always be willing to please her husband and follow his lead. But if his leading fails to consider her needs and orientation, is that love?

A loving husband would either tear up the tickets or call up someone and give them away if he understood the importance of this night to his mate. That is the best scenario she could hope for, but one that would only happen if the husband really had his wife's interest at heart rather than his own. Love requires us to give up our own plans for the good of another, and it works *both* ways. Too often, women are expected to give, submit, follow, and surrender to their husband's wishes without the husband being impelled to serve the needs of his wife. The balance that Ephesians 5 teaches speaks to both sides of this issue. Feminists do not understand this. Unfortunately, many Christian husbands don't either.

This is not a book written for husbands, however, but for wives. I bring up this issue because I see it as a major stumbling-block to women who really do want to give themselves to their husbands. What makes sexual love so thrilling is the giving and the taking, not the giving-giving to another's taking-taking that often happens. It is our responsibility to actively teach our husbands how we feel, what we think, what we know. How can they possibly love us compassionately if we don't? We have as much to offer them as they do to us, and our membership in the kingdom of heaven is just as vital as theirs. How we need one another! From the standpoint of Genesis, a woman's place is next to the heart of her husband as she shares his life as his companion and counterpart. The experience of being made one flesh through the physical joining of our bodies is to remind us how very much a part of one another we are to be.

Consider another example of a stumbling-block to lovemaking: In this situation, a woman's husband is so thoroughly enthralled with lovemaking that he usually gets carried away from the moment they kiss. He heads straight for her erogenous zones every time. He loves to touch the places on his wife's body that have the best sexual connotations for him, and he thinks that this is the way it should be for her too. Often times his wife tries to redirect his hands, and she hints at possible alternatives to his approach. She doesn't know what she wants, doesn't say anything because she thinks *he* should know what she wants, and just keeps assuming he will figure it out for her someday. At other times, she tries to rush through lovemaking because she is too tense or too upset with the situation to enjoy it at all. When her husband asks, "What's wrong, honey?" she thinks it's her fault and either cries or tells him that she is tired.

What does this wife need? What will happen if she keeps on ignoring her needs and expecting her husband to solve her "problem"? If you answered that she will close off her sexuality, you were right. Unless a woman is comfortable with her body and can lovingly guide her husband as she teaches him to view her needs from a feminine perspective, she will always keep wondering why people talk about sex like it's such a great

107

thing. For her, it will be something done *to* her rather than something that springs from inside of herself as she responds to touches that satisfy and stimulate her.

One of the myths discussed in the sixth chapter was that men have a greater sex drive than their wives—period. The wife in this situation has bought that myth instead of learning about her own capabilities for sexual response. She needs to discover what her own erogenous zones are instead of expecting to react like a textbook case. Perhaps these areas for her lie along her neck and earlobes, along the undersides of her breasts and underarms, and next to her clitoris along the inner lips of her vulva. Since every woman responds in her own unique way to sexual stimulation, she needs to describe her reactions to her husband and feel comfortable sharing her responses with him if sex is to be mutually satisfying. It is safe to assume that many women desire to be stroked, caressed, and embraced skin-to-skin with their husbands before, during, and after lovemaking. Unless this need is expressed, a husband is likely to rush into things too quickly, especially if his need is primarily for the release that orgasm and ejaculation bring to him. He is also more likely to turn over and fall asleep after lovemaking, leaving his wife alone to ponder the meaning of it all in the dark.

The solution for this couple lies in the wife's responsibility to explore her range of reactions along with her husband's willingness to be teachable. A good place to start would be for him to give her a complete massage like the one described in Chapter Eight. He could do this for several nights in a row, agreeing not to touch her breasts or genitals for the time being. The goal of this exercise is for the wife to focus on the wonderful feelings that the Lord has designed her body to be capable of and to receive the gift of touch her husband is bestowing upon her. It is likely that he will become aroused during the massage, and she may wish to meet his need for sexual release without penetration after he is finished, or the two of them could agree ahead of time to limit what they are doing to include nongenital touch only. This exercise can work either way and need not concentrate on the woman alone.

When the wife has been able to feel totally relaxed with her bodily responses to her husband's touches, they will want to progress to kisses. They may not have spent an hour just kissing since high school! Kissing within the privacy of one's bedroom is much more fun. The kisses can travel over the surface of the body instead of being confined to the face and neck—whatever is pleasing! Shulamith told Solomon that his kisses were "better than wine," which we can assume means that she found them absolutely intoxicating!

Gradually the couple would progress to caressing the breasts and genitals. A good position for this would be with the wife nearly upright, propped up at the head of the bed with lots of pillows. She could place a rolled up pillow under each of her knees as well so that her legs, buttocks, and pelvic floor muscles would be very relaxed. If she found that she had little natural lubrication at first, a small amount of almond oil on his hands would be sufficient to increase her comfort and enjoyment as well as her husband's ability to feel each area distinctly. She would then guide her husband's hands, helping him to understand the amount of pressure that felt best, the types of stroking to use and what areas to avoid.

Distinguishing the difference between sensations both inside and outside her vagina and the role of her pelvic floor muscles in sexual responsiveness could be determined with her husband's assistance as she consciously pulled inwards and then bulged outwards while contracting and releasing the muscles surrounding her vagina. She might also find that lying on her stomach with a pillow under her hips with her legs relaxed open would increase her enjoyment during vaginal stimulation.

Instead of taking an aggressive role during intercourse, the husband could gently guide his penis with his wife's help into just the outer entrance of her vagina. By using pelvic floor contractions to alternately grip and release her husband's penis, lovemaking could proceed according to the depth and rhythm of the wife's degree of openness. Using her pelvic floor muscles, she would actually be communicating her responsiveness without words in this silent conversation of love. The husband would undoubtedly enjoy these "inside kisses" also. If he was sitting up, supporting his weight by his arms placed to the side and behind him, his wife could easily use her own hip movements to control the tempo of lovemaking. She could also lean back against the pillows and manually stimulate her labia and clitoris in this position. Trying different positions at different times would enable the wife to understand how sensations during lovemaking vary, allowing her to be more expressive and aggressive at times. In these and other ways, this couple would develop their own unique love language over the years as they shared their bodies with each other. Knowing that there is great freedom to privately explore their own distinctive style without feeling the need to perform would remove the pressures of thinking that they had to live up to someone else's standard of sexual finesse.

The Impact of Spiritual Fruitfulness on Sexual Expression

> But the fruit of the Spirit is love, joy, peace, patience,
> kindness, goodness, faithfulness, gentleness, and self-control.
> Against such things there is no law.[5]

The ultimate measure of our thought-life and behavior as Christians is whether the qualities of the Holy Spirit are made manifest in the things that we think, say, and do. If you are unsure about the acceptability of your love life to God, perhaps you need to apply the yardstick of Galatians 5 to measure spiritual fruitfulness in this area of your life.

Paul lists the acts of the sinful nature just prior to spelling out what the fruits of the Spirit are to be in the lives of all believers. By comparing these two lists, we reach a deeper understanding between the two. Asking ourselves the following questions can help us to understand whether our sexual behavior is pleasing to the Lord:

- Is it *loving?*

- Is *joy* expressed in our attitude toward each other? (*Strong's Concordance* defines joy as "calm delight.")

- Do we feel the *peace* of God after we have finished?

- Are we demonstrating *patience* with one another?

- Do we see God's *goodness* manifested in the physical love we share with one another?

- Are we *faithful* to each other?

- Are we being *gentle* with each other?

- Are we able to *control* our thoughts and actions when we are apart? To the extent that we are able to serve one another's needs when we are making love?

If we are to keep in step with the Spirit, we will want to say yes to each of these questions. Our love lives are not set apart from the rest of our walk with God. The time that we spend in lovemaking can be as pleasing, as sanctified, and as blessed as any other aspect of our marriages. This is because of the purpose for which man and woman were created. May God be praised as we learn to enjoy and appreciate the special gift of our sexual responsiveness.

> I am my beloved's, his longing is all for me.
> Come, my beloved, let us go out into the fields
> to lie among the henna-bushes;
> let us go early to the vineyards
> and see if the vine has budded or its blossom opened,
> if the pomegranates are in flower.
> There I will give you my love,
> when the mandrakes give their perfume,
> and all rare fruits are ready at our door,
> fruits new and old
> which I have in store for you, my love.[6]

8

Learning New Skills

Because they have been created by God with equal dignity,
men and women must respect, love, serve, and not despise
one another.[1]

John Stott, *Involvement, Vol. II:*
Social and Sexual Relationships in the Modern World

At this point, you may be thinking: "If sex is a gift of God, why am I often willing to forego the opportunity of experiencing it with my husband?" There are many factors that influence sexual desire and how the body responds to lovemaking. Many of the things that have an impact on this area of our lives were presented in Chapter 4. But what about the things that can get in the way of sexual sharing? For starters, basic physical needs that go unmet—such as the need for good nutrition and plenty of rest—wind up becoming inhibitors to sexual responsiveness. As you can see from Figure 8-1, there are many factors that can detract from your ability to feel interested in lovemaking. Through developing an appreciation of the variety of ways our bodies interact with our emotions, thoughts, culture, and environment, we can learn to understand why our level of interest in sexual sharing fluctuates.

Physical Factors

Try to imagine your body as it directs and "prioritizes" its many activities: providing nutrients to cells for energy and growth; maintaining a steady temperature and metabolic rate; promoting oxygen intake through heart and lung activity; coordinating the complex processes by which our brains and nerves communicate; and removing waste products through our cir-

FACTORS THAT INHIBIT SEXUAL EXPRESSION

Figure 8-1

- Hunger
- Fatigue
- Pain
- Depression
- Alcoholic beverages
- Medications
- Anxiety
- Fear
- Feelings of rejection
- Low self-esteem
- High progesterone levels, hormonal changes
- Illness

- Negative social learning
- Preoccupation with other matters
- Poor body image
- Misconceptions about a Biblical view of sexuality
- Guilt over past experiences
- Fear of pregnancy
- Inability to communicate one's needs
- Not enough time
- Lack of privacy

- Ignorance about how the body functions sexually
- Feeling ashamed or embarrassed about one's body
- Mistrust of husband's motives
- Tension
- High level of stress
- Conflicting sexual needs
- Misunderstanding husband's needs and concerns

culatory and digestive systems. Compared to these essential activities, sexual sharing is relatively unimportant!

To a large degree, our lifestyles can either enhance or take away from our ability to carry out these basic functions. Healthy bodies allow for these physical activities to take place with ease. It is perfectly normal to feel disinterested in lovemaking when we aren't healthy, or when we're in pain, tired, or emotionally drained. We are fooling ourselves if we think it should be otherwise! By acknowledging the reality of how our bodies operate, we can discover ways to be more realistic about what they are capable of. We can also adapt our lifestyles to accommodate our physical and emotional needs and accept our limitations as well as our abilities. It is just good, plain common sense to pay attention to what our bodies "tell" us and meet our requirements for a variety of foods, adequate rest, and refreshing recreation. In meeting these basic needs, nonessential activities such as lovemaking can take place with greater ease.

The Effects of Stress

A major roadblock that stands in the way of satisfying lovemaking is stress. In and of itself, stress is a helpful response on the part of our bodies that enables us to cope with changes in our environment. Over a period of time, however, stress reactions can become chronic and deplete our energy reserve as well as our ability to fight off infection. You may find it easier to understand how this happens if you picture your brain as a "master control center" that must interpret messages that come into the body while adjusting physical responses to match the needs that our environment dictates to us.

Through a complex system of nerves which exit from the spinal cord, our brains carry out the regulation of the many activities that take place within our bodies. From the moment our brains begin to function during the first month of our prenatal development, our nervous systems work to control our vital functions until the last current of electricity disappears and the heart stops beating. The Lord created the brain to direct the work of the body, whether we're asleep or awake, sitting still or running fast. Stop and think for a moment about the last time you tried to match your breathing rate to the oxygen level in your bloodstream when you hurried up three flights of stairs. Get the point? We never have to think twice about such a thing because our brains monitor our oxygen levels automatically. God didn't make our vital functions optional. In order to maintain a "steady state" within our bodies, our nervous systems must be able to keep bodily processes regulated whether we're sleeping, working, thinking, laughing, or doing somersaults.

Within this design, the nervous system also monitors our reactions to incoming information. We are only comfortable within a certain temperature range as a means of protection against chilling and overheating. When the air gets too chilly, we realize we're getting cold and put warmer clothing on. A body position that is held too long causes discomfort and signals us to shift our weight as a way of protecting our joints from damage. A finger that momentarily touches a hot pan is pulled quickly away in order to prevent the skin from burning. In these and many other ways, the nervous system interacts with our environment through our perceptions about how we are feeling at any given moment.

Fear sets our nervous system off like an alarm and provokes a reflex that is outside our control. Called the "fight or flight response," this reflex gears our bodies for activity as a means of helping us to confront the source of alarm or by enabling us to flee from it. The fight or flight response is an important component of our autonomic nervous system that enhances our ability to respond to what goes on around us. It is necessary for survival in a world that can be dangerous to live in.

Think about the last time something unexpected and frightening happened to you, such as when the phone rang in the middle of the night or when a car swerved into your lane and nearly hit your vehicle. Did your mouth dry up? How about your hands—did they get cold and tense? Could you feel your heart pounding away on the inside of your chest? Good! That means you are perfectly normal and that your body is capable of responding to an emergency situation in a healthy way. Like it or not, when the fight or flight reflex is turned on, several things happen: stress hormones are released into the bloodstream that redirect our blood supply away from our inner organs to larger muscle groups, our heart and breathing rates increase, our blood pressure rises, and our emotional state becomes acutely aware of potential danger. What an amazing process this is! We can be thankful for this natural, built-in ability that God has given to us to help us live in an unpredictable world.

113

But what about the times when stress hormones are secreted in *non-threatening* situations? What happens when the *alarm* clock jars you out of a restful slumber? When you drink three cups of coffee shortly thereafter? What does your heart rate do when you lose your cool in a traffic jam on the way to work or when you try to "beat the light" because you're late to an appointment? How about the times you've become angry at the latest bad news on television? Or when you've lost your temper at the kids? These are all examples of things that can *also* stimulate your sympathetic nervous system. Called S.N.S. for short, it is the part of your nervous system that regulates the fight or flight response. Bit by bit, the S.N.S. can be provoked throughout the day, allowing levels of stress hormones to build up without our being much aware of what is happening. If our lifestyles demand that stress hormones be flowing on a continual basis, *chronic stress* results. Since changes in response to daily situations that produce tension are not as exaggerated as those that result in truly dangerous situations, we tend to deny the significance of our reactions. In the long run, the chronic stress that is produced by the challenges of our lifestyle is far more destructive to our health than the acute stress related to an episode that is short in duration.

Happily, the Lord has given us the ability to maintain a balance in our nervous systems (Figure 8-2). While the S.N.S. gears our body for action, the parasympathetic nervous system, or P.N.S., enables us to calm down. The daily stresses of life can and should be counteracted through a period of rest and relaxation at least once *every day*. Even Jesus realized the importance of setting aside time to be alone with His Father away from the demands of the multitudes He ministered to. Each and every one of us needs a time of peace and quiet on a daily basis as well as certain nutrients,

THE NERVOUS SYSTEMS
Figure 8-2

NERVOUS SYSTEM
(Brain, Spinal Cord, Peripheral Nerves)

SOMATIC
NERVOUS SYSTEM
(controls "voluntary" movements)

AUTONOMIC
NERVOUS SYSTEM
(controls "involuntary" activities)

SYMPATHETIC
NERVOUS SYSTEM (S.N.S.)
(gears body for action: fight or flight response)
catecholamines

PARASYMPATHETIC
NERVOUS SYSTEM (P.N.S.)
(gears body for rest: quieting
response) *endorphins*

114

exercise, sleep, and appropriate expression of our emotions. There are five ways that are known to reduce the effects of stress:

A balanced diet: By avoiding excessive sugar, alcohol, caffeine, processed meats, and monosodium glutamate, we can enhance our ability to cope with daily pressures. Several of these substances have been shown to produce changes in heart rate and are not unrelated to other problems, such as tooth decay, obesity, alcoholism, headaches, and nervousness. In addition, drinking six or more glasses of water daily, including foods that are rich in complex carbohydrates (whole grain products, fruits, and vegetables), lowering fat intake, and eating calcium and protein-rich foods promotes health and increases our ability to withstand stress.

Exercise for fun and enjoyment: An exercise program should be fun as well as lively in order to be part of a stress reduction program. Competitive activities or a mind-set that can cause us to push ourselves to the limit may only serve to *increase* the level of stress hormones in our bodies. An activity that is participated in for enjoyment and for fitness is ideal. Cardiovascular fitness activities include swimming, walking, dancing, cycling, running, rope skipping, and cross-country skiing. These are all ways of achieving an improved sense of well-being, especially when engaged in for a thirty-minute period at least three times a week (see Chapter Thirteen).

A regular bedtime followed by uninterrupted sleep: Irregular sleep patterns and frequent changes in bedtime schedules can disrupt the body by interferring with our ability to dream and reach specific brain wave patterns during rest. Dreaming allows us to release tension and anxiety. Our metabolism slows down, and our muscles relax when we achieve a deep sleep state. Since our bodies and minds renew themselves in many different ways when we sleep, getting the rest we need enables us to be refreshed each night.

Appropriate expressions of emotion: God has given us the ability to experience a wide range of emotions. It has been said that if we try to bury the feelings we are uncomfortable with, we bury them alive. Simply denying feelings that we are uncomfortable with doesn't make them disappear. It is only when we face the reality of our emotions and share them with the Lord that we can release them to Him freely. Many of the psalms that David wrote exemplify this principle. As he poured out his heart to God, he was humbled, strengthened, and renewed. This theme is repeated many times throughout the Bible. Psalm 139 tells us that the Lord knows our words even before they are on our tongues and that no matter where we are, in the heavens or in the depths, our God is there. Like David, we too can invite the Lord to know our anxious thoughts[2] and lead us in the everlasting way of His truth. Learning to be open before our Father is an essential part of our relationship to God.

Quiet times for relaxation: We can promote our ability to handle stress on the physical, emotional, and spiritual levels when we take time out to reflect on the majesty of God. Taking fifteen to twenty minutes out of a hectic day to relax in a comfortable positon while setting our minds on heavenly things refreshes our bodies, minds, and spirits. Psalm Twenty-Three describes this well as it paints a pastoral scene of the Lord being our Shepherd, causing us to lie down in green pastures alongside a clear, flowing stream. When we sit with our feet up in a recliner, soak in a warm bath, or lie comfortably on a soft supportive surface, we can help our body relax by releasing the muscular tension that has accumulated during the day. With closed eyes, we can take nice, deep, full breaths as we think about how very much the Lord loves us. Spending time in peaceful communion with Jesus is yet another way to learn about Him. Rather than only asking for His help and intervention, we also benefit from taking the time out to enjoy the ever-present comfort of the Holy Spirit.

Relaxing in this way can stimulate the P.N.S. as a means of countering the effects of stress hormones. When the P.N.S. is switched on, bodily processes slow down and powerful substances called endorphins are released. Endorphins are powerful chemicals that diminish pain and promote a feeling of tranquillity. Also released after times of physical exertion, these substances and the role they play are far from being understood. Our Creator has lovingly granted us the ability to undo the effects of stress if we take the time to draw near to Him in singleness of heart with thanksgiving.

Stress and Sexual Responsiveness

As women, chronic stress inhibits our ability to be sexually responsive in many ways. When the S.N.S. is stimulated by stress hormones, blood flow to the genitals is restricted. This response is much more obvious in a male than it is in a female. Perhaps you have noticed such an event in your husband when you have been caressing one another and suddenly he jumped up thinking someone was at the door. In an instant, all sexual interest was gone as the blood left his genitals and rushed to his legs and arms.

What about other areas? Increased muscle tension in the pelvic floor makes intercourse dreadful, as well as producing discomfort. Instead of feeling sensitive and pleasant, the breasts tighten and feel irritable when touched. Stress hormones are a potent way to delay sexual gratification when danger is present. The S.N.S. in effect "turns off" sexual responsiveness, while the P.N.S. better enables it to become "turned on"!

In addition to relaxation, there are several other ways of stimulating the P.N.S. The response that opposes the fight or flight reflex is called the quieting response. One of the best ways of provoking the quieting response is through touch. Think about the sensations you feel during a back rub or when someone else brushes your hair. Those sensations are

BODY FACTORS AND SEXUALITY

Figure 8-3

BODY FUNCTION	FIGHT OR FLIGHT EFFECTS	QUIETING RESPONSE EFFECTS
Heart rate	Faster	Slower
Breathing rate	Increased	Decreased
Blood pressure	Elevated	Lowered
Sweat production	Increased	Decreased
Metabolic processes	Speeded up	Slowed down
Circulation in large muscles	Greatly increased	Remains steady
S.N.S. activity	Increased	Decreased
P.N.S. activity	Decreased	Increased

ADDITIONAL FACTORS RELATED TO SEXUAL FUNCTION

Blood flow to genitalia	Decreased	Steady (increased when stimulated)
Tension in pelvic floor	Tense	Relaxed
Skin temperature	Lowered	Elevated
Vaginal responsiveness	Sensitivity decreased	Sensitivity increased
Muscle tension	Increased	Decreased or directed to specific areas when stimulated
Breast sensitivity	Reduced	Promoted
Emotional state	Distracted, agitated	Calm, able to focus on pleasurable sensations
Level of sexual response	Greatly minimized	Pleasurable sensations maximized

WAYS TO PROVOKE THE QUIETING RESPONSE

- Massage: back, neck, face, scalp, arms, legs
- Warm shower or bath
- Slow breathing: 6-12 breaths per minute
- Soothing environment: music, candlelight, nature sounds
- Comfortable position with release of muscular tension
- Passive attitude with the avoidance of worry
- Reflecting on the beauty and majesty of God and His creation

related to P.N.S. activity. Loving touch that is aimed at nurturing one's partner in nonsexual ways can be an excellent prelude to lovemaking or as a means of conveying love. Learning the art of massage benefits a marriage in many ways.

117

The Gift of Touch

Have you ever had the luxury of receiving a massage from a registered physical therapist or a certified massage therapist? If so, you are well aware of what a massage can be like when given by an expert. If not, you probably have yet to realize the benefits of a back rub that is professionally administered. I know what you may be thinking . . . that massage has a bad name and how could a Christian even consider going to a stranger for a massage? Well, I admit that I used to think it was pretty strange too until my sister-in-law and one of my best friends (both Christians!) became massage therapists and applied their skills to me one day. It was absolutely wonderful! Now if I could just convince my husband to go through the training . . .

Seriously, I can't think of anything that is quite as relaxing as a back rub that is done well. Part of the reason is that few things stimulate the P.N.S. better. Did you know that we were created with a need for touch *in order to survive?* Babies who receive an insufficient amount of touching actually waste away with a disease called marasmus and *die.* Emotional attachment to our loved ones is promoted through the gift of touch that God has given to us. Loving touch is a means of conveying our attachment, concern, appreciation, sympathy, and involvement toward another person. It does not matter whether the person is two or ninety-two: touch speaks a language of its own.

Consider all of the phrases we commonly use that refer to physical contact:

"I'll be in touch with you soon."

"That scene was really touching."

"Reach out and touch someone."

"Let's stay in touch."

"He really rubs me the wrong way."

"I'll handle that matter for you."

"Is she ever a soft touch!"

Human relationships thrive on touch when it is done appropriately and with respect for another person. We have many examples in the Gospels of Jesus touching those around Him, or of his disciples touching Him. I especially like the references to "the disciple whom Jesus loved" leaning back against Jesus at the Last Supper[3] and when He took the little children in his arms.[4] The "laying on of hands" has great significance throughout the New Testament and continues to be used today in many different denominations during Communion, baptism, ordination, prayers for healing, and requests for special anointing. Through touch we let others know that *we care.*

Between a husband and wife, the gift of touch is as significant as it is in any human relationship. If married partners only touch one another in sexual ways, or in order to attempt to stimulate one another toward sexual arousal, a marriage can suffer. Many women have spoken to me about their resentment of the fact that their husbands only touch them when they want "something in return." It is certainly true that many men have been raised in homes where cuddling, hugging, snuggling, and putting arms around family members was uncommon. Our English heritage is largely responsible for such a "hands-off" approach to family life. Discovering new ways of expressing love through touch can be a growing experience for anyone who was reared in a "low-touch" atmosphere. But learn we must. We cannot afford to abandon the caring communication that *everyone* needs, whether they are aware of it or not. Nonsexual physical expressions of love are a key way of nurturing our husbands and our children within the family. Think for a moment . . . have you ever heard a friend complaining that her husband was giving her too *many* back rubs?

A good way to begin to include more loving communication through touch in your home is by learning how to give your husband a great massage. In this way, your hands will teach him gently about your love for him and will also "tell" him how you would like him to touch you. It is unrealistic to think that your husband will know how to give you a good back rub if he has never received one himself. Taking the time to learn this skill is well worth the time and effort that will be required of you both. Eventually you will have to take turns and may even find yourself trying to think up ways to be the second recipient since it is difficult to want to get up after being the first one to receive the massage!

The principles upon which an effective massage is based are fairly simple to learn and easy to remember. In following these steps, you will rapidly develop a wonderful technique and have your husband expressing his appreciation to you even with your first attempt.

These steps are:

1. *Reduce the friction* that will be caused by your hands with an agent such as cornstarch or oil. The types of oil that work best are vegetable, nut, or seed oils such as peanut, almond, safflower, or corn oil. You may use them alone or in combination with one another. Scented oils may be obtained through some health food stores or specialty soap shops in eight ounce or larger containers.

2. When you are ready to begin the massage, *put on some relaxing music and ask your husband to remove his clothing.* Give him a gigantic terry towel to wrap around himself. When he lays down on his stomach for the back rub, be sure to keep him covered from the buttocks down-

ward. By keeping areas covered that are not a part of the area you are concentrating the massage on, you minimize the fact of his nakedness and keep the focus *away* from his sexuality. Massage can be incorporated into lovemaking at other times. For learning these techniques, and as a means of stress reduction, it's best to agree on avoiding sexual stimulation!

3. *Have him lie on a comfortable surface* at a height that will help you to avoid back strain as you work. If he is lying on his stomach, place a small pillow under his abdomen to reduce back strain for him, if needed. You may also place a rolled towel under the front surface of his ankles to enable his legs to relax. When he is lying on his back, he may enjoy having a doubled up pillow under each knee to reduce back strain as necessary.

4. When you massage, *use strokes that conform to the contours of your husband's body* while at the same time applying pressure that is deep enough to promote circulation, but not uncomfortable in any way. Use your hands to "talk" to your husband lovingly, smoothly, and rhythmically.

5. *Stroke in particular patterns* at speeds described in the text. Rhythm and repetition are essential. Massage without interruption over a specific area until you have completely massaged it.

6. *Pray for your husband while you are touching him.* Let your hands express how you feel about him and view them as a means of conveying not only your love for him, but the Lord's love for him as well. Ask him to do the same for you whenever he gives you a massage—be a blessing to one another!

7. *Obtain feedback from him* to find out what parts of the massage he liked the best and if he would like you to continue by concentrating on specific areas.

8. *Finish the massage one area at a time* by placing your hands flat on the surface that you have completed, pressing in slightly, then lifting up and off the surface. For example, when you have completed the back, place one hand between the shoulders and one hand at the base of the spine, press, then lift both hands at the same time. This is a nice signal that will tell him you are done.

Now that you have learned these tips, you are ready to begin massaging! You may want to begin with just the back and gradually add other areas as your hands become stronger: the shoulders and neck, arms and hands, legs and feet, and scalp and face. Doing a complete massage is time-consuming. You may want to vary the area you massage and how long a time you spend on each, depending on your schedule. When specific areas of the body are tense, such as during a headache or after doing yard work, you may find that concentrating on those areas are a better use of your time.

The circular and patterned movements that are used are directed toward the head and heart, while the long, flowing, relaxing strokes move toward the periphery of the body. In this way, circulation is promoted and relaxation is enhanced. You may want to take the phone off the hook and put on some soothing music to better separate yourselves from the stress of the world outside. This can really be a special time between the two of you, as corny as it may seem. Most of us just get too busy and can use such moments to better appreciate the wonder of our relationships.

MASSAGE TECHNIQUES FOR STRESS REDUCTION

Back:
1. *Circle sweeps:* With your husband lying on his stomach, place both of your hands at the base of his back on his waist. Be sure to have enough oil on your hands so that they will glide smoothly over the surface of his skin. Begin to stroke up along the spine (but not on it), using circular movements that move up, over the surface of the back, toward the sides, then back around to the midline. The strokes are to be six to eight inches in diameter and move in an upward direction until the shoulders are reached. It should take four or five circles spiraling upwards to cover the surface of the back. Once the hands have reached the top, place the hands at the base of the neck, palms down, and apply gentle pressure as they glide down to the base of the back. Repeat this sequence for two to five minutes, or until you feel the muscles in the back release their tension. It may help to think of this counting sequence as you rub: 1 (up), 2 (out), 3 (down) repeated slowly for four or five strokes; on last stroke—1, 2, 3, center, down, 2, 3, 4.

2. *Hands together:* Now you will be focusing your strokes on one side of the back at a time. Place your hands next to one another on the right side of the spine at the base of the back. Put your right hand slightly higher than the left so that your right thumb is nearly over the left thumb near the left forefinger. In this way, your left hand will follow the strokes that your right hand makes, just as if it is imitating what the right hand is doing. Begin stroking using the circle sweeps pattern, making sure to glide smoothly over the skin while applying a greater degree of pressure than before. Continue to rhythmically stroke the right side, including the shoulder, for two to three minutes. Repeat this sequence for the same length of time along the left side, leading with your left hand.

3. *Walk-ups:* Now you will be working closer to the spine, one side at a time. Place the three middle fingers of your right hand next to the right of the base of the spine so that they are almost flat. Then put the three middle fingers of your left hand under the base of your right fingers, with your left hand underlying your right palm. Your fingers will be working as a unit and will be touching the back using the fleshiest part of the fingers. Using circles two inches in diameter, spiral up along the bones of the spine, being sure to avoid putting pressure on the spine itself. You will actually be rubbing only the muscles that lie alongside the bone. The large nerve roots that exit from the spinal cord will be stimulated as well. Each circle can be done in one count, and it will take about sixteen to twenty circles to reach the base of the neck. Continue upwards along the neck using your right hand only, until you reach the skull. Slide back down to the base of the spine with your hands flat and in the same

position you used for Step 2 of the massage. Repeat on the left side, leading with either your left or right middle fingers—whichever is most comfortable. Alternate back and forth in this manner for three to five minutes.

4. *See-saws:* Place your hands parallel to each other over the top portion of the buttocks in a horizontal position. Your right hand should be on top, with your right thumb lying next to the small finger of your left hand. Following the contour of your husband's body, draw your hands out to the sides, then slide them over across the back to the opposite sides. Your hands meet only when at the center of the back. The count would be: 1 (right hand moves left/left hand moves right), 2 (right hand moves right/left hand moves left), 1, 2, 1, 2, etc., until the hands reach the shoulders. The movements are nice and easy, and the count is fairly slow. Slide your hands down along the center of the back, in a parallel position, to resume your starting point. Repeat for two to three minutes.

5. *Thumbs-up:* Now place your wrists about two inches apart, with your thumbs pointing upwards and your fingers directed toward the sides of the back. Your right fingers will be pointed to the right side and your left fingers to the left. With your hands resting gently on the surface of the back, use the pads on your thumbs to press up along the sides of the spine about three inches at a time in wide arcs. The count for this movement is: 1, press, 2, out—a four-count pattern. Lift the thumbs slightly to return to midline after each stroke while keeping the fingers of both hands resting lightly along the sides. It will take ten to twelve strokes from the base of the spine at the top of the buttocks to the base of the skull. (When you reach the neck, you will be using your thumbs only, with your fingers lifted out and away from his neck. Repeat for several minutes.)

6. *Repeat favorite pattern:* Ask your husband which pattern he enjoyed the most and repeat it for a few minutes. Be creative! You may develop several patterns of your own as you discover what he likes best.

7. *The harp stroke:* When you are finished with Steps 1 through 6, you can finish the back rub with downward stroking along the central area of the back. Beginning near the neck, draw the fingers of your right hand down the back in a stroke that begins at the top and lifts off near the buttocks. As the right hand lifts, the left hand repeats the stroke, so that the pattern is continuous. It will take two counts to complete each stroke. Repeat this for one or two minutes. Place your right hand at the top of the back, your left hand at the base, and apply a slight pressure to signal the end of the back rub.

Shoulders and neck

The muscles of the shoulders and neck often carry more than their share of tension compared to other areas of the body. This massage can be done almost anywhere, and it is not necessary to massage skin-to-skin, although it is preferable.

1. *Feather stroke:* You may begin this stroke at the top of the head or under the ears by placing your hands lightly on the surface of the skin. With your hands next to one another, or on opposite sides, smoothly stroke downwards, then outwards. Cover the top of the shoulders, then repeat

this pattern while moving closer to the center of the back each time. It will take three to five strokes to reach the midline. Repeat this sequence for one to three minutes. (You will be stroking downwards to the level of the shoulder blades each time.)

2. *Kneading dough:* Follow Step 1 with a more vigorous massage that will remind you of kneading bread dough. Start with your hands on both sides of the base of the neck with your thumbs pointing toward the spine and your fingers lying across the sides of your husband's neck. Gently squeeze the muscles that lie at the base of the neck while rubbing the muscles carefully between your thumbs and fingers. Move along the muscles that lead from the neck to where the arms are joined to the shoulders. Use circular motions of the thumbs to press his muscles toward your fingers. When you reach the edge of the shoulders, use a long stroke to return back to the neck. Ask your husband how vigorously he wants you to rub, and pray that your hands become stronger! Repeat for several minutes until he indicates that the tension is gone. If indicated, spend time on smaller areas that seem to be especially tender or tense. Rub in this manner along the sides of the neck, if needed.

3. Repeat Step 1. End this massage by placing your hands on your husband's shoulders, applying pressure for a moment, then lifting off.

Arms and hands:

The arms and hands massage is a natural extension of the neck and shoulder massage if you have time to do it. Ask your husband to remove his watch and extra rings that he might be wearing. As with the neck/shoulder massage, this massage can be done with your husband sitting up, with the exception of Step 2, which would necessitate a stomach-lying position.

1. Repeat Step 1 of the neck/shoulder massage, stroking from the crown of the head or the base of the neck all the way down to the fingertips. Continue to stroke this area for about one minute.

2. *Round-the-bend:* If your husband is lying down on his stomach, you may follow Step 1 with this pattern. Otherwise, you will proceed directly to Step 3. Move around to the right side of your husband and pick up his right hand with your right hand, placing his hand in the crook of your right arm. With his right arm extended, use your left hand to stroke up along his upper arm, over his shoulder, around his shoulder blade, and back down the back part of his arm to the wrist. Stroke upwards lightly until you are back up at the top of the arm, then apply a greater degree of pressure so that you feel his arm pulling away from his body as your hand comes down around his shoulder blade and under his arm. Repeat this stroke four or five times, then place his extended hand on your lap or shoulder, depending on how you are positioned. Follow with Step 3 in this position.

3. *Kneading dough:* Move up the arm with the same pattern as Step 2 of the neck/shoulder massage, using gentle kneading strokes until you reach the fleshy, muscular portion of the upper arm. Concentrate the kneading pattern a little longer in this area. When you reach the top of his arm,

place your hands on either side and use a long, smooth stroke to reach his wrist while pulling his arm toward you. Repeat this pattern—kneading up, pulling down—for several minutes.

4. *Hands-on:* Place your husband's right hand in your lap or on a nearby surface, palm up. Hold his hand in both of your own and place your fingers under his hand, as you will be using your thumbs to rub the fleshy part of his hand. Rub in a circular pattern, moving your thumbs up the center of the palm, up and along the base of his fingers, then down across the edges of his hand. After rubbing this way for about a minute, use your right thumb to rub in a small circular motion at the base of his thumb and fingers. Spend about ten seconds on each one, then circle his thumb with your thumb and first two fingers and pull outwards while applying a firm grip, as if you were pulling a tight ring off his thumb. Repeat this pattern until you have done all five fingers.

5-8. Repeat Steps 1-4 on the left shoulder, arm, and hand.

Legs:

Have your husband sit comfortably in a chair or assume a semi-reclining position. The leg massage discussed here is the least appreciated part of a body massage, but is very beneficial for someone who has a desk job and is unable to walk much during the day. Massaging the calves is particularly good for anyone who is on their feet a lot or for those who have participated in cardiovascular fitness activities that are weight-bearing, such as running, stair climbing, rope skipping, or racquetball. (Steps 3 and 4 may be done following a back rub with your husband lying on his stomach.)

1. *Up and over:* Begin by massaging up the center of the legs, using both hands, from along the inside of the knees to across the top of the thighs, and then back down along the outside of the thighs to the outside of the knees. In a large circular motion, press up, over, out, and down with a firm stroke. Repeat for two to three minutes, then cover the entire length of the legs in this fashion, from the ankles, to the top of the thighs, and back down to the ankles again. Be sure that your fingers point up toward the top of the legs on the way up and across the back of the legs on the way down. Repeat for one to three minutes.

2. *Knees up:* Place your husband's right knee over your left hand, wrist, or lower arm and lift it up slightly. Using the three middle fingers of your right hand, stroke clockwise around the kneecap for forty-five to sixty seconds. Be careful not to press on the bones too hard! Place your thumb to the left of his kneecap and your first two fingers to the right of it; then stroke up, lift, and repeat along the sides of the knee for thirty to forty-five seconds. Repeat these two patterns on the left knee, using a counter-clockwise motion on the first stroke.

3. *Calves knead:* Reach around with your right hand to the back of your husband's left leg and begin to knead the muscles of the calf from the back of the top of the ankle to just below the knee. Avoid squeezing the Achilles tendon or the tendon behind the knee. Concentrate on the fleshy, muscular portion of the calf instead. Rub and squeeze in a circular

motion with as much pressure as your husband finds comfortable. When you reach the top, stroke down along the back of the leg until you reach your starting point, then begin moving upwards again. You might find it helpful to hold his leg under the ankle with your left hand and lift it slightly. Repeat this pattern for one to two minutes, then follow with the opposite leg.

4. Repeat Step 4 of the previous section *(Hands On)* with each foot. If your husband is ticklish, adapt the massage so that it is relaxing, or skip this step altogether!

Scalp and face

These areas are important to massage if your husband carries tension in his jaw or forehead. This is one of the best helps to alleviating headaches that I am aware of and can be done using a little cornstarch rather than oil if you prefer. Have your husband sit in a chair, lay his head in your lap, or lie down with you facing the top of his head.

1. *Sleepy head:* Put your hands under your husband's head near the top of his neck. Lift his head up slightly and pull it a little bit toward you. Use your thumbs to hold his head in this position while you use your fingers to do a circular massage pattern along the back of his neck. Move your thumbs very slowly upwards as you continue to rub along the back part of the head until you are about one inch over the ridge that lies at the base of the skull. Slowly press in as you slide your fingers back over the area that you just massaged. When you reach your starting point, move your hands about half an inch toward the ears and repeat the pattern. Continue until you have covered the entire back of the head. Ask your husband if he would like you to do some more of this. If he has chronic neck tension, he may *never* want you to stop!

2. *Chin pull:* Now reach down and put your hands along his jaw so that you are cupping his chin in your fingers. Using a smooth, continuous motion, pull your hands up along the jaw and under the chin, then over the ears to the crown of your husband's head. Lift your hands off and resume this pattern, repeating it several times.

3. *Shampoo:* Pretend you are shampooing your husband's hair, using the broad parts of your fingertips. If you have long fingernails, trim them before you begin any massage, but especially before this part! With circular patterns, rub his scalp rhythmically for about a minute, covering every square inch of his scalp. Apply as much pressure as he indicates is comfortable.

4. *Tiny circles:* Use the three middle fingers of both hands and massage with gentle pressure from just above your husband's temples to the base of his jaw. The pattern is made up of circles about an inch in diameter that spiral slowly downwards over the temples, cheekbones, up into the hollow of the cheekbones, over the jawbone to the midline of the chin. When completed, slide your hands back up, using a slight pulling motion, and start over, with your hands about one quarter of an inch farther forward than they were the first time. Repeat the pattern four or five times.

125

5. *Facial stroke:* It may seem strange to you to be giving your husband a "facial," but he will probably find it delightful! With your hands placed lightly on the surface of his forehead, you will be stroking from the center of the face, outwards to the sides, and lifting your hands off the surface of your husband's face after you go over each part of it to return to the middle: the forehead, eyebrows, eyelids (don't press!), nose/cheekbones, underneath the cheekbones, up along the front of the jaw and over the edge of the jaw, up across the temples to the top of his head. Repeat this pattern until you hear him snoring . . .

Personal Organization Strategies

This chapter would be incomplete if it ignored the importance of developing a "stress plan" as a means of coping with stress. In addition to the skills presented thus far, an active management scheme must be included. You will need to make an assessment of your personal life, identify the things that produce the greatest time, energy, and financial conflicts, and then develop a plan by utilizing strategies that will help you to resolve these conflicts. Many sources of tension—a baby with colic, a strong-willed toddler, a limited budget—are definitely not going to go away overnight. Simply dreaming about "better days" that may never arrive is not a constructive way to deal with the here-and-now aspects of the areas of your life that cause you the most tension.

What happens within your body when you are confronted with conflict or tension in your environment? Do you notice your reaction immediately, or does your stress response tend to accumulate over a period of hours or days? What are your stress symptoms? Look over the partial list below to identify the ways that your body reacts to stress:

HOW DO YOU HANDLE STRESS?

MONITORING YOUR STRESS RESPONSES AS THEY RELATE TO TIME-RELATED EVENTS

Figure 8-4

STRESS RESPONSE	TIME/DAY	REASON, IF KNOWN
Hot flashes or chills		
Neck pain or tenderness		
Rashes or hives not caused by allergies		
Frequent headaches		
Insomnia		
Irritable bowels		
Cold, clammy hands		
Upset stomach		

STRESS RESPONSE	TIME/DAY	REASON, IF KNOWN
Heartburn or acid indigestion		
Teeth grinding		
Excessive sweating		
Twitching		
Inability to concentrate		
Constant daydreaming		
Frequent crying spells		
Tenderness under cheekbones		
Outbursts of anger		
Nightmares		
Overeating		
Lack of appetite		
Forgetfulness		
Withdrawal from others		
Frequent sore throats		
Lowered resistance to infection		
Heart palpitations		
Hyperventilation or feelings of breathlessness		
Lack of energy		
Inability to relax		
Nervous laughter or giggling inappropriately		
Biting fingernails		
Alcohol or drug abuse		
Chain smoking		
Dependence on caffeine to achieve sense of vitality		
Constipation		
Nausea		
Dizziness		
Sense of feeling directionless		
Suicidal thoughts		
Self-criticism		
Other:		

When you experience stress-related signs and symptoms
do you care about yourself enough to say

STOP

????

127

Obviously, these symptoms are not *only* related to stress, but could be caused by a variety of other physical and psychological illnesses. In the absence of a medical diagnosis following a thorough examination by a qualified physician, however, each of the symptoms listed has been identified as a possible stress reaction. Each and every one of us has a limit to the amount of stress we can deal with before our bodies and our minds react. And some of us just cannot handle as much stress as the next person. We are *not* all created equal when it comes to the ability to withstand the pressures and demands that are placed upon us. As the uniquely created individuals that we are, we each need to determine what our "stress tolerance level" is and avoid exceeding it on an everyday basis.

Delegating responsibilities at home, at church, at work, and within our extended families can be an invaluable stress management skill. In fact, this technique is the most widely used stress management practice among top business executives today. By delegating responsibilities, we can decrease the amount of overload we feel and thereby reduce our stress level. Take a long, hard look at your responsibilities and see what you can come up with in terms of a list. Write everything down that you are responsible for in each dimension of your life. We are all managers at some level, just as we are all workers on other levels. Each of us are responsible for how we manage time, money, and other resources, as well as for possibly managing other people.

Now that you have made at least a broad category list, skim through it and put a check beside each item that could be delegated. Taking out the trash is an example of a duty that might be delegated; nursing the baby is not. With any task that could be delegated, try to pick out a handful of those that might be the easiest to delegate and start there. Who else could do it? How could it be done more simply? Could it be done less often? Are you a perfectionist who cannot bear the thought of someone else doing the task less capably? Delegate anyway . . . or you will end up driving yourself, and everyone else, crazy. One person cannot do everything. Jesus knew that! He trained His disciples to minister effectively and "delegated" much responsibility to them.

The next point to tackle is deciding whether you need to *alter your work or home environment through learning to monitor your stress level and helping others to accommodate your needs for quiet times, rest, recreation, and relaxation.* Choosing a job outside the home that places an unbearable amount of pressure upon you will make you an unbearable person to live with. The saying that "something's gotta give" certainly applies here. If your job places demands on you that prevent you from being a loving, emotionally available wife and mother, why are you keeping that job? If it is because there are no others available, might you be able to alter your work environment so the stress level is reduced? If you are in school, could you take fewer classes and delay graduation a semester or two?

When you are at home, do others recognize your need to unwind or do you go right from the frenzied pace of an outside job to a similar pace at home? Do you have a tendency to keep giving out to others when you desparately need to be taking *in* something to nourish your mind, body, and spirit? Stop! Learn to monitor yourself and say that four-letter word that appears on red signs all over town. Just simply say, *Stop*. The best managers do, and so can you, whether the budget you are working with is one hundred and twenty dollars or one hundred and twenty million dollars. Take your stress tolerance level into consideration when you take on new responsibilities, a new career, or a new position in women's ministry at your church. In discovering what price you pay for pushing yourself too hard, you may also find that you don't have to pay that price anymore.

Creative problem-solving and decision-making involve using your thought processes, your ability to picture outcomes, and your intuition as you come up with ways to change your lifestyle. Keeping in mind the benefits of a more responsive and relaxed approach to life will help motivate you. After all, good nutrition, exercise, and a sound night's sleep provide us with *more* energy to face each day. Knowing the results of stress management skills helps us to actively pursue a lifestyle that will enable us to be more vibrant as well as more energetic. The Lord has given us the Holy Spirit to help guide us. As we pray for discernment, let us keep our ears open for that "still, small voice" that often causes us to hesitate before we pursue our latest idea of what will fulfill us or make us "more complete" in Christ through trying to earn God's acceptance.

Organizing oneself requires the use of time management and goal-setting. Setting up a series of steps help us to accomplish our goals in an orderly fashion. In this way, amazing things can be accomplished. A major goal may only be reached by setting up a sequence of smaller prior goals. The really big achievements of our lives will elude our grasp if we are unwilling to take the steps that are necessary to reach them along the way. On some days, setting just one or two goals for that day is all we can handle. When we are ill, when we have several preschoolers running around the house needing attention, when we have guests staying in our home, or when any one of a number of situations find us wondering how to cope, it may be that we have an unrealistic expectation of what we can actually accomplish on a given day. Taking the time to begin our days with prayer and reflection on God's Word is an invaluable means of starting with an outlook that enables us to be better able to understand what aspects of our lives are the most important to the Lord.

There are so many pressures that face us as women today. Stress is a reality as we confront the demands of our responsibilities, whether we have willingly chosen them or been placed in a position of needing to face and accept them as God has brought them into our lives. Within our churches, we need to better support and learn to love one another as sisters in the Lord instead of trying to determine which one of us is the most "spiritual" or the best example of what it means to be a "godly woman." Walking out the truth of what it means to be redeemed and forgiven is a path that we must follow *together* as we respect one another's differences and celebrate our similarities. We can do much to decrease the stressful aspects of our lives if we learn the skill of compassionately sharing one another's burdens while at the same time doing what we can to carry our own.

> Let the morning bring me word of your unfailing love,
> for I have put my trust in you. Show me the way I should go,
> for to you I lift up my soul. Rescue me from my enemies, O
> Lord, for I hide myself in you. Teach me to do your will, for
> you are my God; may your Spirit lead me on level ground.[5]

9

Our Cyclical Nature

One reason why Christian women have such a hard time
accepting themselves, including their bodies, is because the idea
still prevails that the spiritual and mental areas of our lives are
somehow closer to God, more pleasing to him and more
"Christian" than the physical realm. The Bible, which calls the
body the "temple of the Holy Spirit," says the contrary: the more
authentic our faith is, the more we are able to live at peace with
our bodies. The more I succeed in accepting myself as a physical
creature, the more I am able to live in harmony and peace with
myself.[1]

Ingrid Trobisch, *The Joy of Being a Woman*

In the healthy female body, there are six reproductive functions that take place once puberty has ushered in its changes. Each function is accompanied by its own set of physiological events. Only two of these functions involve the sexuality of our husbands in a direct, physical way.

Menstruation, the monthly shedding of the lining of the uterus, is the first function to become evident. About half of all American girls are thought to begin menstruating between the ages of twelve and a half and fourteen and a half. The onset of one's menses follows approximately two years of breast development and other physical changes. This process continues until menopause, which usually takes place between the ages of forty-seven and fifty.

The second function, *ovulation*, involves the release of a mature egg, or ovum, from an ovary and doesn't usually begin until about one year after a girl's periods start. As a female moves into adolescence, genital changes prepare her to participate in the third function, *sexual intercourse*, when the mons pubis (the fleshy area covering the pubic bones) becomes more prominent and the labia majora (major lips) develop and become fuller, covering the rest of the external genitalia that are normally visible throughout childhood. Also, the labia minora (inner lips) develop and grow, and the Bartholin's glands on each side of the vaginal opening become capable of releasing fluid to lubricate the vagina during sexual arousal. The clitoris, a small sensitive organ that is mainly composed of erectile nerve tissue, develops an extensive system of blood vessels at this time, and the vagina changes in color to a deeper red. The mucous lining of the vagina becomes thicker and remains so except during lactation and after menopause, when it becomes considerably thinner and drier. Even the secretions of the cervix change, becoming more acidic than in the past.

Sometime between the ages of ten and twelve, the uterus begins to grow fairly rapidly, until it is doubled in size, usually between the ages of sixteen and eighteen. Once it has reached its mature size, the fourth function, *gestation* or pregnancy, may safely take place. Pregnancy in turn prepares the maternal body for the fifth function: *partuition,* or childbirth. After giving birth, a woman's body triggers the onset of *lactation*. Through the amazing process of breast-feeding, a baby can be completely nourished by the mother's body after she gives birth until sometime around the middle of the first year of life.

These six functions comprise the range of reproductive activities that the Lord designed to take place within the female body. At times, not all of these functions are capable of performing normally, and medical assistance is needed to diagnose and treat the difficulty. Most of the time, all six functions appear in the developmental sequence that I have briefly described.

Each of these reproductive activities are dependent upon the secretion of chemical substances called hormones, which are produced within the body and carried in the bloodstream to the specific sites they are designed to stimulate. Hormones are capable of acting as messages to cells as a means of increasing their functional activity.

The primary "sex hormones" that are secreted by the female body are estrogen and progesterone. Both are produced by the ovaries. The principal sex hormone for males, referred to as an androgen, produces masculine characteristics and is called testosterone. Sex hormones are responsible for a wide range of reproductive functions and for our "secondary sexual characteristics," which we closely associate with our ideas of femininity and masculinity: the amount and location of body hair growth, breast development, sex drive, location of body fat deposits, deepening of the voice, development of muscle tissue, and changes in external genitalia.

The Female Reproductive System: An Inside View of The Menstrual Cycle

At a very early stage during our prenatal development, a group of cells were organized in response to hormonal stimulation to become our ovaries. Also referred to as gonads, ovaries are the sex glands of females that secrete estrogen and progesterone. Male gonads are called testes, which begin to secrete testosterone by the seventh or eighth week after conception. In the developing female, the gonads begin to change into ovaries by the tenth or eleventh week and develop high in the abdomen near the kidneys. They descend downwards and outwards before birth and end up being located closer to the brim of the pelvis.

Each ovary is approximately one inch wide, one and a half inches long, and one quarter of an inch thick, resembling an almond in shape and appearance. In younger women, the ovaries are smooth and pink; in older women, the ovaries are shrunken, pitted, and grey. This change is the result of repeated discharges of eggs, or ova, through the surface of the ovaries, causing them to become wrinkled up and puckered looking as scars form. The ovaries have two responsibilities: to produce ova and to secrete female sex hormones.

At birth, each ovary contains about one quarter of a million small saclike structures called primary follicles. Within these follicles lie immature ova. By puberty, all but approximately ten thousand of these primary follicles degenerate. During our reproductive lives, about three hundred and seventy-five of these remaining follicles expel ova; the remaining follicles degenerate. By the age of fifty, most have disappeared.

Around eight years of age, females begin to secrete a "hormonal messenger" from their pituitary glands that signals the ovaries to begin to prepare their bodies for other reproductive functions. The pituitary gland steps up its secretion of hormones between the ages of eleven and fourteen, and these hormones bring about the time of puberty. During puberty, the ovaries begin to release estrogen into the bloodstream in response to the stimulation that they receive from the pituitary glands. Estrogen is the key ingredient responsible for further developments in the female reproductive system. It is estrogen that stimulates the oviducts (Fallopian tubes), the uterus, and the vagina to mature, increasing their size and ability to function in a reproductive capacity.

The secondary sexual characteristics that are produced by estrogens include the broadening of the pelvis so that its outlet changes from a narrow funnel-shaped opening to a broad oval outlet; the development of smooth, soft skin; the formation of an elaborate duct system in the breasts; the deposition of fat in the breasts, buttocks, and thighs; the growth of pubic hair that has a flat upper border; and early uniting of the growing end of long bones within the bone shaft to limit height.

The primary follicles in the ovaries are stimulated to develop and mature by two hormones released from the pituitary gland: follicle stimulating hormone (FSH) and luteinizing hormone (LH). Ovulation may not take place when the release of these hormones is inhibited by disease or the use of oral contraceptives. FSH is responsible for the early growth of immature ova and the enlargement of the primary follicle. This process of enlargement is due to an accumulation of fluids in the follicle that is similar to the formation of a skin blister. Fifteen to twenty immature follicles are stimulated to grow every month. Of these, only one bulges outward, like a balloon in the wall of the ovary, developing to full maturity. This mature follicle is called a graafian follicle; the other follicles simply degenerate.

In the surface of the graafian follicle is a small, nipplelike protrusion called a stigma. As the stigma develops, the pituitary gland ups its output of LH. As the level of LH rises, the stigma disintegrates and causes the graafian follicle to burst. Some women feel this happen—it is called *mittelschmerz* after a German term that means "pain in the middle." It is a sharp sensation felt in the midabdomen towards either the right or left side, depending on which ovary has released an ovum through the graafian follicle.

The ovum that escapes from the follicle is very fragile and requires nourishment and protection as it travels down the oviduct. It can be fertilized for only twelve to twenty-four hours after ovulation. The cells that remain in the graafian follicle that has just released the ovum are then stimulated by LH to become a temporary gland called the corpus luteum (yellow body). The corpus luteum secretes two important hormones that prepare the oviducts and the uterus to receive the ovum.

The oviducts are trumpet-shaped structures that lie close to the ovaries and extend to the upper corners of the top of the uterus. They are three to five inches long. It is not yet completely understood how the ovum enters the oviducts, but it is thought that at the time of ovulation the muscles within the walls of the oviduct begin to contract and create suction to draw the ovum into the inside of the tube. The ligaments that support the oviducts from the uterus draw the fingerlike ends of the tube, called fimbria, toward the ovary as a means of directing the ovum into the oviduct.

The inside walls of the oviduct are covered with tiny hairlike projections called cilia that create a constant current by beating in a direction that encourages the egg to move toward the uterus. It is as if they are all working in unison as they cry out, "Come on down!" The ova from the right ovary normally enter the right oviduct and those that are released from the left side are directed into the left tube. Many cases have been recorded, however, that show it is possible for a crossover to occur, with the oviduct of the right side, for example, moving over to the left ovary to "pick up" an egg.

When the graafian follicle ruptures, a discharge is released with the ova that contain "nurse cells," called cumulus cells. A cumulus is a cloud that is especially billowy looking, with heaped-up masses. That is exactly how these cells look as they surround the egg, helping to sustain it during its journey to the uterus. As the ova passes through the oviduct, the ever-beating cilia partially separate the cumulus from the ovum as the mass passes through the tube.

Down to the Uterus

Upon entering the tube the ovum, with its nurse cells, is moved through the duct by wavelike muscular contractions similar to those that take place in our intestines. This motion, called peristalsis, presses the cluster of cells down the tube until it reaches the uterus. The ovum is transported at a leisurely pace, arriving at the uterus three to seven days after ovulation.

If the egg is fertilized, this would be most likely to happen while the ovum is still in the upper third of the tube. This means that the sperm must travel an incredible distance to reach the ovum—only the strongest can survive the distance required! Because the egg must be fertilized during the first twelve to twenty-four hours following ovulation, conception must take place at the far end of the tube if it is to happen at all.

Progesterone, which means "in favor of gestation," is secreted by the corpus luteum during this time, causing the glands that lie inside the oviduct to secrete a fluid that nourishes the ovum.

The uterus, or womb, is a hollow muscular pouch that is pear-shaped and lies in the pelvic cavity between the bladder and the rectum. It is about three inches long and two inches wide at the top. It becomes narrow at its base, where it is normally about a half to one inch across. The size of the uterus varies, depending on the age of the female and her reproductive state. At birth, a baby's uterus is enlarged due to hormones that she receives from the mother while still in the womb. The uterus becomes smaller during childhood because it lacks this hormonal stimulation. As discussed earlier, the estrogens that are secreted at puberty signal the uterus to grow until it reaches its mature size. After childbearing, it reaches its largest dimensions; it remains large until after a woman experiences menopause, or the cessation of her menstrual cycle.

The uterus is divided into three portions. The fundus of the uterus is the upper division, lying at the top between the oviducts. It is extremely muscular and is responsbile for the strong contractions that press the baby down through the pelvis during childbirth. Below the fundus lies the body of the uterus. The fundus and the body expand enormously during pregnancy to accommodate the baby's growth. The body of the uterus narrows near its base at a place called the isthmus. The isthmus thins out and lengthens during pregnancy and aids the body of the uterus as it grows. The isthmus is often not considered as a separate part of the womb, but is merely seen as the dividing line between the body of the uterus and the cervix, or neck, of the uterus. The cervix is the lowest part of the uterus and is attached to the front wall of the vagina. The cervical canal is about an inch long. The cervix has fewer muscle cells than the rest of the uterus and more collagen fibers. Within the canal is a mucous membrane, with glands that secrete a fluid that changes in appearance and chemical composition prior to ovulation.

The uterus is normally maintained in its position by the muscles of the pelvic floor and is capable of a wide range of movement. The only immovable, or fixed, portion of the uterus is the cervix. The remainder of the uterus is free to expand, contract, tip forwards or backwards, be pushed upwards by a full bladder or downwards by the rectum if it is distended. During lovemaking, the uterus changes its position several times and contracts during the phases of sexual arousal that accompany orgasm.

A fertilized egg, called an embryo after the third week of its development, usually implants itself in the body of the uterus a good distance away from the cervix. This is the ideal place for the ovum to attach, because it allows for the greatest degree of expansion and the most developed blood supply.

The two layers that make up the uterus are the myometrium and the endometrium. The myometrium, which means "muscle layer," consists of many interwoven fibers of muscular tissue. It makes up seven-eighths of the thickness of the walls of the uterus and has the capacity to expand greatly in size. There are three layers of muscle: an inner layer of circular fibers, a thick intermediate layer which has fibers laid out in a figure-eight pattern that surround the blood vessels that contract to stop the flow of blood after a baby is born, and an outer layer that extends lengthwise across the uterus like wide rubber bands. The outer layer is four times more plentiful in the area of the fundus, to aid it in the expulsion of a baby.

The Build-up of the Uterine Lining

The endometrium, or "inside layer," lines the body of the uterus and is richly supplied with blood vessels. It is about five-eighths of an inch thick and made up of soft tissue that grows for about two weeks prior to ovulation in preparation for the possible implantation of a fertilized ovum. During menstruation the superficial layer of the endometrium is shed, like the peeling off of a layer of wallpaper.

The menstrual cycle consists of four distinct phases that mainly affect the tissue structure of the endometrium. The regenerative phase begins as soon as menstruation stops and lasts for two days. At this time, the glands and cells that are left start to multiply and rebuild the endometrium. Any blood that remains is absorbed, as in the healing of a wound. The proliferative phase (notice the word prolife here!) begins two days after menstruation ceases and lasts until ovulation, for about fourteen days. To proliferate means "to grow rapidly in the production of new cells." This is just what happens as estrogen stimulates the lining of the endometrium to rebuild itself until it is about an eighth of an inch thick.

The premenstrual phase, or secretory phase, starts after ovulation when progesterone that is secreted from the corpus luteum causes further growth in the cells of the endometrium, an increase in the blood supply to the lining of the uterus, and the secretion of fluid from glands that have developed in the lining of the uterus. The endometrium reaches a thickness at its peak of about a quarter of an inch. The lining of the uterus actually is a glistening red at this point after having been so well prepared to receive the awaited guest, a fertilized ovum.

The high levels of estrogen and progesterone at this time in the cycle inhibit the release of any more FSH or LH so that no new primary follicles start to mature. Progesterone keeps the uterus quiet by acting on the myometrium, or muscular layer, of the uterus as a precaution against the possible expulsion of a fertilized egg. It also begins to stimulate growth in the ducts of the breasts, which some women experience as tenderness and/or swelling in this area.

When fertilization does not take place, phase four, or the menstrual phase of the cycle, is initiated. The corpus luteum is active for about ten to twelve days following ovulation, during which time it is secreting estrogen and progesterone to prepare the endometrium to prepare itself to receive a fertilized ovum. If fertilization doesn't occur, then the corpus luteum begins to disintegrate and the amount of estrogen and progesterone that is being secreted falls. The corpus luteum ends up as a white scar, called the corpus albicans (white body), eventually becoming a wrinkled indentation on the surface of the ovary. About two days before the end of the normal menstrual cycle, the corpus luteum stops secreting hormones altogether and the level of estrogen and progesterone sharply falls, bottoming out on about the twenty-sixth day of a thirty-day cycle.

The Lining Is Discarded

When hormonal stimulation of the endometrial lining stops, the cells in this area shrink to about two-thirds of their normal size. About one day before the onset of menstruation, the blood vessels that supply the lining of the uterus are closed off. In the absence of a blood supply, the cells that line the uterus die and separate from the rest of the uterus. These dead cells, along with a small amount of blood that is released from the capillaries (tiny blood vessels) of the endometrium, are expelled by contractions of the uterus as the menstrual flow. During menstruation a little more than an ounce of body fluid and the same amount of blood leave the uterus in a flow that lasts for about five days. Menarche is the term that is used to describe the first menstrual cycle and menopause is the term for the last.

An abnormally large amount of menstrual flow is called menorrhagia. This condition can be caused by disorders of the glands that secrete hormones affecting the menstrual cycle, various diseases, or abnormalities of the reproductive system. Any excessive bleeding should be reported to a physician so that it can be diagnosed and treated.

COPING WITH MENSTRUAL CRAMPS

Figure 9-1

Menstrual cramps are not a figment of the imagination, but are instead linked to *real* causes. Treatment for painful menstruation, or dysmenorrhea, has become more effective through the use of antiprostaglandins which act to inhibit contractions of the uterus. This type of medication, ibuprofen, is available over the counter in the form of 200-milligram tablets or by prescription in 400, 600, or 800-milligram dosages. A woman who is suffering from painful cramps due to endometriosis, fibroid tumors, or ovarian cysts may find that this medication offers little or no relief. The advantage of using antiprostaglandin medication for normal menstrual cramps is that it can be taken as needed (as opposed to every day with birth control pills or hormones) for as little as one day a month. Other prostaglandin inhibitors are: fenoprofen (Nalfon), mefenamic acid (Ponstel), naproxen (Naprosyn), and naproxen sodium (Anaprox). Discuss these medications with your physician, and be sure that you understand the benefits and risks in taking them.

Other methods of relieving uncomplicated menstrual cramps are:

- using a heating pad
- massaging the lower abdomen
- taking a warm bath
- experiencing orgasm to relieve pelvic congestion
- doing stretching exercises to relieve tension
- drinking red raspberry leaf tea; peppermint tea for digestive upset
- having a baby

Amenorrhea is the absence of menstruation and can be primary, meaning that menstruation has never occurred, or secondary. Secondary amenorrhea is normal during pregnancy and lactation. It can also be the result of poor nutrition, anorexia, stress, intense and prolonged physical exertion, medication, a low percentage of body fat, and hormonal disorders. Primary amenorrhea can result from some of these same conditions or from malformed or underdeveloped reproductive organs. Medical assistance should be sought when prolonged amenorrhea exists.

Mild discomfort often accompanies the onset of the menstrual flow. Low back pain, tenderness in the lower abdomen, diarrhea, and cramping of the uterus are not uncommon during the first twenty-four hours. The difference between mild discomfort and painful menstruation is whatever a woman explains it to be. No one outside a woman's body can determine how much pain is present, because pain is whatever a person says it is! It is a subjective experience that can't be measured as you would one's heartbeat or temperature. A competent health care provider will avoid saying something nonsensical like "The pain is all in your head." Pain is *always* "in our heads" as well as our bodies, because it is the brain that tells us we are hurting!

Dysmenorrhea is the term for painful menstruation. It can be caused by inflammation of the pelvic cavity or reproductive system, constipation, a hormone imbalance, emotional stress, and substances secreted by the body called prostaglandins. The actual causes of painful menstruation are poorly understood at this time, however. If a woman's menstrual cramps are not relieved by mild painkillers or become disruptive to her daily schedule, dysmenorrhea is said to exist.

The two types of dysmenorrhea that are related to a hormonal imbalance are called spasmatic dysmenorrhea and congestive dysmenorrhea. Spasmatic dysmenorrhea is caused by an imbalance of progesterone, with too much of it being secreted in relation to the level of estrogen. This condition can be treated with hormones, and is likely to be less severe after a woman bears a child. It is most common between the ages of fifteen and twenty-five.

Premenstrual Syndrome Isn't Just a State of Mind

Congestive dysmenorrhea is associated with premenstrual syndrome, or PMS. It is probably caused by too much estrogen in relation to progesterone. The symptoms include a feeling of heaviness due to fluid retention in the breasts, ankles, and abdomen. It usually begins during the week prior to the onset of menstruation and can include many other symptoms: headache, breast soreness, a craving for sugary foods, fatigue, depression, irritability, dizziness, complexion changes, and forgetfulness. PMS was used successfully by the defense in the trial of two different women accused of murder in England, who were freed when their lawyers stated that hormonal influences had made the women abnormally violent. In the past few years PMS has come to be viewed as a serious problem that is disruptive to women's lives. The fact that PMS was used as a legal defense makes it a feminists nightmare! For those who deny that "biology is destiny," who assert that a woman's reproductive anatomy has little to no effect

THE MYSTERY OF WOMANHOOD

on her ability to actively participate in her chosen career—be it gymnastics, modeling lingerie, or being the president of a large company—the PMS phenomenon is of great concern.

The actual causes and best treatments for PMS are still undergoing debate. Some say that it isn't caused by a deficiency of progesterone, but by vitamin or mineral deficiencies, low blood sugar, low thyroid function, or poorly functioning prostaglandins. A few doctors treat PMS with drugs that are ineffective or actually harmful. Diet and vitamin therapies have relieved the symptoms of PMS for many women. Based on a diet for hypoglycemia (low blood sugar), whole grains, no caffeine, lots of water, no sugar, and small, frequent meals are recommended in addition to taking anywhere from 300-800 milligrams of vitamin B_6 daily during the week before the onset of menstruation. Other women have found that their symptoms are only relieved by taking progesterone in its natural form, which is derived from yams or soybeans and made into a powder that can be absorbed from vaginal or rectal suppositories. Complete studies on premenstrual syndrome have yet to be done; the Food and Drug Administration has yet to recommend suitable doses of progesterone for use in treating PMS.

The controversy over PMS will continue until adequate studies are performed by accredited institutions that clearly demonstrate what it is and how best to treat it. Until then, we will be besieged by quacks who, as usual, are looking to make "a fast buck" off women who are suffering from the very real symptoms of PMS. Consumers should be careful about taking progesterone or vitamins in large amounts until the effects of such substances on the human body are known. In the meantime, a diet that is low in sugar seems to be a good way of helping the body withstand the onslaught of hormonal changes before menstruation. Caffeine, alcohol, nicotine, nitrates and nitrites, salt, monosodium glutamate, chocolate, and artificial sweeteners should be avoided as well. Getting the proper amount of rest, eliminating sources of stress, and managing the stress that can't be eliminated are also important ways to decrease the severity of PMS symptoms.

It is estimated that nearly 80 percent of all women experience PMS to some degree. That makes PMS a fact of life for the majority of women, if this is accurate. One of the most effective ways of learning how to cope with the mood swings and physical symptoms of the last week of the month is to understand our own cycles and realize that the hormonal fluctuations we experience are *real*. It isn't as if most women are *looking* for excuses to hide behind or gain sympathy for. The ovary literally explodes with ovulation each month, and the reproductive system is actively engaged in performing its responsibilities every day. We don't often think about all of the things going on inside us, but we need to accept that the things we can't see are producing changes that affect our *entire* body.

Our cyclical nature is an integral part of who the Lord created us to be. We need to learn creative ways to deal with aspects of our sexuality that are difficult to cope with rather than denying how much we're affected by our bodies at times!

As we look over the complex process of the menstrual cycle, we can either be amazed at the balance of its design, or deny the wisdom at work in our bodies; we can be realistic about making plans that fit in with what our bodies are doing at specific times of the month, or work at full-steam, only to collapse with fatigue; we can eat nutritious foods that will strengthen our bodies, or follow our cravings for junk food and exaggerate premenstrual tension; we can be honest with our husbands about how we're feeling and why, or pretend that everything is fine because we don't want to be seen as "the weaker sex." To live in harmony with the way the Lord has created us means we can acknowledge the fact that our bodies' cycles *do* affect us. We can live with our cycles while consciously helping our bodies cope with the changes we experience from month to month. Our sexuality encompasses so many things! Being a woman can be a joyful experience when we understand and accept the fullness of our identity.

Menstruation and Levitical Law

> When a woman has her regular flow of blood, the impurity of her monthly period will be seven days, and anyone who touches her will be unclean till evening. Anything she lies on during her period will be unclean, and anything she sits on will be unclean. Whoever touches her bed must wash his clothes and bathe with water, and he will be unclean till evening. . . . If a man lies with her and her monthly flow touches him, he will be unclean for seven days; any bed he lies on will be unclean. . . . You must keep the Israelites separate from things that make them unclean, so they will not die in their uncleanness for defiling my dwelling place, which is among them.[2]

In 1986, it is difficult to imagine what it was like to be a woman living in the desert, with no running water or flush toilets, no packages of sanitary napkins or tampons to buy, and no soap or deodorant. The Lord in His wisdom gave His people a set of laws, recorded in Leviticus, that comprise the first public health code to be used by a group of people in history. Our Creator, who had made the human body, was intimately familiar with every cell, every process, and every organism that could thrive within us. The fifteenth chapter of Leviticus speaks directly to the contaminating properties of bodily discharges; the menstrual flow is included in this category.

141

It was not until the mid-1800s that Ignaz Semmelweiss discovered the importance of soap in preventing the cross-contamination that results from not washing between examining a person who has just died of an infectious disease and examining a laboring woman. Soap is a relatively new "invention," and the concept of cleanliness in preventing disease was not widely accepted until the 1880s. Dr. Semmelweiss was ridiculed for his theory of why soap deters infection and was ostracized by his profession. It is often only in retrospect that such discoveries make sense to us. Today we can't even imagine what hospital wards must have been like without antiseptics, clean sheets, and sterile instruments, just as we can't imagine life without disposable toilet and menstrual paper products!

The menstrual flow is made up of body fluid containing cells that have sloughed off the endometrium and blood from the capillaries of the lining of the uterus. This discharge leaves the body in a clean state. Once it becomes exposed to air, however, it becomes an ideal medium for bacteria to grow in. With no soap to keep the vaginal area cleansed and little water available to even rinse off the menstrual flow, we can easily understand why these verses in Leviticus emphasize the danger that would be inherent in such situations. If we were to be this cautious today about sexually transmitted diseases and their symptoms, we could quickly curtail the rate at which such infections are spread—especially if monagamy was also embraced! AIDS would cease to be a public health menace; genital herpes would be curtailed; and gonorrhea would no longer be making thousands of women sterile each year. The Lord was explicitly clear about the dangers of discharges and skin lesions and informed the Hebrew nation of what He knew in very specific language.

The laws we find in Leviticus are further proof of the Lord's sovereign nature. We can read these chapters today and marvel at the way in which the Lord provided practical help and protection to preserve the health of His people. Now that we understand more about microbiology, we are able to reasonably protect ourselves from many diseases and infections that can be curtailed through proper hygiene. Menstruation is no longer a cause for separation from everyday life and need not be considered filthy in any way. Daily bathing or showering with soap and water has made all the difference in how we can approach this aspect of our lives.

The toxic shock syndrome scare that linked the deaths of women using superabsorbent tampons to a fatal disease reminds us of the power of micro-organisms to multiply and devastate. Toxic shock syndrome, or TSS, is a recently identified disease caused by a bacteria called Staphylococcus aureus. Research is being done to find out more about this disease and why the use of tampons is associated with it. It has been estimated that fifteen out of every one hundred thousand girls and women who are menstruating will get this disease each year. The Food and Drug Administration has offered the following guidelines: the low risk of getting TSS can be almost entirely eliminated by not using tampons; the risk can be reduced by using tampons on and off during the menstrual cycle (such as wearing them during the daytime only) and by not leaving a tampon in for more than four hours at a time; about one in every three females who have had TSS get it again and should not wear tampons until more research has been done. The warning signs of TSS are: 1) sudden fever that is usually 102 degrees or higher and 2) vomiting or diarrhea. If these signs should occur during a period, the tampon should be removed and a doctor called right away. Other symptoms include a sudden drop in blood pressure accompanied by dizziness and a rash that looks like a sunburn.

AVOIDING TOXIC SHOCK SYNDROME

Figure 9-2

If you choose to wear tampons rather than sanitary pads during your period, you can reduce the risk of developing toxic shock syndrome by:

- washing your hands before and after inserting a tampon
- washing the external genital area twice a day while menstruating
- not leaving a tampon in place for more than four hours
- alternating tampon use with sanitary pads for a twenty-four-hour period
- wearing tampons only when you are flowing heavily
- avoiding superabsorbent brands of tampons, which are more likely to cause tiny cuts in the skin of the vagina when inserted

---

Making love during menstruation may be uncomfortable and unaesthetic for many women, but in a healthy woman there are no medical contraindications to having intercourse during one's period. It is important to know that pregnancy can result from lovemaking during menstruation, unlikely as it may seem. Many women prefer to not have intercourse when they feel discomfort or are self-conscious about what they consider to be messy or malodorous lovemaking. This is not an ideal situation for a woman to be fully sexual responsive, and each couple needs to be completely frank with one another about their feelings regarding sexual expression during menstruation. Alternative expressions to intercourse might be preferable, for instance, or seminudity instead of full nudity to enhance a woman's feeling of attractiveness. Some couples choose to view menstruation as a break, a time for "courtship activities": going out for a date, playing Scrabble, or walking in the park hand in hand. All women benefit from having times like this, whether for the purpose of avoiding intercourse during menstruation or not!

Other women experience a heightened desire for lovemaking during their periods, especially when the flow tapers off after the first few days. Be open about your level of interest with your husband if this is true for you. If he is unresponsive, find out how he feels about making love during this phase of your cycle. Your husband may just not be informed enough to know that bathing before going to bed sufficiently cleanses you and that on light days there is only a trace of evidence that you are menstruating. He may be pleasantly surprised to discover that this phase of the month can be a time of increased responsiveness for *both* of you!

Be confident in determining your own preferences and needs as a couple in this area, knowing that there is no single "correct" way to approach the subject. What matters is how the two of you feel about lovemaking during menstruation.

The rhythms of regeneration, proliferation, ovulation, the premenstrual phase, and menstruation form a pattern that repeats itself several hundred times during a woman's fertile years. These cycles form a framework within which other reproductive functions may be expressed and experienced. Learning to live with our fertility and making decisions about how we will come to terms with it at various points of our lives will be our next consideration.

> In the life of each of us, I said to myself,
> there is a place remote and islanded, and given
> to endless regret or secret happiness.
>
> Sarah Orne Jewett, *The Country of the Pointed Firs*

144

10

Living with
Our Fertility

*Marriage is to produce children and make the earth fruitful for
God. Christian marriage, in other words, is God-centered
(producing what God wants) rather than me- or us-centered
(meeting my or our desires). As with all God's designs, our needs
do get met, but by the route of faith. First we do what God
commands; then to our surprise we find ourselves blessed. First we
deny ourselves and take up our cross, and then we find the
burden light and pleasant. Then we find ourselves. Then we find
our hearts set free, and the love of God shed abroad in our
hearts, and our marriages blossoming and blooming.[1]*

Mary Pride, The Way Home

Throughout early Biblical history, God's blessing was often associated with the desire that His people be fruitful, increase in number, and replenish the earth.[2] Even when the descendants of Abraham, Isaac, and Jacob had multiplied to the point that they were "as many as the stars in the sky," Moses replied to the apparent population explosion by saying:

May the Lord, the God of your fathers, increase you a
thousand times and bless you as he has promised![3]

Contrary to current trends, the Bible *never* portrays childbearing as an unwanted or negative side-effect of marital sexuality. Indeed, God's Word always views children as the *expected* fruit of the marriage union. If we are to be sincere in our evaluation of contemporary responses to the way our Creator designed our bodies, we must be willing to open our eyes to the truth of Scripture and remove the lenses through which we have grown accustomed to viewing our capacity for fruitfulness.

First of all, we need to recognize how our dependence on medical technologies associated with controlling fertility has promoted the view that conception depends on our personal decisions and actions alone. The truth is that, ultimately, it is God who imparts life to each human being.[4] Physical fruitfulness springs from the hand of God as an integral expression of our sexuality. Although the *frequency* of ovulation appears to be a consequence of the Fall ("I will greatly multiply thy sorrow and thy conception"),[5] the *fact* of our ability to bear fruit for God was established before sin entered the world.[6] In learning to live with our fertility, we must once again affirm the Biblical norm of fruitfulness and avoid compromising or undermining it.

As Christians, how we respond to God with our bodies matters. If we claim to value children as gifts from the Lord and yet employ technologies and adopt attitudes and behaviors that make it impossible for children to enter the world, we contradict ourselves and the clear message of Scripture. If we oppose abortion based upon the claim that it is God who forms life within us and yet deny that the Bible states that the Lord considers *conception itself* to be a blessing, are we faithfully representing the *complete* picture regarding childbearing within Scripture? Have we consistently resisted the compulsion to choose socially acceptable alternatives to fruitfulness? Apparently many of us have not. Believers as well as nonbelievers have adopted the reproductive norms of our culture and have willingly embraced artificially induced barrenness as a valuable "reproductive alternative" in the absence of sound teaching about Biblical norms dealing with this important aspect of our lives. As childless marriages, genetic engineering, amniocentesis, two children/zero population childbearing, and the abandonment of fertility through elective sterilization continue to increase in popularity, the evangelical church seems to be at an impasse as to how to interpret the collective impact of these trends. In the meantime, Christians by the thousands are allowing their posterity to be excised from their bodies. Consequently, the view that children are "a heritage of the Lord" is vanishing from many churches across Western Europe and North America.

The Affirmation of Human Life

We need a revolutionary message in the midst of today's relativistic thinking. By revolutionary, or radical, I mean standing against the all-pervasive form which the world spirit has taken in our day. This is the real meaning of radical. God has given his answers in the Bible—the Bible that is true when it speaks of history and of the cosmos, as well as when it speaks of religious things. And it therefore gives truth concerning all reality.[7]

If we are to approach female sexuality from a truly Biblical perspective, we will most assuredly be in opposition to current world views that are expressed within Western culture. Taking such a stand will be radical, even revolutionary. But I believe that our bodies have become a battleground upon which a war of great proportions is being waged. Consider this: *it is only through women's wombs that human life enters God's creation.* If our Maker does in fact care for each child as a loving Father, could He ever *bless* us with sterility? No! Although His Word makes this very clear, somehow we've missed the mark on this point.

It is not enough to believe that marital sexuality is simply a beautiful expression of love within marriage when it is also undeniably the garden in which human souls are sown and nourished while being brought to fruition beneath the loving hand of God. As a mother and father, two people make a significant contribution to the kingdom of God through creating a family in which God's presence dwells.

We need to learn to view our fertility from an *eternal perspective* instead of only considering the trials and troubles that will face us when we are obedient to God in this area of our lives. The Bible makes it abundantly clear that human life is not disposable. *Each and every child that is conceived possesses a life that Christ may enter into and live within throughout eternity.* Bringing a child into the world affirms this. When a couple says yes to their ability to be vehicles through which this amazing event takes place, a unique individual is given the opportunity to experience what it means to be created in the image of God. Think of it! You and I are here today because our parents did not say no.

Our Father has graciously given us His Holy Spirit to sustain us while we rear each little one on His behalf. We are not alone as we live out the day-to-day reality of mothering our children. God is able to comfort and guide us as we journey toward our final destination. Our lives—each life—has significance beyond the grave because we are loved by a God who is there. One day we will be made new as we stand in His presence. Every tear will be wiped from our eyes.[8] Along with our children, we are moving through time toward the moment when we will stand together praising God as we finally see Jesus face to face. What a gift! What an opportunity—to experience what it means to be alive. . . . to have become a part of the kingdom of God and to have our children share in this with us! *This* is the reality of what the Bible says about the value of human life to the Lord.

May God give us the strength to stand in this present age as we share His truth with a dying world.

Jonathan's Story

1980 will be a year I will always remember. It was to be the year that I graduated from college after ten years of part-time attendance, the year of launching out after spending eight and a half years of my life pregnant or breast-feeding (or both!) without a single break. The youngest of our

147

three children was finally weaned and toilet-trained, and we were celebrating the fact that there would be no more diapers to wash at our house.

I met with an adviser at the university to prepare my entrance into a graduate program in medical education, looking forward to an eventual career in teaching health professionals how to become better educators. Suddenly I became ill with an infection and was unusually tired and irritable.

At the end of an office visit to my family physician, I asked him if he thought my period might be delayed as a result of the illness. As he wrote out a prescription he told me we had better check to see if I was pregnant. "But I couldn't be," I replied to his preposterous proposal. "Don't even suggest it!"

I'll never forget the feeling in the pit of my stomach as he shared the results of the test with me. My head was reeling. I did *not* want to have another child, not then, not ever. I had had enough of nausea and heartburn and labor pain.

My previous pregnancies had been filled with joy and anticipation, but now I felt only guilt because I was angry and deeply depressed. I read certain Psalms repeatedly, especially Psalm 51. I wept off and on for nine months. When friends from the university would hear of my impending "bad fortune" (an unplanned pregnancy), they would ask me what I was going to do about "the situation." I told them that abortion was not a consideration. Silence inevitably followed, and they would look at me as if I had suddenly turned into a mindless reproduction machine.

During labor I still felt distant from the baby that my body had nurtured for so long. As I propped myself up on my elbows to watch Jonathan's eight and a half pound body slip out into the world, I was amazed at my reaction. He was beautiful! Joanna and Katherine and David had a new brother! Here was our second son! I was meeting a new person only God had seen before, greeting a life that He had determined would join our family.

More tears began to flow, but they no longer tasted bitter because they sprang from a thankful heart. Over the months that followed, my heart opened up to receive Jonathan's love until I eventually felt as strong a bond with him as I had with our previous children. Leaving the university was a small price to pay for the benefits we reaped from Jonathan's arrival. The long days of full-time mothering and breast-feeding enabled me to draw closer to the Lord than I ever had been before, causing me to reevaluate my roles as a wife and as a mother. "The steadfast love of the Lord never ceases . . ."

When I look at Jonathan today, I can't believe that I was so blind to the beauty of his conception or that I ever considered him to be anything *but* a blessing. He has been such a gift to me! Had I felt differently about abortion, I would have missed one of the greatest opportunities for growth the Lord has ever provided us. You see, God *knew* that Jonathan would enrich our lives even though we didn't welcome his conception. Proverbs states that "In his heart a man plans his course, but the Lord determines his steps."[9] So it was for us. As we laid our plans aside, we were broken through this experience for the glory of God.

I share this story not to condemn others who might have reacted differently than I, but as a way of expressing how very important it is to be responsive to the will of God even when it hurts—and sometimes *especially* when it hurts. Just when we think we have it all together, Jesus beckons us to come closer to the Cross, to go further in our walk, to more deeply share with Him. The sacrifices of God really *are* a contrite heart and a broken spirit.

Becoming a mother in today's culture is a humbling experience. Lifting the restrictions we have placed on our sexual fruitfulness is scary, risky. But being agreeable to bringing new life into the world enables us to respond in faith to a way of life in which we lay down our own needs for the sake of expanding God's creation. I urge you to reflect on the significance of this.

The Myth of the Natural Mother

Nowhere in the Word of God are we told that God "calls" only *some* married women into motherhood. Most of us at one time or another have probably heard someone say, "Well, of course children are easy for *her* to have. She's naturally gifted to be a mother." Are there really two kinds of married women in the world—those who are natural mothers and those who are not? The truth is that the idea of the "natural mother" is a myth. There are no natural mothers! Motherhood is not a peculiar talent, inborn trait, or special gift which some women have and others don't. Being a mother is *a way of life, open and available to all married women.* It depends upon one's willingness to make the necessary commitment and the sacrifices associated with laying down one's life for the love of one's children along with one's husband. Who in their "natural" minds would *want* to spend their time wiping dirty bottoms, preventing siblings from killing one another, doing tons of laundry, or sitting up all night with a hospitalized child? As we serve the little ones the Lord entrusts to our care, we know that what we do unto them we also do unto Christ our Savior.

If you doubt this, look around you. Who are the mothers and fathers that exemplify fruitfulness and dedication to the task of nurturing their children? Are they the parents with an overiding commitment to a worldly value system and who always seem to "have it all together"? Or are they the ones who usually sit at the back of the church near the aisle so they can make a fast exit in case of a toileting emergency? You know, the ones that

149

look tired yet somewhat amused as their kids take turns snuggling up next to them, wriggling around, and slouching down as far as possible during the worship service . . .

As opposed to a natural call, the ability to be parents comes in the doing of the tasks and the opening of our hearts that enables us to love our children as we surrender our time, resources, and energy to promote the growth and health of another human being. It doesn't take a college degree to learn how to do these things, just lots of prayer, patience, and calling out to God for help in times of need. (Like at least half a dozen times a day!) This requires no special talent—it requires brokenness and self-denial!

Paul wrote that those who marry "will face many troubles in life."[10] In 1 Corinthians 7:32-35, he went on to say that an unmarried man or woman can be more fully concerned with the Lord's affairs than can those who are married. Yet there are many Christians today who want to have it *all*: full-time ministry, marriage, parenthood, financial ease, *and* the chance to do the Lord's business. Perhaps Paul was right. Those who wish to serve the Lord more fully might be better off remaining single and celibate, as the apostle recommended, rather than imposing infertility upon their marriages "for the sake of Christ." It seems that the evangelical church has lost the concept of being single unto the Lord and has promoted barrenness as a result. Children are *not* simply optional elements in a marriage that add pleasure and meaning to our lives.

As we yield ourselves to the Lord in His service with thankful hearts, let us remember how Paul urged believers in Rome to respond to God's gracious gift to them:

> . . . I implore you by God's mercy to offer your very selves to
> him: a living sacrifice, dedicated and fit for his acceptance,
> the worship offered by mind and heart. Adapt yourselves no
> longer to the pattern of this present world, but let your
> minds and your whole nature be thus transformed. Then you
> will be able to discern the will of God, and know what is
> good, acceptable, and perfect.[11]

The Pattern of This Present World

Did you know that the world's experts do not fully understand how many of today's contraceptives work? Increasingly it is becoming evident that many methods of birth control allow conception to take place and interrupt a pregnancy *after* it has begun. Such drugs and devices are actually technologies that induce abortion during the early weeks of pregnancy. These methods are abortifacients rather than contraceptives, since the word *contraception* literally means "against conception."

Postfertilization methods of preventing birth from taking place include the following technologies which are used regularly on a continuous basis or as needed to interrupt a pregnancy:

- Intrauterine devices, or I.U.D.'s, which in some way render the lining of the uterus incapable of receiving an egg. An estimated 240 million abortions per year are induced by the use of I.U.D.'s.[12]
- Oral contraceptives, which employ backup mechanisms that prevent implantation should an egg become fertilized. There is no way of even being able to begin to estimate the number of silent abortions that the Pill is responsible for each year.
- Morning-after pills which use DES (diethylstilbestrol) to force menstruation to begin. There are no statistics kept as to how many women are put on these pills, which were designed to induce abortion following intercourse.
- Prostaglandin suppositories, which stimulate uterine contractions in an effort to expel "the products of pregnancy"
- Intramuscular injections of prostaglandins or progestogens
- Vaginal silastic devices containing prostaglandins
- Vaginal rings and implants containing progestin
- Menstrual extraction or "once a month" pills
- Vacuum aspiration

I strongly urge you to protest the concept of *birth* control because *it presupposes that births may be prevented through technology at any stage of prenatal development as well as after birth through the refusal to medically treat children who are viewed as "defective," "subnormal," or "less than human."* We must be very clear about making the distinction between what it means to control *birth rates* compared to what happens when we act to *prevent conception.* This is because the moment of fertilization is a line of demarcation, the incredibly significant boundary between independent cellular life and the permanent fusion of genetic information that sets the pattern of a person's life in motion.

It is important for those who seek to guard the rights of unborn children to understand how contraceptives function and whether or not a particular method can be *guaranteed* to prevent conception as its *sole function.* We must confront physicians by asking for complete information on the modes of action of various methods of family planning. Just asking, "Does it prevent conception *100 percent of the time* or does it prevent birth in some other ways?" should enable health care providers to more honestly represent these technologies to their clients.

An interview with Malcolm Muggeridge in *Christianity Today* contained his perspectives on the relationship of contraception to abortion. With a great deal of foresight, as well as hindsight, he stated that he thought the wide acceptance of birth control methods makes it "ridiculous to talk about abolishing abortion," claiming that "if you have contraception, you will have abortion." Prochoice advocates have said exactly the same thing as they have claimed that an increased acceptance of contraception in the sixties paved the way for abortion rights in the seventies. Is this far-fetched, or is there in fact a direct link between the two? Considering the invasiveness of the methods just outlined, it would seem that the boundary lines are becoming increasingly difficult to distinguish.

Muggeridge went on to say that if we "divorce eroticism from its purpose, [we] create the sort of conditions out of which come abortion and euthanasia. . . . If marriage is erotic satisfaction, then it is clear that monogamy won't meet that need. It only meets that need if it represents something more than that. . . . If you say, 'I demand sexual gratification, irrespective of any institution, and I demand the right to prevent its consequences,' then I know what will happen to man. Namely: unhappiness. The busting up of the Christian way of life will soon follow."[13]

Why Not the Pill?

It was just fifty years ago, in 1937, that the hormone progesterone was found to prevent ovulation in rabbits. Further research discovered that a synthetic substance derived from a type of yam growing wild in Mexico could produce the same effects as naturally secreted progesterone.

In 1956, a related substance called progestogen was combined with estrogen to produce a hormonal contraceptive that could be taken orally on a daily basis. The addition of estrogen to progestogen assured a normal menstrual flow at the end of each "cycle" even in the absence of ovulation. This sequence of events, accompanied by a wide social acceptance of contraception, led to the mass marketing of what became known simply as "the Pill."

There are three major types of oral contraceptives (OC's) available today: those combining estrogen and progestin; phasic pills that utilize doses of both hormones to more closely duplicate a woman's cycle; and progestin-only minipills. OC's that contain low levels of estrogen or progestin alone pose the least risk of serious side effects, but may suppress ovulation *as little as 40 to 50 percent of the time, allowing for possible repeated fertilization of ova.*

OC's alter the physiology of the menstrual cycle by:

- inhibiting the production of the hormones FSH and LH, which are needed for the maturation of an egg by the ovarian follicles;
- hastening the migration of the egg through the fallopian tube. If the egg is fertilized, the Pill also acts by:
- causing the ovum to arrive before the uterus is ready to receive it;

- altering the lining of the uterus to render it less fertile and
- causing cervical mucus to become heavier and act as a barrier.

The exact number of these mechanisms functioning at a given time cannot be accurately predicted. Health professionals cite the primary advantage of taking OC's as an effective form of contraception because it has a theoretical use-effectiveness* of greater than 99 percent and an actual use-effectiveness of 96 percent. This type of medication, they claim, can also improve acne, regulate irregular menstrual cycles, provide relief from menstrual cramping, decrease the amount of menstrual flow, and reduce the length of one's periods. The Pill is also popular because it allows for spontaneity in lovemaking since there are no devices or spermicides to apply.

Since few men visit their wife's or fiancee's physician at the time an OC is prescribed, they tend not to be well informed about how the Pill acts or the problems that are directly linked to OC use, which take up page after page in the *Physician's Desk Reference* guide to prescriptive medications. If men were more aware of these things, I doubt that many of them would want their partners to use the Pill in spite of its relative "benefits."

The many side effects of OC's are well documented. This is thought to be the major factor behind a trend away from their use. In 1973 the National Center for Health Statistics reported that 36.1 percent of all married women between the ages of fifteen and forty-four stated a preference for the use of OC's. In the decade that followed, Pill use dropped to nearly half that amount.[14]

More than one-third of those women who take OC's reportedly experience such irritating side effects as:

- Fluid retention
- Swollen gums
- Weight gain
- Chronic vaginal or urinary tract infections
- Breast tenderness
- Painful intercourse
- Nausea
- Mild headaches
- Hair loss
- Chloasma, or darkening of the skin around the forehead, upper lips, and under the eyes

- Increased amount of body hair
- Alterations in thyroid function
- Swelling of the cornea, resulting in contact lens irritation
- Worsening of acne
- Spotting between periods
- Unusual fatigue or weakness
- Loss of appetite or weight loss
- Abdominal cramping
- Extreme fluctuations in sexual desire
- Diarrhea
- Moodiness

*The effectiveness of a contraceptive if it is used completely accurately 100 percent of the time.

153

The use of OC's also increases the risks of developing hypertension (high blood pressure), impaired liver function, gallbladder disease, thromboembolism (the formation of a clot within a vein), cerebrovascular disease (stroke), and certain types of heart disease. It is now known that OC's cause blood platelets to mass together and adhere to the lining of blood vessels, a condition that favors the formation of clots. Since OC's also seem to inhibit the system that breaks down small clots, the combination of these two factors increases the risk of diseases related to internal clotting. Because of the risks that are associated with taking OC's, there are over thirty-five conditions that contraindicate their use.

A recent comparison of IUD users to OC users found that women who use the Pill had a higher rate of cervical cancer. For this reason, women who take the Pill are advised to arrange for Pap smears once or twice a year. Fifteen percent of those women who use OC's also develop diabetes or develop a prediabetic condition and are asked to be tested for glucose intolerance on an annual basis. Related sugar imbalances in the vagina create a medium for the growth of yeast, making treatment for *candida albicans* a far from uncommon occurrence.

Women who take the Pill also are likely to acquire vitamin deficiencies. OC's deplete levels of vitamins B_6, B_{12}, C, E, and folic acid. In addition, body levels of trace minerals, including zinc and magnesium, may be lowered as well.

Considering the way the Pill changes so many body functions, why would women want to take it unless it was absolutely indicated to correct a serious medical problem? As evidenced by the dramatic decline in Pill use since the early seventies, fewer and fewer women do. Then what *are* couples using that has been so effective in lowering the birth rate to an all-time low?

The "Easy" Way Out: Permanent Sterility

Elective sterilization has become the single most popular form of contraception. Sterilization does the job of preventing conception better than any other method. Current health science texts cite sterilization as being second only to abortion in its ability to control the birth rate in the U.S. One third of all sexually active men and women have been sterilized, and it is estimated that *one-half* of all married couples have chosen this method of contraception. Vasectomies and tubal ligations have been performed by the millions in the last fifteen years. Are there any drawbacks, or is this method really the escape from fertility that so many have longed to find throughout history?

Now wait a minute . . . do I actually mean to imply that our ancestors would have been anxious to tie their tubes too? I certainly do! We are, after all, living at a time in which fewer women and babies die during pregnancy and childbirth than ever before, are we not? And we do have more wealth, more labor-saving devices, and better shelter than those that preceded us, don't we? *Rather than taking advantage of these factors, we are abandoning reproduction in record numbers.* The long-term consequences will have a tremendous impact on the Western world, a world that our children will inherit.

Speaking of this trend, noted French demographer Pierre Chaunu observed: "The rejection of [marriage and the family] is a recent phenomenon. For the moment, it is limited to the sixth of the world that constitutes the developed nations, the eight hundred million men and women who have decided to commit the strangest collective suicide of history."[15]

In West Germany, birth rate figures are catastrophic, having reached an average of 1.27 children per family. By the year 2020, West Germany's population will be cut in half, from sixty million down to thirty million, if this rate continues. Professor Chaunu claims that the difference between West Germany's rate and that of France, Switzerland, and our own country's is simply the difference between "imminent collapse and slow death."

It does not take an expert on population growth to help us predict what the impact of a rapidly shrinking work force would have on the federal budget. As our generation faces retirement, who will be supporting the Social Security system? (That is, if it doesn't collapse in the meantime!) Will we see a revival of Hitler's "useless eaters" propaganda as a way of encouraging the aged and disabled to lighten the tax load through euthanasia?

Zero population caught on so well that it became practically an overnight sensation, but let's not fool ourselves that it is because we are all morally committed to controlling overpopulation. As a childbirth educator, I know better! Over the past five or six years, more and more women feel comfortable informing other class members that "this child we're expecting is our second and our last" as they introduce themselves at the beginning of a refresher series. *None* have ever said that it was because they were afraid of overpopulation. But I have heard a variety of *real* reasons as I've listened to their statements. They have included:

> "I'm so glad I don't have to go through *this* again—twice is *enough*."
> "Our car only holds four people."
> "We want to have the ability to travel."
> "We decided that our incomes would only support two kids."
> "I can't wait until they are all in school!"
> "God wants us to be responsible stewards of our resources."
> "I really hate being pregnant. And besides, children are much more interesting than babies."
> "Too many sleepless nights . . ."

I have yet to hear any mothers say they won't be having any more children due to health reasons, genetic concerns, or absolute poverty. The thinking seems to be more along the lines of "I don't mind having two since I can get through this stage pretty quickly and get on with the rest of my life sooner." Two children are manageable; with three, you're outnumbered; four have become almost an embarrassment ("Gee, Mom, look at that huge family sitting over there!"); and if you have five or more, forget it—you are a bona fide phenomenon.

When a couple decides that they would prefer to adopt a comfortable lifestyle rather than conform to the Biblical standard of fruitfulness, these attitudes often are the result. But what is more important? From an eternal perspective, does a parent's ability to provide private music lessons, a college education, and a wide assortment of material goods mean more than providing life itself to a child? If having four or six or eight children requires that those children sleep three or four to a room instead of having the luxury of rooms of their own, will that really matter in the long run? Could it be that fruitfulness in fact promotes a simpler, less materialistic approach to life that is easily lost within a society fed by consumerism?

The Sermon on the Mount runs counter to everything that material excesses represent. Providing for our wants is very different than the type of stewardship that enables us to meet our basic needs. In sacrificing fruitfulness for the sake of maintaining a certain standard of living, families may miss the opportunity to more fully embrace Jesus' teachings. Walking in obedience before God in this area of life can open up new horizons to Christians who have been raised in our culture. For example, having a third child may mean saying no to a second car. With the fourth, an athletic club membership and cable television may need to be canceled. Five may prevent annual out-of-state vacations unless the family learns camping skills. Many of the things we spend money on are optional from a Biblical standpoint; children are not. Laying down our lives for the sake of bringing new life into the world forces us to come closer to adopting a way of life that keeps us nearer to the Cross. Could this be one of the reasons fruitfulness is so clearly represented as a blessing in God's Word?

Sterilization poses medical as well as spiritual risks. The relative safety of sterilization causes couples to decide that a "one shot deal" is well worth the risks involved. In exchange for convenience and effectiveness, fertility is completely abandoned. The mortality rate for female sterilization is 1 to 10 per 100,000 women. Depending on the type of procedure used, the rate of complications varies from 1.6 to a high of 13.3 percent, including such conditions as wound infections, bowel burns, uterine perforations, and bladder injuries. For men, problems associated with vasectomy surgery run about 5 percent.

Dietrich Bonhoeffer wrote: "The most radical way in which unwanted births can be prevented is by sterilization. . . . In order to assess this problem justly, one must above all not conceal oneself from the gravity and the seriousness of this interference with personal life. The human body possesses an inherent right of inviolability. Neither I nor anyone else can lay claim to an absolute right of free disposal over the bodily members that have been given to me by God."[16] He extends this same argument against suicide as well.

I think Bonhoeffer's comparison of suicide to sterilization is an appropriate one. The ultimate statement that a person is the master of one's fate is to choose one's own death. Sterilization is similar in that men or women seize control over what has been given to them by God and seal the fate not only of their fertility, but of any future offspring with which the Lord may wish to bless them. Do we in fact have the right to this type of control? Do we have the right to commit reproductive suicide?

The flipside of fruitfulness is barrenness. Within Scripture, there are numerous references to the Lord "shutting" women's wombs. Barrenness, or infertility, is consistently viewed as *the absence of God's blessing*. In Hosea, the extreme example of this is demonstrated in the prophecy that "Ephraim's glory will fly away like a bird—no birth, no pregnancy, no conception. . . . wombs that miscarry and breasts that are dry."[17] In this passage, barrenness represents God's judgment, a punishment inflicted because of a people's disobedience.

Jesus Himself referred to barrenness just prior to His crucifixion. On the way to the Cross, He turned to a group of women who were mourning for Him and said, "Daughters of Jerusalem, do not weep for me; weep for yourselves and for your children. For the time will come when you will say, 'Blessed are the barren women, wombs that never bore and the breasts that never nursed.' "[18] His statement clearly refers to the desolation He had spoken of to His disciples just prior to His arrest, predicting the calamity that would befall the inhabitants of the earth at the end of the age.[19] In telling these women that barrenness would one day be viewed as a blessing, I believe Jesus was underscoring the devastation of humanity that would take place in the end times. To women of His time, I am sure this seemed hideously twisted and unbelievable. Barrenness a blessing? Breasts that would not nurture? Sadly, it is very difficult for us to relate to how this must have sounded, because as a culture, we now consider it normal, even desirable, to become barren.

I am, of course, here speaking about "elective barrenness"—not about couples who wish to bear children but are unable to do so. Nor do I mean to imply that in any specific case involuntary infertility is a curse of God's judgment. Barrenness is surely a consequence of the Fall, as, for example, disease is. But just as we do not think of someone who has cancer as being under God's judgment, neither should we think of involuntarily childless couples in that way.

Responding to a Biblical View

It is time that Christians begin to give very careful consideration to the question of conception control through studying the Scriptures, earnest prayer, and asking their pastors and others in positions of leadership to provide a positive Biblical basis for its practice. Conception control has usually been justified along the lines of the "Bible doesn't forbid it" type of argument, which is an argument from silence, and which is notoriously

TOWARD A CHRISTIAN ETHIC OF FAMILY PLANNING

Figure 10-1

CONTEMPORARY VIEW OF REPRODUCTIVE RIGHTS

A. My body belongs to me; therefore:
- I have the right to decide what to do with my body.
- I am responsible to myself alone for my decisions and my actions.

B. In regards to my sexuality, this means:
- I am free to express my sexuality in any way I choose.
- I alone will decide how many children I will bear, if any, and when I will bear them.

C. This in turn allows me to:
- abandon any marriage contract that violates these rights.
- refuse to bear children that I do not want to bear.
- terminate any pregnancy that I deem undesirable.
- live my life according to what I think best suits my needs.

"We recognize the right of the individual, married or single, to be free from unwarranted governmental intrusion into matters so fundamentally affecting a person as the decision whether to bear or beget a child. That right necessarily includes the right of a woman to decide whether or not to terminate her pregnancy." (Supreme Court decision on abortion, January 22, 1973)

BIBLICAL VIEW OF FRUITFULNESS

A. My body belongs to God (1 Cor. 6:19, 20); therefore:
- It is my responsibility to live in harmony with the Holy Spirit (Rom. 8; Gal. 5:16-26; Eph. 5:15-21; Phil. 2:1-11; Col. 3:1-17).
- I am responsible to God for my decisions and my actions (Ps. 139; 51; Matt. 16:27).

B. In regard to my sexuality, this means:
- I am to present my body as a living and holy sacrifice to God and not be conformed to worldly patterns of sexual behavior (Rom. 12:1, 2; 1 Cor. 12:20; Eph. 5:1-5).
- As a married woman I am called to be physically fruitful for God (Ps. 128; Prov. 31; 1 Tim. 5:14; Titus 2:3-5).

C. This in turn constrains me to consider that God's Word:
- views fruitfulness as a blessing (Gen. 1:28; 9:1; 17:6, 20; 28:3; Exod. 1:7; Deut. 1:10, 11; Ps. 107:37-43; 127:3), never as an unwanted burden.
- considers children to be an implicit part of family life and the expected fruit of the marriage union (see above references).
- approaches human life as having eternal significance to a personal Creator.

"Behold, children are a gift of the Lord; The fruit of the womb is a reward." (Psalm 127:3, NASB) suspect logically and ethically. Evangelical Christians need to completely reevaluate the ethic of conception control in light of the Bible's normative picture of the family.

A possible way of approaching this is to compare a contemporary view of reproductive rights to the Biblical view of fruitfulness.

From this model, I believe it is easier to understand how the basic assumption that "My body belongs to me" violates the Biblical view of fruitfulness and what the natural consequence of this approach has been. I pray that you will have the courage to say, "My body belongs to You, Lord. Help me to understand how to respond to my capacity for fruitfulness."

Fertility Awareness and Family Planning

If the frequency of conception is in fact a result of the Fall, fruitfulness need not be equated with unlimited fertility. Just as it is wise and prudent to seek treatment for disease, which was also a result of the Fall, it also may be wise and prudent to remain fertile and yet temporarily avoid conception at times.

Recent developments in the field of reproductive biology have contributed a method of conception control to the field of family planning that is effective and yet poses no medical risk to either partner. We now have the means to help us space our children as the Lord leads without drugs, surgery, or vaginal devices. Couples who choose to be responsive to the Lord in this area of their lives can learn to share the responsibility of living with their fertility through using a method based on fertility awareness. It is the least invasive form of conception control and is based upon learning to recognize the symptoms of ovulation during a woman's menstrual cycle. The objective of using fertility awareness as a means of contraception is to schedule lovemaking around the natural rhythm of the wife's body and the signs of fertility that accompany it.

Although many women tend to ovulate about halfway through their cycle, this is not true for every woman. Timing intercourse by the calender alone is an ineffective means of avoiding conception for this reason. The effectiveness of fertility awareness methods results from more specific observations that are taught by trained instructors through natural family planning classes, now available around the world. Taking a series of classes and attending follow-up sessions is essential if a couple wants to increase the effectiveness of this form of conception control.

A key principle of this approach is that a couple's relationship may be enhanced as each partner responds to the wife's patterns of fertility. It requires that each partner be committed to understanding the recurring rhythms of the menstrual cycle. Communication is essential. In living with an awareness rather than a denial of fertility, the possibility of conception is open-ended, granting the Holy Spirit room to prompt a couple from one month to the next. *This method is entirely compatible with the physical reality of our sexuality and acknowleges the value of ongoing responsiveness to the Lord as He leads each couple to affirm the dignity and worth of human life.*

Fertility awareness methods may be used to either prevent or achieve a pregnancy by allowing couples to know the exact time of the month that a woman is likely to conceive. There are two methods taught in natural family planning classes: the Ovulation Method, which involves observing the changes taking place in a woman's vaginal secretions, and the Sympto-Thermal Method, which combines mucus observation with temperature and cervical assessments. Both methods require recording observations on a chart and an initial cycle of abstinence so that secretions following lovemaking are not mistaken as a sign of fertility. Each method is highly effective when learned from a qualified instructor and followed conscientiously.

Within the neck of the uterus there are hundreds of "crypts" that act as a storage area for sperm after ejaculation where the sperm are nourished and kept alive for up to five days; over this period, the sperm are continuously circulating to promote the possibility of conception. This "time-release" action ensures that healthy sperm will be in the ovum's vicinity during the six- to eight-hour period following ovulation in which fertilization must occur. Because sperm can travel very fast, they can make the trip up to the oviducts in less than an hour. They cannot, however, make this journey unless the woman's body has begun to secrete a special substance known as fertile mucus. Within this solution, the sperm are able to migrate to their destination in the oviducts where an egg may be waiting. Most eventually miss their mark and end up landing in the abdominal cavity. This incredible system is designed to promote conception through an interwoven set of biological mechanisms that attempt to link an egg cell and a sperm cell together when they are at their peak. We take this very much for granted, and yet it is a process that is absolutely mind-boggling.

Since the mucus that is manufactured by the crypts in the cervix varies in consistency, appearance, and chemical composition during the menstrual cycle, it is possible to know when fertilization would be most likely to occur. The mucus that is secreted reflects the levels and types of hormones that are present in a woman's body at any given time; so becoming familiar with mucus patterns is a viable way of either planning or preventing pregnancy. Because sperm cannot live long in nonfertile mucus, fertility is just a temporary state that exists for only one phase of the menstrual cycle. One of the real benefits of natural family planning is that neither partner needs to use drugs or devices of any kind during the infertile phases of the cycle.

After menstruation, cervical secretions tend to be thick and rather dry, appear opaque (yellow or white), and have the consistency of thick paste. When viewed under a microscope, a maze of meshlike formations that are tightly woven together are seen. This mucus acts as a plug within the cervical canal, acting as a natural barrier to sperm and is referred to as the "Basic Infertile Pattern of mucus." Some women do not notice any mucus at all after having a period. This is called the "Basic Infertile Pattern of dryness."

The secretion of infertile mucus continues for several days until there is a change in the pattern: a sticky threadlike mucus after dry days or a sensation of moistness after tacky mucus has been present. As the days go by, the cervix secretes a thinner, clearer type of mucus in increasingly larger amounts. This is accompanied by a sensation of wetness in the vaginal area. The fertile mucus pattern that is smooth in consistency, watery, translucent (colorless or yellowish), and cloudy begins about six days prior to ovulation. When placed on the thumb and forefinger, it remains smooth on both fingers and can be stretched up to an inch between them.

The fertile pattern of mucus provides a woman with a signal that ovulation is approaching, giving her ample warning to abstain from intercourse. Because sperm live three to five days in this type of secretion, intercourse must be avoided whenever a fertile pattern is observed unless a couple has chosen to conceive.

The last day of the fertile mucus pattern is the "Peak Day" of fertility during the menstrual cycle. Mucus on the Peak Day is shiny, slippery, and lubricative. This type of mucus resembles raw egg whites and may be stretched an inch or more in length. Under a microscope, it reveals long channels through which sperm may rapidly travel. Estrogen is responsible for this change.

Menstruation taking place fourteen days after the Peak Day confirms that ovulation accompanied the "Mucus Peak." Once ovulation has taken place, the mucus once again becomes sticky, cloudy, and dry, resuming a Basic Infertile Pattern. When the Basic Infertile Pattern has continued for three days in a row, it may be assumed that ovulation has occurred and that the ovum has perished.

Exceptions to these mucus signs are covered in natural family planning texts and classes. Breast-feeding, vaginal infections, illness, approaching menopause, and secretions related to sexual arousal and intercourse all affect mucus observation, but have been studied extensively so couples may learn how to respond to these conditions. Participating in a class and obtaining individualized counseling is *essential* to understanding how to apply this method to one's own circumstances.

Many physicians are not trained to teach this method and are therefore unable to either appreciate it or recommend it. When asked about natural family planning, the average doctor assumes that a woman is

FERTILITY AWARENESS DURING THE MENSTRUAL CYCLE

Figure 10-2

PHASE:	MENSTRUAL/ POSTMENSTRUAL	OVULATORY	POST OVULATORY
SECRETIONS:	MENSTRUATION DRY DAYS: INFERTILE MUCUS PATTERN Sensation of dryness in the vaginal area. Sperm cannot penetrate this type of mucus.	FERTILE MUCUS PATTERN Dry sensation ends. Mucus begins—sensation of wetness in the vaginal area. Mucus now supports the life of sperm cells. Conception may occur from any genital-to-genital contact on mucus days prior to ovulation. P E A K 1-2-3 Clear, slippery mucus; highly stretchable and lubricative. Ovulation follows. Count 1-2-3 days after peak is fertile.	LATE DRY DAYS: INFERTILE MUCUS PATTERN From the fourth day after Mucus Peak this cycle is infertile until the next cycle begins except under special circumstances.
TEMPERATURE:	LOW ⟶	RISING ⟶	HIGH ⟶
CERVIX:	Low, firm, and closed.	High, soft, and open.	Low, firm, and closed.
DURATION:	Highly variable, lasting from days to many weeks or even several months.	Somewhat variable, lasting from seven to eleven days in most women.	Least variable, lasting about ten to fifteen days in 90 percent of all women.
ABILITY TO CONCEIVE:	Woman is infertile. Genital contact will not cause pregnancy.	Woman is fertile. Genital contact makes conception likely.	Woman is infertile. Genital contact will not result in pregnancy.

asking him about rhythm. Usually, he hasn't the expertise required to advise her of the benefits or the actual effectiveness of this form of conception control. Frankly, it is much easier to prescribe a pill than to provide guidance in fertility awareness, and few medical schools teach students to fully understand this method.

The Sympto-Thermal Method includes temperature observation as an additional means of determining fertility. After the ovum is released, the progesterone level in a woman's bloodstream rises, which in turn causes a rise in the temperature of the body when it is at rest. Progesterone also acts upon the reproductive system by suppressing further ovulation and drying up fertile mucus.

When the resting, or basal, body temperature rises, it serves as a confirmation that ovulation has taken place. A woman cannot become pregnant once she has entered the high-temperature phase of her menstrual cycle.

The basal body temperature (B.B.T.) changes slightly throughout the cycle and tends to be one half of a degree lower before ovulation occurs. Following ovulation, temperature recording confirms infertility until menstruation begins.

The B.B.T. is taken upon waking after sleeping for at least three hours. Many women keep their thermometers by their beds and simply take their temperatures first thing in the morning before getting out of bed. Most drugstores carry B.B.T. thermometers, which have larger numbers and record a much smaller range in temperature than regular thermometers. For this reason, a B.B.T. thermometer cannot be used when a fever is present and should be washed in only cool water to avoid breakage. Because a B.B.T. thermometer is specially calibrated for accuracy and ease of reading, it is worth the extra couple of dollars that it costs.

The B.B.T. may be taken orally, vaginally, or rectally. Because the oral temperature is generally lower than a vaginal or rectal reading, the same route should be used throughout an entire cycle to maintain consistency. Oral temperatures need to be taken for eight to ten minutes, while taking the temperature vaginally or rectally requires only five minutes. Falling asleep during the reading might incur breakage; so it is advisable to set a snooze alarm or timer for the required period and *then* go back to sleep. The thermometer should be stored away from heat sources such as radios, lights, radiators, and heat vents and should be shaken down after the temperature has been recorded.

Emotional stress, illness, restless sleep, medication, electric blankets, and alcohol consumption the previous night can create higher than normal temperatures and are known as disturbances. These factors can be accommodated once a woman understands their significance in relationship to other signs of fertility.

The third way of determining fertility is by examining the cervix each day. This method has not been studied for its effectiveness and is of greatest benefit to those women whose mucus is very scanty or who experience a fairly continuous mucus discharge. It may also be useful when one's temperature has been affected by stress or illness.

When the cervix begins to rise, soften, and open, it may provide additional evidence that the ovulatory phase has started. Checking the cervix is no more difficult than inserting a diaphragm or cervical cap. As long as a woman's hands have been washed thoroughly and her fingernails have been trimmed, there is little risk of injury or infection.

The cervix feels very similar to the tip of one's nose when it is in a closed position. It may be checked by inserting one or two fingers upwards with the pads of the fingers aimed toward the pubic bone in front. Near the top of the vagina on the front wall lies a round protrusion with a dimple in it. This is the cervix. (After a vaginal birth, the dimple turns into a smile!) If the vagina is too dry to insert the fingers into comfortably, water may be used as a lubricant. Other substances should not be used because they may mask the presence of slippery mucus. During infertile phases of the menstrual cycle, the cervix is easily reached when a woman is sitting on a toilet or standing with one foot on the edge of the tub or toilet stool. As fertility approaches, the cervix feels softer and recedes higher into the vagina, sometimes becoming nearly impossible to reach. Comparing the cervix as it changes from day to day provides additional proof of when ovulation occurs.

The theoretical effectiveness rate of these methods when used as a means of child spacing is approximately 99.6 percent or nearly as effective as oral contraceptives. Actual use-effectiveness, according to a leading authority in the field of natural family planning, Dr. Thomas Hilgers at Creighton University, is 94.8 percent.[20] The book *Contraceptive Technology* rates the effectiveness of the cervical mucus method at 98 percent when it is used consistently and effectively.[21] Considering these statistics, why aren't more couples using this method? When we consider the alternatives, *fertility awareness is the only method of family planning that is safe, effective, and does not impair our ability to be fruitful for God.* In addition, there are no barriers within the vagina to the one-flesh union created by genital-to-genital contact during lovemaking and no chemicals to prevent sperm from merging with a woman's body following intercourse. It is truly remarkable that the one method of conception control that allows us the greatest freedom to respond to the Holy Spirit is based upon symptoms that our Creator has built into our sexuality!

> Surely God is my salvation; I will trust and not be afraid.
> The Lord, the Lord, is my strength and my song; he has
> become my salvation.[22]

Opening Up
to the Experience
of Childbearing

*Instead of understanding ourselves by what was given in our
inheritance, we understand ourselves by what we become in
creating new life. Self-love is barren, infertile. Love is fertile. Self-
love is attached to the familiar, the cozy: possessions and customs.
Love is detached from the cloying clutter and therefore open to
fertilization by the new, open to the ecstasy of intercourse and the
act of reation. Attachment is closed up and walled in.
Detachment opens out and grows up.*[1]

Eugene H. Peterson, *Earth and Altar*

The test has confirmed it: a new life has begun! Within the womb a baby
is growing. The news is staggering in its proportion, yet is something
that is heard around the world every day. So incredible is this tiny miracle,
yet so common. A most human event has entered into a man and woman's
relationship as God's creation is affirmed once again.

The nine months of pregnancy bring many changes to a marriage. As
questions surface and new responsibilities are anticipated, a couple is likely
to feel ambivalent as well as overjoyed. They wonder: Who will this baby
be? What kind of parents will we make? How will we manage to pay all the
bills? Will our relationship be changed forever? Will we be able to give up
our relative independence? How will it feel to be so tied down? Getting
married involved a step toward maturity and away from one's childhood;
becoming parents is a more drastic move in the direction of growing up.
Regardless of their ages, two lovers are now expectant parents. Naturally,
they spend a great deal of time thinking about how the arrival of their
baby will change what exists between them.

Before there is time to think about it, however, the baby makes his or
her presence known. The moment the ovum is fertilized, a process is set

into motion that alters the mother's body in significant ways. Although she cannot feel this little one, her body quickly becomes aware that this cycle will be different. Progesterone levels remain high after ovulation and signal the uterine lining to remain ready for the egg's arrival. While traveling through the fallopian tube, the rapidly dividing cluster of cells issues a substance that begins to prepare the mother's breasts for lactation. In an amazing way, the baby is actually ensuring his future supply of nutrients.

Once imbedded in the uterus, the embryo sends another messenger into the mother's bloodstream called HCG (human chorionic gonadotropin) that is capable of producing a feeling of queasiness for days on end. It is now thought that nausea is in fact a positive indication of the baby's secure attachment to the wall of the uterus since a connection has been established between vomiting, "morning sickness," and the extent of implantation. Nevertheless, it is difficult to appreciate this sign when having an upset stomach that may last from dawn until dusk. Women who experience this discomfort find it discouraging and are not likely to be completely thrilled with being pregnant. Daily nausea definitely can have a negative effect on one's outlook on life!

All hope for a romantic maternity vanishes when fatigue sets in and a woman becomes ruthless about getting sleep. Even before the first missed period, napping, dozing off unexpectedly, and early bedtimes start to become a way of life. The transformations going on inside the uterus are neither seen nor felt, but are taking place at a brisk pace nonetheless and the demand for energy and nutrients is high.

Mood swings may become commonplace as well. It is not unusual for an expectant mother to vary from one extreme to another as she reflects on her situation. "Honey, I feel so special being pregnant," she might say as she wakes up, but before she leaves the bathroom she may find that other feelings overwhelm her as last night's dinner threatens to make a hasty exit from her stomach. In a rush of tears and doubt, she may admit she is sick and tired of feeling tired and sick, and may wonder, "Why did I ever want to be pregnant anyway?"

Ambivalence—excitement mixed with apprehension—joy flipped over to reveal fear—a time of evaluating and sorting through *many* feelings. Pregnancy reflects all of these things. The passage from being a couple to becoming parents is one of life's most meaningful, and challenging, events.

It is easy to wonder what the Lord had in mind when He designed this strange process. During pregnancy, a woman's body must undergo tremendous physiological changes as it carries a baby to term. For forty weeks this waiting period continues, producing opportunities for emotional as well as physical growth. In responding to these changes in their own unique ways, couples can develop resources that will enable them to be more closely knit together as husband and wife before the baby comes. If they are willing to open their hearts up to one another, all sorts of interesting things may happen: frustration can lead to the development of patience; fear can dissolve into the triumph of trust; fatigue can provoke the elimination of nonessential activities; and a fragmented lifestyle may be restructured on the basis of family-centered priorities.

Rather than be confused and surprised by the negative aspects of childbearing, a couple can creatively cope with the challenges they are confronted with. Crisis becomes a chance for teamwork and intimate sharing. In this way, pregnancy becomes a time marked by a deepening of the bond that a man and woman share as their marriage reaps a harvest of spiritual dividends.

The Apostle Peter seems to have understood this principle of progressive growth well. It appears that he knew that the depth of our walk with the Lord is based on a series of steps as the Lord leads us from one place to the next. Much of our growth in things of the Spirit depends on our willingness to respond to God's desire for our maturity in a wholehearted and obedient manner. Consider the way Peter expressed this as you think about how this passage might also be applied to the strengthening of your marriage:

> His divine power has given us everything we need for life and godliness through our knowledge of him who called us by his own glory and goodness. Through these he has given us his very great and precious promises, so that you might participate in the divine nature and escape the corruption in the world caused by evil desires. For this very reason, make every effort to add to your faith goodness; and to goodness, knowledge; and to knowledge, self-control; and to self-control, perseverance; and to perseverance, godliness; and to godliness, brotherly kindness; and to brotherly kindness, love. For if you possess these qualities in increasing measure, they will keep you from being ineffective and unproductive in your knowledge of our Lord Jesus Christ.[2]

Pregnant Pauses

In addition to the obvious physical changes that occur during pregnancy, a more subtle change begins to take place. Up until now, a woman's reproductive tract has been primarily receptive in its sexual function. But as the child within her grows, a woman is faced with changing the way she views her sexuality. The womb that has always been empty is now occupied. The breasts that were a source of mutual pleasure to herself and her husband swell as glands develop that will eventually produce milk for the baby. The vagina that has caressed her husband's penis in lovemaking prepares to take on its birth-giving role. In a culture that views the female body as a sexual object, these transformations can be perplexing indeed. Our society has made the 38-22-34 figure into an icon. As a result, men and women alike are confused about how pregnancy, birth, and breast-feeding affect sexual activity.

During pregnancy, a couple's feelings and attitudes about female sexuality will converge with their feelings and attitudes about childbearing. In some relationships, the blending of these two dimensions of life will produce serious conflict: a husband might be unable to be aroused by his wife's enlarged body; a woman may find it difficult to mesh her maternal and sexual roles; both could find it strange to have a "third person" nearby during lovemaking. On the other hand, there are couples who find that childbearing expands their ability to love and care for one another, both in bed and out of it. A mutual commitment to satisfy one another's sexual needs, express affection frequently, and share in numerous ways together enriches the marital bond immensely, while a refusal to really listen to each other and spend time together will threaten to tear a marriage apart.

A series of pauses affect virtually every couple's sex life during the nine months of pregnancy and the three-month adjustment period that follows it. For the span of a year, changes that are basically biological in nature sweep into a couple's relationship, greatly increasing the need for understanding and communication.

Progesterone, the hormone that quiets smooth muscles during pregnancy, has an enormous effect on a woman's desire for sexual expression, and it is nearly impossible to predict how a given woman will respond to the demands placed upon her mind and body. Each woman is unique and needs to be open to her own way of reacting to the experience of bearing a child. There are no clearly marked road maps to follow along this route, even though countless women have traveled this road before.

The physiological changes brought about by childbearing and breast-feeding are, however, predictable for the most part in spite of the wide variety of individual responses that are possible. The personalities of the man and woman involved, along with their one-of-a-kind relationship, will influence how they meet the challenges they face. Becoming informed about what takes place during pregnancy, birth, and lactation reduces the mystery and provides a factual framework to base decisions upon.

Unless there has been bleeding or a history of miscarriage, lovemaking may continue as it did before pregnancy for the most part. Many couples find that freedom from using a contraceptive enhances intercourse. There will need to be an ongoing revision of lovemaking positions throughout pregnancy and during recovery afterwards for the sake of promoting comfort. Deep penetration and intercourse that is too vigorous may be uncomfortable due to a greater amount of blood in the vessels within the pelvic area.

It is helpful to look at the common elements in each of the four trimesters or three-month periods of pregnancy and postpartum. Each is influenced by a characteristic set of body changes that influence sexual response and the desire for sexual activity. Remember: no two women are exactly alike in which symptoms they exhibit or in the way they respond to what is happening within their bodies.

SEXUAL RESPONSE DURING PREGNANCY

Figure 11-1

DESIRE
- Changes in body image greatly influence a woman's sexual responsiveness.

- Desire for lovemaking fluctuates with moods, energy level, discomforts experienced.

EXCITEMENT
- Time required for arousal may be shortened due to increased blood supply to pelvic area.

- Vaginal lubrication develops more rapidly and more extensively than when not pregnant.

- Breast enlargement may have a positive effect on women who had felt that their breasts were too small.

- Breast and nipple stimulation may relieve tension in breast tissue in some women; others may find contact painful or uncomfortable.

PLATEAU
- Marked enlargement of the outer third of the vagina may enhance sexual response.

ORGASM
- Orgasmic frequency may result from heightened pelvic tension due to increased blood supply.

- Spasms of the uterus, called Braxton-Hicks contractions, may replace or accompany orgasmic contractions in the pelvic floor muscles.

RESOLUTION
- Vasocongestion of the pelvic area is frequently not relieved by orgasm; feelings of fullness may remain.

169

- Length of this phase may be increased, resulting in a degree of discomfort in the pelvic area.

- Some women find it easier to become aroused again and may experience multiple orgasms.

- Braxton-Hicks contractions may not subside immediately.

The First Trimester

For many women, an increased need for sleep, digestive changes, urinary frequency, and breast tenderness are the trademarks of early pregnancy. Participating in lovemaking may take real effort! It is important to avoid using pregnancy as a way of neglecting the need for sexual sharing even though one's sex drive may seem to be at an all-time low.

Beginning a pregnancy with the commitment to remain sexually responsive is a key to avoiding problems later on. It may help to discuss specific concerns with a health care professional who is trained in sexual counseling. Not all physicians are. In fact, some tend to be just as prone to embarrassment as you or I would! Addressing the emotional aspects of sexuality may be something that a doctor feels inadequate to deal with in comparison to the anatomy and physiology involved. For this reason, it is important to realize that one's choice of a health care provider, whether it be an obstetrician, a family practice physician, or a midwife, plays a central role in the way a woman responds to her childbearing experience. Choosing a person who is skilled in the art of counseling as well as in maternal-child health care is well worth the extra time and effort it may take to find someone who has both of these skills.

It is not unusual for a pregnancy to seem more real to the mother than to the father initially. After all, none of these changes are apparent from the outside until the fourth or the fifth month. One of the best ways to deal with this is by keeping lines of communication open. If a woman takes the time to share and express her reactions to her pregnancy, she can enable her husband to feel more included in the experience. An especially meaningful moment may be attending a prenatal visit together and hearing the baby's heartbeat for the first time. If the dad is not able to be there, the baby's heartbeat can be recorded on a cassette tape to share later on, if possible. If an ultrasound becomes medically necessary, the father can also accompany the mother and have the opportunity to see the baby's image displayed in full view. (An ultrasound should not be arranged for the sole purpose of seeing the baby, however, since the long-term effects of this procedure are as yet unknown.)

Many wives feel an increased need for touch and receiving nurturing from others as pregnancy progresses. When a husband creatively responds to this need, it is easier for his wife to relax and enjoy her sexuality in spite of being pregnant. Helping with housework and cooking, encouraging his wife to eat well and get plenty of rest, and finding many ways to express affection and say "I love you" go a long way in promoting sexual harmony. Through assuming an active role as the spiritual leader in the home, prayer times and shared Bible study are important ways a husband can help his wife respond to the demands of childbearing. Also, being willing to learn about a factual view of sexuality during this time allows a couple to deal with concerns about the effects of lovemaking on pregnancy.

There are a number of things that a woman can also do to enliven her marriage by developing habits that will enhance the quality of her pregnancy. Being attentive to one's appearance through selecting clothes that are attractive as well as functional can really be a self-confidence booster. Wearing support hose lessens the chance of developing varicose veins, as does taking a regular walk every day. Taking one or two showers daily, with particular attention to rinsing off secretions around the genital area, will eliminate body odors that make some women self-conscious. Eating nutrious foods provides the mother's body, *and* the baby's, with the nutrients that are necessary for the growth and maintenance of all of the cells that are working and developing at this time. Giving oneself permission to rest is also an important way of providing energy to the many processes that are taking place.

Increasingly, women are finding that regular exercise reduces the feeling of lethargy that often sets in during pregnancy. Exercise can help the body adapt to gestation through strengthening the muscles that are affected by the baby's growth and decreasing the discomforts related to carrying a baby. Types of fitness activities that are fun and contribute to a sense of vitality are important, as is checking with one's health care provider prior to participating in any exercise program. Walking, swimming, and low-impact, low-intensity aerobic dancing are all excellent forms of exercise that promote cardiovascular endurance. Including a basic routine of stretching and conditioning exercises suited to pregnancy will contribute to achieving a well-balanced approach to maintaining physical fitness. Including one's husband in regular walks together is an example of a way to stimulate sharing as well as to encourage a healthy attitude toward pregnancy. Being creative about structuring time together can by physically *and* emotionally beneficial!

The Second Trimester

By the fourth month of pregnancy, the initial adjustment period is over. Consequently, a renewed feeling of interest in lovemaking is not unusual. As the developing fetus grows, the mother's abdomen expands to accommodate the increased need for space. By the sixth month, her breasts begin to make a substance called colostrum until breast milk begins to be produced about forty-eight hours after the baby is born. Tissue within the

171

vagina becomes increasingly more elastic, and a feeling of fullness in the pelvic area results from the large amount of blood that is now circulating there. Nausea may persist throughout pregnancy, but the majority of expectant mothers have greater difficulty coping with indigestion, heartburn, and/or constipation at this point.

It is not unusual for sexual responsiveness to increase dramatically as the early discomforts of pregnancy subside. Most women continue to want reassurance of their partner's love and acceptance of their changing bodies through affectionate gestures like cuddling, hand holding, and back rubs. Making love is enhanced because of an increased amount of lubrication in the vagina, but may be decidedly uncomfortable unless a couple is willing to experiment with new positions for intercourse. Positions that avoid putting pressure on a woman's abdomen and allow her to control the depth of penetration are preferable, such as lying side-to-side (either facing each other or with the husband behind his wife), having the husband kneel in front of his wife, or a woman sitting astride her husband.

Some women find that they begin to experience multiple orgasms during this phase of pregnancy due to the increased amount of vasocongestion present. This can be stimulating for one's husband, but can actually be somewhat alarming for the wife. Being open to one's body during pregnancy is just as important as at other times in life. Talking through some of the things that may be confusing prevents misunderstanding. Otherwise, a husband may interpret his wife's withdrawal from the strength of her responses as a rejection of his sexuality. There can be no replacement for communicating one's thoughts and feelings if lovemaking is to be mutually enjoyable.

The Third Trimester

As the baby's due date approaches, a decrease in the frequency of intercourse is commonly reported. Medical advice ranges from warning parents to avoid intercourse for the last six or eight weeks to giving the go-ahead to participate in lovemaking until labor begins. Some health care providers even recommend making love as a way to stimulate the onset of labor. One study found that semen and nipple stimulation actually may help to "ripen" the cervix in preparation for birth, while others have suggested nipple stimulation as a way of stimulating labor.[3] Unless the amniotic sac is broken, the baby is normally well protected within the uterus up until the time of delivery.

Many women notice that they have uterine spasms, called Braxton-Hicks contractions, following orgasm. This tends to be particularly true of women who have given birth previously. These contractions vary in intensity, feel muscular rather than cramplike, and do not develop a regular pattern. They also become weaker over time rather than stronger or closer like true labor does. Another difference in sexual response that is

172

commonly reported is that the pelvic area continues to feel full and tense after orgasm during the resolution phase. Instead of a feeling of relief as blood leaves the area, the vessels stay congested as a normal consequence of late pregnancy. It can be helpful to soak in a warm bath or gently massage the lower abdomen if this becomes a problem.

Toward the end of a first pregnancy, the fetus descends into the mother's bony pelvis any time from two to six weeks before delivery. This event is referred to as lightening or engagement. The cervix is pressed down when this happens, making the vagina less spacious. Rectal pressure may also be felt. If a couple wishes to continue to make love up until the baby is born, they will find it challenging to find positions that will be comfortable for the mother. Alternative expressions to intercourse, such as petting, are often found to be preferable to penetration. It is a time when acceptance of the process of the body's preparation for birth is essential.

The Sexuality of Giving Birth

Creating a child is a most intimate act. The birth of that child is no less intimate as a woman's total being becomes absorbed in the process of giving birth. Labor is not just something that happens to you: it is the fundamental effort required to bring new life into the world. The Lord has designed this process to take place at the center of female sexuality as a baby emerges from the mother's body. The ability to actively participate in giving birth brings the act of marriage full circle, and when shared, becomes a landmark in the history of a marriage.

It is true that love has the power to cast out fear—even the fear of childbirth. Preparation for birth that allows two people to come to terms with the fruition of their sexual relationship can draw them together in profound ways. As a childbirth educator, I have had the privilege of witnessing the admiration with which many men regard their wives. It is a beautiful thing to behold! A man and woman choosing to bring forth their child together are blessed in many ways as they realize the differences in their sexual natures with a greater appreciation than they may ever have realized before.

Giving birth is a process involving hard work and, in most cases, a certain amount of pain. Having realistic expectations about the effort involved can reduce feelings of anger afterwards. Looking to the Lord for strength is the most valuable birth technique that exists. Breathing and relaxation, prayer and listening to music, and strategically applied back rubs also contribute to the body's healthy adaptation to labor. As the baby moves through the birth canal, the vagina stretches to make room for the little one's passage. The muscles of the pelvic floor separate as the baby presses through. A woman is likely to feel completely absorbed in what she is doing, unable to do anything but push with her entire being as the baby

173

prepares to leave her body for life outside her womb. Suddenly, the head appears . . . then the ears, and whooshhh . . . there is the darling face! In one more contraction, the shoulders fit through and the body quickly slips out in a rush of warm fluid. The umbilical cord is still beating as the mother and father may reach to touch their son or daughter for the very first time. This is the result of that special moment shared nine months ago. It is nothing less than a stupendous accomplishment and they are, understandably, very proud. As tears of joy streak down their cheeks, they praise God for the miracle of life they see before them. And what an awesome thing this time together is . . .

Opening up to birth a baby requires a willingness to trust God for the way He has designed the sexual function of our bodies. Labor is a powerful thing as the uterus works to accomplish the task of opening the cervix and pressing the baby out of the womb. There is little in today's world to prepare us for such a task. But the Lord has given something that will teach us much about what is required of us during this process: His love. Our Father's love is the underlying theme upon which His creation is founded. Thanking God for the wonder of our bodies enables us to appreciate the amazing tasks they are capable of. Trusting Him to lead us *because He loves us* helps us to cast off fear and put on acceptance. We are not here by accident. The way our bodies function is an intergral part of His pattern for our lives.

The Fourth Trimester

The six weeks that follow a baby's arrival are a continuation of childbirth as the uterus shrinks to its previous size and the process of breast-feeding is established. Within minutes after a baby's arrival, the placenta detaches from the wall of the uterus. Immediately the blood levels of progesterone and estrogen plummet. As the infant is placed at the mothers' breast and begins to suckle, a hormone called oxytocin is released that causes muscle cells in the uterus and breasts to contract. This in turn encourages the uterus to reduce the amount of bleeding from the place where the placenta was attached and the glands within the breasts to begin the initial phase of lactation.

Another hormone, prolactin, begins to be secreted by the pituitary gland, triggering tissue in the gland cells of the breast to begin milk production. Although breast milk will not appear until some time between thirty-six and seventy-two hours after birth, colostrum is secreted in the meantime. It is the perfect substance for a baby's early feedings, consisting mainly of proteins, antibodies, water-soluble vitamins, and minerals. This highly select blend of nutrients also contributes to the health of the baby's intestinal tract, protecting him from the bacteria and viruses that are present in the birth canal and associated with other human contact. It is becoming increasingly clear that breast milk is the ideal food for human infants and is also responsible for a more rapid recovery on the part of the mother. This wonderful diet for newborns is actually a liquid tissue that is alive with many beneficial organisms. It is also species-specific and cannot be duplicated. Appreciating the qualities of breast milk enables a mother to get through the early adjustment period more easily because she knows that she is giving something to her baby that no one else can provide.

During the first few weeks after giving birth, both mothers and fathers are faced with interrupted sleep, a need for time spent alone together, and a transition period that involves the adjustment of family relationships and sexual roles. At times, one is likely to feel overwhelmed by the changes taking place. This period is actually quite similar to a honeymoon in that the parents are spending time "falling in love" with their new baby during what has been called the "babymoon." Just as pregnancy may be compared to courtship and giving birth to the wedding ceremony, the postpartum period is similar to the intensity of the days following one's marriage celebration. A great deal of emotional energy is spent on forming a bond with the baby that will serve as a foundation for a lifetime of parenting. It is an exhausting effort.

In the midst of this upheaval, the mother's body is healing from the strain of childbirth. A discharge from the uterus, called lochia, continues until the womb has returned to its normal state. The breasts swell and fill with milk, and tend to leak periodically for several weeks. The pelvic floor must regain its strength. Her abdominal muscles initially feel soft and saggy until they resume their regular tone. Stretch marks are apparent at various places where skin has stretched to accommodate the baby's growth. If an incision was made in the perineum during delivery, it will gradually heal, leaving scar tissue that may initially produce a feeling of tightness in the vagina. Considering this assault on a woman's body image, is it any wonder that she is likely to fear becoming pregnant again? Having intercourse with her husband may be the *last* thing on her mind! It is common for women to temporarily think that they will never be sexually desirable or responsive again.

It is difficult for a man to understand what is going on within his wife's mind and body at this time. After all, *his* body has felt none of the pregnancy or the birth. He can never know what it is like to have milk secreted from his body. The only way for him to understand what is happening to his partner is if she verbalizes her feelings to him. In his mind, the experience of sex will always be associated with the release and excitement of ejaculation. But in his wife's mind, sex produced these *un*comfortable feelings in addition to joy. It may take her some time to sort through her feelings about what has taken place within her body. Resuming intercourse may be delayed for several weeks to several months as her body and mind begin to feel comfortable with making love again.

During this time, a woman benefits from hearing that she is loved and appreciated just for who she is. Expecting her to be a super mom and a great lover places an intolerable burden upon her shoulders. It is easy to think that things will never return to normal and wonder how all the pieces will ever fit together in the future. Taking time out to rest, nap, get out for brief periods of time, and spend time in leisure activities (such as taking a long bath or listening to music with headphones on) will restore a woman's appreciation for life if she is depressed, fatigued, or suffering from feelings of isolation.

Sexual expression can become a natural outcome of taking the time to touch and talk. If intercourse is painful or seems to be temporarily undesirable, alternative forms of lovemaking may be employed. Lying naked together by candlelight will help a woman feel less self-conscious about how her figure may appear. Agreeing to mutually satisfy one another without the expectation of penetration will relieve anxiety, if present, about making love. It may be that a wife just wants to be held or touched affectionately for the time being. Her husband's desire for sexual release, when present, may be met through close body contact that allows both to share in his experience of orgasm. This is a perfectly natural way to enable a couple to meet each other's physical needs.

PROMOTING SEXUAL HARMONY DURING TIMES OF STRESS

Figure 11-2

Most husbands and wives find that any crisis or stressful event affects all aspects of their relationship. Sexual sharing and expression are also affected. When intercourse is undesirable during pregnancy or recovery after birth, vaginal penetration may be missed less if alternative forms of lovemaking are employed. Kissing, hugging, massage, and petting are all ways a couple can bolster sexual harmony. Being open to each other's feelings and understanding that *love, time, and patience* are needed will enable a couple to weather the changes in their lives more easily. Remember that the reasons underlying the desire for sexual expression are because it was created to be:

- *a means of conveying and sharing love.* Many women feel isolated and emotionally vulnerable during pregnancy and after giving birth. Sexual sharing can be an important way of reassuring a woman that she is still sexually attractive even though her body looks and feels different.

- *an affirmation of one's sexual identity.* It is not unusual for a woman to have conflicting feelings about her body's sexual functions. Sharing these reactions with one's partner can enable a woman to accept her capacities for giving birth and breast-feeding while at the same time recognizing that she is able to respond to her need for sexual expression through lovemaking.

- *a relief from the stressful aspects of marriage.* Most men and women feel refreshed and relaxed after they experience orgasm. The stresses of childbearing and parenting place taxing demands on the marital relationship. Intimate contact helps a couple to be a source of pleasure to one another in the midst of responsibility.

- *an exclusive part of the marriage relationship.* Sexual sharing is an important means of daily reestablishing this exclusive aspect of a couple's relationship. It can serve as a way of reminding a husband and wife of the special attraction they have toward one another. While sex cannot solve *all* problems, it can be an important means of saying, "I love you. You are still the most important person in my life."

When the wife feels that she wants to begin having intercourse again, she will benefit from taking a warm, relaxing bath beforehand. Starting the second week after giving birth, she can help her vagina and perineum to heal by doing 100 Kegels (pelvic lifts) daily in sets of twenty-five and applying a small amount of Vitamin E oil to this area. This may be done by putting a few drops of the oil on her first two fingers and gently rubbing it into the walls of the vagina after it has healed. Then additional oil may be massaged into the perineum, which is the area lying just behind the vaginal outlet toward the anus. Care should be taken to avoid rubbing from the the rear forward, as the vagina may be contaminated with germs from the rectum in this manner. The application of Vitamin E oil may help these places to heal and will help the skin to be more resilient and stretchy. It may take about six to eight weeks of doing both of these things regularly to reach a point where the vagina feels truly responsive once again.

A mixture of one tablespoon of almond oil may be mixed with several drops of Vitamin E oil as a lubricant for the penis prior to making love. A commercial product that is designed for the purpose of lubricating the vagina and is water soluble may be used instead.

It is important to be sure that the penis is slippery before guiding it into the vagina. The vaginal lining is likely to be dry and tender initially, and the application of a lubricant will make intercourse more enjoyable. The wife should be the one to place her husband within her body and must be sure to expand her pelvic floor muscles by bulging them outwards as she does so. This will widen the vaginal opening and relax the P.C. muscles, which tend to become constricted when a woman is anxious or fearful about lovemaking. If attempting intercourse is still uncomfortable, the woman may also find it helpful to ask her husband to gently insert two clean, well-lubricated fingers into her vagina and rotate them while exploring this area to encourage relaxation of the P.C. muscles and identifying possible areas of discomfort. Tender, delicate stimulation of the clitoris is more desirable than ever. The woman should guide her husband's hands to indicate what pleases and arouses her.

If there are areas of tenderness within the vagina, assuming a different position for intercourse that allows the wife to control the depth of penetration is advisable. Also, guiding the penis away from irritated areas may be achieved through the use of positions that change the angle of intercourse. The woman-astride position, with the wife either facing toward or away from her husband's torso, may be particularly comfortable. If this position makes her feel she is too exposed, lying in a semisitting position propped up on pillows with her husband either sitting or kneeling in front of her may help. A rear-entry position with the wife leaning over a chair or dresser covered with a pillow while standing up is preferable to the use of this position while kneeling because penetration will be considerably less deep.

Making sure to include adequate time for pleasuring before intercourse will enable the woman's mind and body to be aroused enough to feel receptive to making love. An additional advantage to this can be that her husband will require less time to ejaculate after entering her so that excessive rubbing of the vaginal tissue may be avoided. If lovemaking proves to be painful in spite of trying a variety of things to relieve discomfort, the couple may resume touching without penetration as a way of fulfilling their desire to be sexually close to one another. Each woman varies in the length of time it takes to recover from giving birth, with some feeling ready to resume intercourse two to three weeks following delivery and others still feeling pain a year or more afterwards. A consultation with a health care provider who is skilled in providing counseling and diagnosis for a long-term difficulty should be consulted if pain is still present after four to six months, providing a woman has been doing Kegels and applying Vitamin E oil on a regular basis.

When a woman is breast-feeding a baby, her body secretes prolactin in large amounts, which produces a feeling of tranquillity. Many women report that this feeling of tranquillity is *not* conducive to promoting a desire for sexual expression since the sexual response cycle is based on a feeling of *tension*. Because prolactin levels are highest during a feeding and for the period immediately following it, nursing a baby two to three hours before lovemaking may help. This is precisely the *opposite* of what many books and articles recommend, however. That is because research in this area has been done quite recently and most authors are relatively unaware of the role prolactin is thought to play in a woman's sexual responsiveness. Most sources suggest nursing just prior to going to bed so the mother's breasts will be fairly empty and less likely to leak. It all depends on one' point of view: would you rather feel more responsive and leak milk occasionally during lovemaking or feel unresponsive and experience less leaking? Lactation consultants jokingly suggest that the husband should bring some cookies to bed with him as a way of taking a lighter look at this phenomenon! A woman may also wear a bra with cotton nursing pads to absorb leaking if she feels self-conscious about her milk supply. Having a waterproof mattress pad under the sheets with an absorbent towel to lay on can avoid extra laundry. Leaking does not tend to continue past the first six weeks and in those women who continue to experience it, most have usually become accustomed to it by this time.

If a couple is using fertility awareness as their method of family planning, they will need to receive special instructions about how breast-feeding affects the mucus sign. Frequent nursing tends to produce a lack of ovulation and menstruation for an average of fourteen months following a baby's birth if the mother refrains from using bottles and pacifiers, continues to nurse at least every four hours around the clock, and avoids starting solids until the baby is six to eight months old. If this ecological pattern of breast-feeding is not practiced, a woman's fertility is likely to return much earlier. If a couple wishes to avoid pregnancy in either case, she will need to become familiar about how to check for fertility while she is lactating.

Mothering an infant can be a tremendously satisfying experience. Babies benefit from having frequent, regular contact with their mothers, and breast-feeding is an ideal way to provide for this need. It is not unusual, however, for mothers to notice that they feel like they have ministered to their baby, and other children, all day out of their emotional energy reserve. When it comes time to share sexually, they may feel there is nothing left to give. Breasts that have been repeatedly stimulated by the baby's sucking may feel as if they need a break. Having a husband who is sensitive to the physical and emotional demands being placed on his wife will enable him to minister to her in a mature way through praying for her, accepting the way she feels, meeting her need for adult companionship, and being committed to sharing himself with her in love. When a woman feels loved and accepted, she is unlikely to feel sexually unresponsive, unless she is so ill, hungry, or tired that her body is physically unable to function as it should.

Bearing one's first child involves a sexual passage in all women's lives. It is safe to assume that most couples are challenged by the events they are faced with during this unique time. Moving through the phases of pregnancy, childbirth, and breast-feeding can draw a husband and wife closer together or it can drive them farther apart. Much depends on their ability to listen, to care, and to understand one another's needs and desires. No one passes through this time without experiencing difficult moments. With the Lord's help and a commitment to love each other in spite of what may happen, the bond that a man and woman share can become stronger, offering a couple the opportunity for a fresh discovery of one another and the chance to explore new dimensions of their sexuality.

Thy lovingkindness, O Lord, extends to the heavens,
Thy faithfulness reaches to the skies.
Thy righteousness is like the mountains of God;
Thy judgments are like a great deep.
O Lord, Thou preservest man and beast.
How precious is Thy lovingkindness, O God!
And the children of men take refuge in the shadow of Your
    wings.
They drink their fill in the abundance of Thy house;
And Thou dost give them to drink of the river of Thy
    delights.
For with Thee is the fountain of life;
In Thy light we see light.[4]

FACTORS AFFECTING SEXUAL EXPRESSION
DURING THE CHILDBEARING YEAR

Figure 11-3

FIRST TRIMESTER

Every woman's pregnancy is unique and presents an opportunity for emotional growth as new experiences are encountered. Before the pregnancy is even confirmed, hormonal changes alter the mother's physiology in many ways. Sexual expression is influenced by these changes in the reproductive system, and most couples find themselves faced with unexpected challenges and significant surprises.

PHYSICAL:
- Fatigue, increased need for sleep

- Nausea, indigestion, vomiting

- Breast tenderness

- Feeling of fullness in pelvic area

- Possible spotting—frequent urination, possible leaking

EMOTIONAL:
- Bond created by baby's conception

- Ambivalent feelings about the experience of pregnancy

- Feelings of self-protectiveness

- Concern about weight gain, body image

- Pregnancy may seem more real to the mother than the father

WHAT TO EXPECT:
- Change in lovemaking frequency

- Revision of lovemaking habits to avoid discomfort

- Increased vaginal lubrication

- Less abandonment with greater degree of gentleness

- Increased tension in pelvic area during sexual arousal due to increased blood supply to that area

WIFE'S RESPONSE:
- "Touch and talk" before sexual sharing

- Commitment to satisfy husband's sexual needs

- Discount what friends may say about their experiences

- Discuss specific concerns with health care provider

- Avoid using pregnancy as an excuse to refrain from lovemaking if there are other reasons why sexual sharing is bothering you

- Express affection in a variety of ways

HUSBAND'S RESPONSE:
- Willingness to accommodate pregnancy through creative problem solving

- Help with housework, encourage wife to rest

- Lots of "tender pats," fewer passionate caresses if wife is less responsive

- Commitment to understand wife's emotional and physical needs

- Develop a factual view of lovemaking during pregnancy, deal with fears regarding harming the baby during intercourse

- Find many ways to say "I love you"

- Spiritual leadership, shared prayer, and Bible study

SECOND TRIMESTER

During this trimester, the initial adjustment to pregnancy has been made. Nausea and fatigue may be greatly diminished and the chance of having a miscarriage is greatly reduced. Until the sixth month, the baby and the mother's abdomen are not yet large enough to present much of an obstacle to lovemaking, but a woman may feel awkward and unattractive to her husband due to her changing shape.

PHYSICAL:
- Possible vaginal and nipple tenderness

- Swelling of the vagina and labia

- Less relief following orgasm due to pelvic fullness

- Nausea may persist

- Indigestion, heartburn, and constipation are common throughout the remainder of pregnancy

- Increased vaginal lubrication

EMOTIONAL:
- Fear of harming baby or provoking a miscarriage may persist

- Feeling of fetal movements may be a distraction or an impediment to lovemaking

- Feeling of well-being may be a boon to sexual expression

- Sexual response may increase dramatically due to pelvic congestion, nipple sensitivity

WHAT TO EXPECT:
- Increased energy reserve

- Fluctuations in desire for lovemaking

- Desire for reassurance through cuddling, hand holding

- Greater sense of stability

- Need to revise positions for lovemaking as baby grows

- Increased feelings of femininity

- Increased feelings of dependency on husband

WIFE'S RESPONSE:
- Acceptance of maternal role

- Increased bonding with baby as movements are felt and interpreted

- Willingness to feel comfortable with expanding waistline and breast changes

- Commitment to improve nutrition and promote fitness through appropriate exercise

- Continued commitment to include husband in pregnancy

- Acceptance of changes in sexual response

HUSBAND'S RESPONSE:
- Create opportunities for courtship activities

- Support necessary lifestyle changes through own involvement in wife's activities

- Continued patience and understanding will be much appreciated

THIRD TRIMESTER

Sexual activity declines for most couples as the baby's due date approaches. Discomfort during lovemaking is a reason that is commonly given for this decline, especially during the ninth month. Unless a couple is told that lovemaking is contraindicated, intercourse may continue during this period and may even be beneficial, preparing the cervix for birth.

PHYSICAL:
- Fatigue, insomnia, restlessness

- Increased pressure within pelvis

- Lower back discomfort

- Braxton-Hicks contractions

- Enlarged abdomen

- Frequent urination

- Colostrum secretion

- Increased vaginal discharge

EMOTIONAL:
- Anxiety about labor and birth, becoming parents, baby's health

- Excitement about receiving a new person into the family

- Need for recognition of baby, self

- Changes in body image

- Worry about husband's opinion of weight gain, decreased ability to be active, productive

- Increased feelings of vulnerability, need for protection

- Need for nonsexual nurturing

WHAT TO EXPECT:
- Established patterns of lovemaking are challenged and subsequently modified

- Decreased vaginal space after baby engages in pelvis

- If interested in lovemaking, creative positions and gentle movement may be preferable

- Intercourse may be too tiring or uncomfortable to be enjoyable

- Rate of orgasm often declines

- Uterus may stay hard for several minutes after orgasm

- Husband may be attracted to (or perplexed by) elasticity of vaginal tissue and amount of lubrication present

WIFE'S RESPONSE:
- Discuss concerns with husband

- Share openly with the Lord, pour your heart out to Him

- Trust in the Lord's ability to strengthen and uphold you

- Prepare for giving birth, breast-feeding

- Avoid comparing yourself to others, accept own uniqueness

- Satisfy husband's sexual needs without penetration if intercourse becomes painful

- Be thankful for the life within you, for your body's amazing ability to care for your baby

- Pray often and avoid worrying

HUSBAND'S RESPONSE:
- "Get in touch" with your wife every day through back rubs, hand holding, putting your arms around her, and cherishing her

- Accept her decreased sex drive, if present

- Realize that this is a temporary state of affairs

- Participate in birth preparation together

- Find new ways of expressing your appreciation

- Encourage communication

- Welcome the opportunities for growth that God gives you

FOURTH TRIMESTER

Adjustments in lovemaking habits accompany a baby's arrival as part of a larger transition period that includes many changes in social and family roles. With each child that is born, relationships shift to include a new family member. The mother's fatigue and time-consuming involvement with the baby challenge others to support and understand her during the time her body returns to its normal state. There is no replacement for communicating each other's needs through talking and taking time out to openly share concerns, fears, and the emotional response that follow the end of pregnancy.

PHYSICAL:
- Fatigue

- Healing of the uterus, pelvic floor, and perineum

- Adjustment of the breasts to lactation

- Vaginal dryness and tenderness

- Vaginal tightness

- Leaking of milk

- Fluctuations in desire for sexual interaction

- Stretch marks, change in measurements from prepregnancy

EMOTIONAL:
- Fear of pain during intercourse

- Feeling that episiotomy site may be damaged during intercourse

- Postpartum "blues"

- Engrossment with baby as bonding takes place

- Possible fear of pregnancy

- Distracted during lovemaking by baby's presence in house

- Disappointment in lack of muscle tone or weight loss

- Frustration at not being able to get more things done

- Possible jealousy and resentment of baby taking up so much of wife's time

WHAT TO EXPECT:
- A period of transition and readjustment that is temporary

- Decreased vaginal lubrication and elasticity

- Mood swings

- Need for patience while healing is completed

- Restructuring of social life and responsibilities to allow for rest, time alone as a family

- "Babymoon" that differs from the everyday routines

WIFE'S RESPONSE:
- "Mothering the mother": accept help, allow others to nurture you

- Encouragement to eat well and get plenty of rest

- Pelvic floor exercises and Vitamin E oil to promote healing

- Be sensitive to husband's needs and concerns

- Accept the transition period as a unique time in life

HUSBAND'S RESPONSE:
- Gain satisfaction through providing and caring for wife and child(ren)

- View fatherhood as a full-time commitment

- Plan to take time off for the "babymoon"

- Do not pressure wife to resume intercourse if pain is present; employ alternative expressions of lovemaking

LACTATION

The process of breast-feeding a baby involves a mother in the care of her baby that produces a unique relationship between the two of them. The intensity of the bond that exists enables a woman to nurture her infant physically as well as emotionally. The love that is poured out into the mother-child relationship through the giving of one's milk is a significant gift and one that is not without its costs. The baby's father can express his love for his child best by loving the mother and helping her to feel that what she is contributing to the family is very valuable indeed.

PHYSICAL:
- Fatigue, an increased need to rest and take naps

- Full, possibly leaking breasts

- Probable lack of ovulation and menstruation for a significant period of time if fully breast-feeding

- Vaginal dryness due to decreased estrogen levels

- Frequent stimulation of the breasts through nursing

EMOTIONAL:
- Increased feelings of femininity

- Pleasure through nursing after the initial adjustment period

- Possible sexual feelings produced during feedings may cause concern if not understood and accepted as normal

- May feel emotionally and physically drained at times

WHAT TO EXPECT:
- Sexual stimulation causes release of milk

- Return of desire for lovemaking will occur earlier in women who are experiencing a high degree of sexual tension, later in those who are struggling to cope with new demands and investing a large amount of energy in forming an attachment to the baby

- Most women find nursing to be a pleasurable experience

WIFE'S RESPONSE:
- Acceptance of pleasant feelings produced by baby's sucking

- Commitment to meet own needs for nutrients and rest

- Share feelings with husband

- Time nursings, when possible, to avoid feeding the baby in the late evening before going to bed or time lovemaking earlier in the evening to coincide with baby's schedule

- Keep a sense of humor about leaking and take measures to make it less bothersome

HUSBAND'S RESPONSE:
- Encourage wife to have some time to herself each day: warm baths, time to do something creative, go for walks, etc.

- Affirm wife's sense of dignity by recognizing that she is nurturing and caring for your child

- Express your love in practical *and* romantic ways

/ *12* /

Entering into
the Fullness of Life

Let patience have her perfect work. Statue under the chisel of the sculptor, stand steady under the blows of his mallet. Clay on the wheel, let the fingers of the divine potter model you at their will. Obey the Father's lightest word: hear the Brother who knows you and died for you. . . . We die daily. Happy those who daily come to life as well.[1]

George MacDonald, in
George MacDonald: An Anthology by C. S. Lewis

Aging, menopause, wrinkles, and gray hair? Or wisdom, maturity, and a wealth of life experiences? When we think of growing older, which do we think of first?

What does it mean to be marble in the hands of a Master Sculptor over one's entire lifetime? Can we trust Him to chisel His life within us as we seek to conform to His image? How do we become clay that responds smoothly to the firm hands of the Potter as He molds and shapes us over the years? If we love Jesus, we will give Him the freedom to carve His ways into our minds and hearts. Through surrendering our need to be in control of our lives, we may enter into the fullness of life by dedicating each day to the Lord on a moment-to-moment basis. None of us can do this perfectly, but with God's grace we will be able to remain headed in the right direction. Learning to trust Jesus through *all* of the seasons of our lives allows Him to teach us about the extent of His love for us. And what is His love like?

As we walk with Him from day to day, we will find His love to be the bread that sustains us when we are tired and weak. It will come as living water as it rushes into our souls to cleanse away sin and satisfy our thirst for forgiveness. At times, it will be the still small voice that reminds us not to worry, that each day is sufficient unto itself and to trust God to provide for our needs. When we look at a waterfall or gaze at the stars on a clear

191

summer night, we will joyfully feel the majestic nature of our Creator's love as it is manifested in His handiwork. Perhaps our response will be to whisper, "Jesus, Your people rejoice in You!"

We believe in Jesus not only because of what He did two thousand years ago, but because of who He is today and because of what He continues to do in the lives of millions every day. The miraculous source of life that turned water into wine, fed five thousand people with five loaves of bread and two fish, healed people of incurable diseases, raised the dead, and rose victorious from the grave is represented in us through the Holy Spirit. For Christians who actively follow Jesus, aging is not so much the loss of youth as it is the opportunity to discover new dimensions of our walk with the Lord.

As Christian women, we each have something to offer to the Body of Christ. *What we do with our time matters.* Do you believe that? Whether we are younger or older, sick or healthy, shy or outgoing, we can serve our Lord. This will be true whether we lead a choir, write letters to prisoners, organize a food bank, serve on the mission field, or care for children. The Lord has told us that it is what is in our hearts that counts!

Why does it seem to catch so many people by surprise that they have just turned forty or sixty? Perhaps the mid-life crisis we so often hear about is more a symptom of modern lifestyles than a necessary component of growing older. It seems that if people were to abide by Christ's teachings from the Sermon on the Mount, there would be little cause for dismay upon exiting from youth.

Recently a woman told me that she felt that she didn't quite fit in anywhere now that she is in her late forties. Her children are all married or in college; her parents and one of her brothers have passed away; she works full-time outside the home in a Christian environment among people in their twenties and thirties; and she directs women's ministries at her church. She has been married for twenty-nine years to the same man, with whom she continues to enjoy a lovely sexual relationship. Role models in her life, however, are sadly lacking. In what women's magazines, she asked, are there fashion layouts and articles which realistically offer ideas that she could adapt to her unique lifestyle? In combining ministry, marriage, professional skills, and an interesting job, she is not a typical career woman who "dresses for success." Now that her children have grown, she is searching for an identity that affirms her past while opening up new horizons for her future.

Since the turn of this century, the average life expectancy for women has gone from age forty-five to close to eighty years of age. Until recently, few women had the luxury to contemplate how to spend "the rest of their lives" like women today do. My friend, and those of us like her, must consider choices that will allow us to expand our abilities in ways that

192

conform to our need to serve Christ in contemporary life at the end of the twentieth century.

Building for the Future

The life patterns and habits that we acquire during the early years of adulthood lay a foundation for the way we will live during the later years of our lives. There are no demarcation lines that divide "youth" from "middle age" or "middle age" from "old age." Our histories develop on a day-to-day basis, with each event that we encounter being added to our experience of what it means to be alive. We cannot say, until we look back, that this or that day will be any more significant than any other. We also do not feel ourselves jump from being young into being old. *Aging is a natural process that is merely a continuation of who we already are.* You and I will not be different people ten or thirty years from now. We will just be *more* of who we are today.

If we refuse to acknowledge the fact of our mortality or the probability that we will live to be at least seventy years old, we will find it difficult to head into the future gracefully. But if we begin early to build for the future in a positive way through adjusting the way we view aging, we will be more likely to have positive things to contribute to the world around us as we grow older. Expecting to look and feel the same way at sixty-five as we did at twenty-five denies us the honor and dignity that should be accorded to those who have a lifetime of learning behind them. Our perspective on aging must be different than that of the world's if we are to shape our identity in conformity with God's will for our lives.

Growing older in the years that are allotted to us permits us to mature in faith and hope. The accumulation of time spent in Bible study, prayer, ministry, and Christian service builds up a treasure that can never be taken away from us. We will *never* lose the time and resources we invest on behalf of the gospel. The kingdom of God that Jesus taught about requires that we use our gifts and talents wisely rather than for the sake of material gain alone.

When we meet older people who drain our energy through their bitterness and dissatisfaction, we are seeing a harvest being reaped from seeds that were sown over the span of a person's lifetime. What a joy it is to meet people who are radiant with Christ's love in the later years of life! In contrast, they continue to minister God's strength to others even though their natural strength is waning. It is a privilege to be with a man or a woman whose faith has become deeply rooted in his or her heart after weathering the trials of life.

When my husband and I first became Christians, we went to a church that was pastored by a man in his late sixties. Ted and Myrna Mosies were godly figures to those of us who flocked to the services conducted in the cinder-block building that Ted constructed on his own. We were able to feel that we were a part of the Body of Christ in an active way through this loving couple's acceptance of our countercultural lifestyle, when no other church would have been comfortable having us even walk in their front door!

On Sunday mornings, youth from miles around would come to hear Brother Mosies teach. He never seemed to notice the beards, long hair, blue jeans, and sandals that most of the congregation wore. On the other hand, few of us ever thought of Ted as "old." We loved to hear him teach in his Dutch accent and listen to him sing "In the Garden." In a world where there seemed to be an abundance of bigotry and hate, Leach Road Church offered us a taste of paradise.

It was comforting to be around our pastor and his wife. They lived in a simple one-bedroom house in the midst of a working-class neighborhood. They always had something to give to others, yet never seemed to be lacking in any way. Ted *always* picked up hitchhikers. The Mosieses were constantly feeding people, helping people, and ministering to people, all in the name of Jesus. How they let their lights shine . . . and all at an age when they should have been slowing down and retiring!

Over the years, Ted's health deteriorated. He developed diabetes and lost all of his teeth because of a massive infection. As he became increasingly weaker, he continued to trust the Lord to sustain him. At about the same time, each of us moved away from that phase in our lives, either in an actual or a symbolic way. Ted retired from active pastoring. Not too long afterward, he went to be with the Lord when his body ceased functioning. It was as if he realized that he finally could "retire" once his ministry to us was over. Myrna had a devastating stroke that left her partially paralyzed and unable to speak. She now lives in a nursing home and is confined to a wheelchair.

Even though I had not seen her in eight years, I wasn't surprised to see the beauty of the Lord resting on Myrna's face when I greeted her at my sister's wedding last summer. With pure white hair and eyes that sparkled with Christ's love, Myrna's physical debilitation is not what caught my attention. It is rare to see such incredible sweetness resting upon an older person's face. I could not look at her without feeling touched in a powerful way by the joy of the Holy Spirit.

When I think of what it means to grow older, I will always think of Ted and Myrna Mosies. I will remember the things they taught me about the God who lives and the Son He sent to save us. Like Mary of Bethany, these two precious people were not content to store up treasure for themselves when they could share it with Jesus. Like them, I hope to be able to reject the notion that growing older means growing inward.

With God's grace, each of us can become a light that shines forth

God's love if we set our minds upon Him. Paul wrote that "the mind controlled by the Spirit is life and peace" and that "if the Spirit of him who raised Jesus from the dead is living in you, he who raised Christ from the dead will also give life to your mortal bodies through his Spirit, who lives in you."[2] These words apply to *all* believers, regardless of how young or old they are. We must reject the current cultural mind-set that makes women afraid of growing older.

The Dignity of Maturity

> She is clothed with strength and dignity;
>   she can laugh at the days to come.
> She speaks with wisdom,
>   and faithful instruction is on her tongue.
> She watches over the affairs of her household
>   and does not eat the bread of idleness.
> Her children arise and call her blessed;
>   her husband also, and he praises her:
> "Many women do noble things,
>   but you surpass them all."
> Charm is deceptive, and beauty is fleeting,
>   but a woman who fears the Lord is to be praised.[3]

Menopause is not a disease.
Growing older is not an illness.
"Crow's feet" are *not* caused by a lack of moisturizer.
Believe it or not, we *can* laugh at the days to come when we realize where we're heading! Myths about aging are rampant in our society. Here are a few of the more prevalent beliefs that influence the way women view the effects of aging on their sexuality:

MYTH #1: *No matter what happens to a woman in midlife, menopause is the culprit.*

FACT: Just as getting married and childbearing involve sexual passages, passing through menopause involves changes that have an impact on a woman's life. However, it is the other changes that occur in most women's lives at or around the time of menopause that have a much greater effect on their everyday activities and priorities. A number of events happen between the ages of forty-five and sixty that involve changes in a woman's role and status as well as on her body. These are:

- Life patterns shift as children grow up, leave home, get married, and possibly start a family of their own.

195

- A number of family members and friends become chronically ill; loved ones close to the family die.

- Working adults prepare for retirement; many women make career changes or return to school for a first or second degree.

- The issue of death is faced more realistically from a personal standpoint.

- Minor changes occur in sexual function that involve a readjustment in attitudes and practices related to lovemaking.

- A change in the metabolic rate reduces one's caloric requirements by about 200-300 calories per day.

The concept of the "midlife crisis" is relatively new to the field of mental health. Crises can occur at any time in life when new roles are assumed and a person moves through a period of transition from one phase of life to the next. We each respond in our own unique manner as we cope with life changes during adolescence, college graduation, getting married, childbearing, or the experience of losing a loved one. Actually, *any* event that rearranges our lives can precipitate a crisis. For a life crisis to occur, there must be a noncoping response to a particular situation, such as bouts of sadness, withdrawal from others, or outbursts of anger. Each of these symptoms should be responded to on an individual basis if and when they occur.

When a woman prepares ahead for midlife by anticipating the changes she can expect to happen, the likelihood of one of these events producing a long-term disruption in her life would be unusual, with the exception of becoming a widow. For instance, if a woman *expects* to fall apart when she stops menstruating, then that will be a real possibility. Much depends on one's outlook and ability to recognize stressful periods that require special attention to one's diet, need for rest, recreational activities, and time spent drawing near to God through prayer, fellowship, and Bible study.

MYTH #2: *A woman is not the same person after she goes through her "change of life."*

FACT: Menopause is part of God's design for our lives. It is the time when a woman's ovaries no longer produce changes in the uterine lining that cause monthly bleeding in the absence of conception. For most women, the process of the *climacteric* begins between the ages of forty-five and fifty. Menopause, or the stopping of menstruation, is just one part of this process.

During the climacteric, the production of estrogen recedes and progesterone secretion is phased out almost entirely. Most women do notice that they will tend to gain weight more easily unless they exercise and reduce their caloric intake. The majority of women, however, do *not* experience the distressing symptoms commonly associated with menopause, such as depression, insomnia, headaches, and skin changes. Of those that do, it is unclear which of these things are associated with factors other than a reduction in hormone levels.

It has been estimated that as few as one in ten women experience "hot flashes" or the sensation of heat spreading over various places on the body. The exact cause of hot flashes is unknown; some women seem to have a similar sensation in the week following childbirth. This is a physically harmless experience that varies in frequency, strength, and duration in the women who report having it.

Treating this symptom as if it is a sign of a disease seems uncalled for. It is usually a temporary irritation that is often best managed by using stress management techniques such as relaxation and slow breathing, and reminding oneself that it will produce no harm to the body.

Instead of becoming a *different* person after menopause, a woman is likely to feel that she is passing into a phase of her life that will allow her to express *more* of who she is. The care and nurture of children and teenagers involves doing certain tasks to the exclusion of participating in activities that demand large amounts of time and energy away from the family. During the years that a woman concentrates on raising her children, valuable skills are developed that later lend themselves to ministry within the wider community she lives in. Child-rearing is a magnificent training ground for the development of time management skills, creative approaches to getting jobs done, learning to be patient in the midst of multiple demands, and finding ways to express one's gifts in a multitude of situations.

For example, I have learned to have my "quiet time" with the Lord while doing dishes, making beds, doing the laundry, and vacuuming the rug. It seems like the more I concentrate on Him, the less aware I am of the routineness of my tasks. This habit has helped me to avoid becoming resentful on many occasions, and at the same time, has made it easier to carry the Lord's presence with me wherever I go, into whatever I am doing. Other women have shared that they have developed a rich prayer life under similar circumstances. I wonder where the church would be today without the countless women who devote hours of prayer to the building up of the church while doing mundane things like fixing sack lunches or scrubbing out bath tubs.

The point to remember is this: the things you are doing today will follow you into the future. We shall reap what we sow. Our early adult years can be a time of learning disciplines that will be put to good use in the years ahead. Our youth will never be "taken" from us if we spend it on the Lord's behalf.

MYTH #3: *A woman's desire for sex is greatly reduced after menopause.*

FACT: Some women desire sexual sharing less after menopause, but the majority find their love lives relatively unaffected by menopause. Hormone levels vary from woman to woman, and it is not known to what extent a decrease in desire may be related to biological (as opposed to psychological) factors.

What *is* known is that one half of all menopausal and postmenopausal women report no change in their desire for sexual activity and one quarter say that they experienced an increase after menstruation stopped.[4] Since most men find that their sexual response becomes slower with age, an interesting thing takes place in many marriages: the husband is likely to require a longer time to become erect, which means that the time spent during the excitement and plateau phases of lovemaking must be significantly longer. It is as if the Lord designed these changes into our bodies to enliven the sexual dimension of our lives at a time when communication and mutual understanding are more important than ever. Changes in physical responses to sexual arousal can become an opportunity for a couple to discover new ways to approach this aspect of their relationship.

The primary change that a woman must learn to cope with is the reduction of cervical mucus that causes the vaginal lining to become thinner and drier. This is similar to what happens while a woman is breast-feeding, but will be more pronounced and involves gradual changes in the entire reproductive tract. The use of vaginal creams containing estrogen should be carefully evaluated to compare the risks and benefits associated with their use. Estrogen cream is rapidly absorbed into the bloodstream through the skin of the vagina. Until further research is done, it is not known what the long-term effects of such treatment are. If a woman chooses to avoid applications of estrogen, Vitamin E may be useful. Spending a longer time arousing one another, using positions that enhance comfort, and stroking a lubricant onto the husband's penis will also make intercourse easier. Frequent lovemaking actually "exercises" vaginal tissue and keeps it healthier than when regular intercourse is avoided.

MYTH #4: *Mental instability is a natural part of menopause.*

FACT: The belief that emotional instability is the cornerstone of menopause is inappropriate because it focuses on a single facet of a woman's life, causing her to view a normal process as an abnormality. Rather than attempting to understand the underlying causes for emotional expressions, blaming "The Change" for her reactions becomes an easy way to explain every nuance of her behavior. Considering the other changes that are likely to be going on in her life, it is likely that a woman will encounter feelings that she may find difficult to deal with at times.

Living in a society that places a premium on leanness and suppleness is likely to threaten a woman's self-esteem. If she has built her sense of worth around her external appearance rather than on the eternal bedrock of Christ's love, she will find that she has built her house on sinking sand. Active involvement in following Christ does not produce this type of neurosis. As an endless number of celebrities parade their face-lifts and tummy-tucks before us, we can view the quest for endless youth with compassion instead of envy.

At any time in life, imbalances can occur within the level of chemicals in the brain that produce depression, erratic behavior, or outbursts of anger in stressful situations. A thorough physical examination should be conducted whenever a woman feels she has lost joy in living, experiences memory loss, or cannot control her anger. There may be physical causes for these symptoms that can be treated with medication. As Christians, we sometimes forget this well-known fact. We may fall into a way of thinking that causes us to value the medical treatment of our bodies, but denies treatment for the mind. In light of current research this is unwise. There are now medications that can correct imbalances in the brain. These treatments for depression and anger can bring entire families out from under the oppression of one member's struggle to cope. It is irresponsible to refuse to get professional help and try to "go it alone" when certain emotional states become overwhelming. It is not normal to be suicidal, listless, or out of control. Blaming menopause for such reactions prevents a woman from getting the help she needs and deserves.

MYTH #5: *Menopause is an experience that fills most women with dread.*

FACT: Are you kidding? Most women are through with being fertile *long* before their bodies are. Many women have had hysterectomies in their thirties and forties, experiencing the loss of menstruation far in advance of their biologically determined date for this event. For the rest of us, can any of us claim to have ever been particularly fond of menstruating? Of course not! Having one's period simply is not the highlight of the month for any woman, unless it is seen as proof that a pregnancy has not taken place.

The only reason menopause might be a source of concern for a woman is if she does not know the facts about it. Because of the mystery and folklore that surround menopause, many women are unclear about what it actually involves.

The last period in a woman's life usually occurs between the ages of forty and fifty, but can happen as late as sixty. In the years preceding menopause, a woman's menstrual cycle is disrupted. Her periods are likely to become irregular as a result. About one quarter of those women who experience menopause notice no other changes except the cessation of their periods. Half notice slight physical and/or emotional changes. The remaining 25 percent have symptoms ranging from hot flashes to joint pains. Any troublesome symptoms that might be experienced do not pose a threat to a woman's health unless they are associated with other causes. Because disease may occur that is unrelated to menopause, it is important to discuss any health concerns with one's health care provider. Signs that warrant immediate medical attention are:

- bleeding between periods

- prolonged or excessive menstrual bleeding

- a period six months or more from the period that seemed to be the last

These symptoms could indicate a life-threatening malignancy, such as cancer of the uterus, and must be evaluated to determine the reason behind them.

The most common treatment for irritating symptoms associated with menopause is hormone replacement therapy. The hormones used may be a combination of progesterone and estrogen, or estrogen alone in the form of vaginal cream or oral tablets. There are various drugs besides hormones that act to decrease the severity of symptoms associated with menopause. Alternative medical treatments consist mainly of tranquilizers, antidepressants, or sleeping pills.

Estrogen therapy is associated with cancer of the uterus, and its use should be thoroughly evaluated by a woman and her husband along with the woman's health care provider. The advantage of taking estrogen is that it does lessen the severity of symptoms related to menopause, including osteoporosis, but it does not usually slow down or stop the aging process. For many women, a healthy diet and vigorous exercise may be better than swallowing estrogen tablets. Exercise keeps bones strong and reduces or eliminates depression if participated in on a regular basis (three or four times per week), while sound eating habits provide the body with nutrients needed by the body at this time.

MYTH #6: *Life becomes less interesting for women after menopause.*

FACT: By this point, you should already be able to determine the inaccuracy of this statement! The last thing a woman needs when experiencing this transition is pity. Entering these later years of one's life is fulfilling and meaningful for most Christian women, who find themselves feeling more aware of God's love than ever before.

Although a mother's responsibility to her children changes when they leave home, she does not cease to be a mother. Her children will *never* outgrow their need for encouragement, reassurance, affirmation, and love. If she is blessed with having grandchildren, there will be numerous ways for her to contribute to their lives. Our society seems to be running short of grandmas who have the time, or the inclination, to make life truly special for their grandsons and granddaughters.

Most importantly, the church never loses its need for those who are willing to serve Jesus. One of my favorite stories in the New Testament is about a disciple named Dorcas, who "was always doing good and helping the poor."[5] She was beloved by many. When she became ill and died, Peter was called to her bedside, where he found many women weeping over her body. Dorcas had made robes and other clothing for the widows who were mourning there, which they showed to Peter as he entered the room. After sending them out, he got down on his knees and prayed, and then turned toward the figure lying on the bed. After speaking her name and telling her to rise, Dorcas opened her eyes and sat up. It is easy to imagine the joy that broke forth in her town that day as her many friends praised God for sending this precious woman back to them.

Who claims that life is less interesting after menopause?

> Trust in the Lord with all your heart,
> And lean not on your own understanding;
> in all your ways acknowledge him,
> And he will make your paths straight.
> Do not be wise in your own eyes;
> fear the Lord and shun evil.
> This will bring health to your body,
> and nourishment to your bones.[6]

/ 13 /

Choosing a
Healthy Lifestyle

*Heavenly Father, I am glad to be alive. I pray for the courage to
face my past intelligently. Help me to understand my shape and
my shaping. Where I can never be different, teach me acceptance.
Where others influenced me in the negative, make me merciful.
Where you and I together can rework me, show me my part.
Thank you for giving me life in any form. Amen.[1]*

Charlie Shedd, *The Fat Is in Your Head*

The belief that we are loved and accepted by God encourages us to
develop lifestyle habits that conform to His design for our lives.
Knowing that our bodies belong to God enables us to care for ourselves
with an attitude of thanksgiving rather than of pride. With the Lord's
help, we can choose not to abuse ourselves with alcohol, drugs, or tobacco.
Learning to balance our need for exercise and rest teaches us to avoid the
extremes of either a sedentary existence or a fitness-crazed mentality.
Living a healthy lifestyle becomes a *positive* addiction because the more
one lives in accordance with what is good for the body, the more wholesome and delightful it feels!

Have you ever noticed how just breathing clean, fresh air is an invig-
orating experience when there is a sense of appreciation for living? Being
able to leap and dance and sing is an exhilarating event if we have joy in
our hearts. Fixing meals that are meant to provide for the physical needs
of one's family can become a way of also refreshing their spirits as everyone sits around the table to talk and eat together. Some of the best things
in our lives are related to the physical dimension of our existence. That is
why there is such a fine line between enjoying health and pursuing sensuality.

The impact of our personal habits on our daily lives has far-reaching
consequences. Our bodies have been created to play intricately orchestrat-

203

ed harmonies with our minds and spirits. When one of these parts slips out of tune, the entire symphony is affected. We must avoid emphasizing only the externals. How we look is only *one* aspect of who we are.

Health is a state of mental, emotional, physical, and spiritual well-being, not simply the absence of disease. By this definition, no one is ever perfectly healthy! Within this model, well-being becomes the goal at the end of a long continuum. Each of us is at our own unique place along that line between total health on one end and premature death on the other:

Figure 13-1

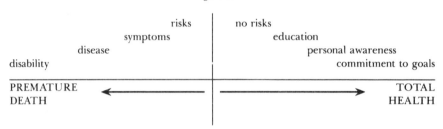

According to this model, the most physically fit athletes can be unhealthy. Though someone may *appear* to be well, looks are deceiving. As Christians, we are aware of how sick a person may become spiritually and still be considered "healthy." Current standards of fitness often fail to address this key principle.

The central reality in our lives must rest upon our acceptance of Jesus Christ as our Lord and Savior and the finished work of the Cross. Without this belief, living a healthy lifestyle is irrelevant. But let's make no mistake—our Creator wants to transform us from the inside out. The way we live is to be a reflection of our faith in *every* dimension of our lives. Bit by bit, God is restoring us as we "put on the new self, which is being renewed in knowledge in the image of its Creator."[2] In a culture that measures health by body fat percentages and oxygen uptake measurements, it is easy to overemphasize calories and workout schedules rather than the condition of our hearts.

In this book, I have addressed areas of our lives as women that are more deserving of our energy and attention than achieving the ideal weight or coordinating a wardrobe in the right "season." It really boils down to determining our priorities and taking care of first things first. In a sense, this chapter is less important than most of the others, but its topic plays a significant role in our lives nonetheless. When we feel good because we are taking care of our bodies, we will feel more energetic in the sexual dimension of our lives as well.

The Importance of Exercise

Our bodies were designed to function best when they are challenged by physical activity and given the opportunity to rest regularly. Too much of one or the other throws us out of whack! Some people are genetically equipped to run faster, stretch farther, or work longer than others. When these abilities are put to good use, it amazes the rest of us. (We need to remember this when we attend an aerobics class and see the instructor do a perfect open straddle stretch, and if that weren't enough, follow it up by casually leaning forward and leaning her elbows on the floor. The average woman just isn't built that way!) We *are* structured, however, to benefit from regular exercise that places an appropriate amount of stress on our hearts and lungs to help them work more efficiently. The degree of effort that each woman should expend will depend on her age, weight, current health status, and other related factors.

Cardiovascular fitness is brought about through large muscle activity that is done rhythmically and continuously for a period of at least twenty to thirty minutes every other day or for a minimum of three days per week. By stimulating the heart to beat faster and the lungs to breathe more air, the body's ability to carry and use oxygen is enhanced. The term *aerobic* combines two Greek words, *aero* (air) and *bios* (life), to describe types of exercise that produce cardivascular fitness. Swimming is the best form of aerobic exercise because it allows all our major muscle groups to work while at the same time reducing the strain that gravity places on us. Cross-country skiing, brisk walking, cycling, stair climbing, rope skipping, jogging, running, and aerobic dance are other excellent forms of exercise that condition the heart and lungs. Dr. Kenneth Cooper's book *The Aerobics Program For Total Well-Being* is a complete guide to developing aerobic fitness and represents the accumulation of many years of research that Dr. Cooper has performed in this area. I recommend that you read it before beginning a vigorous exercise program.

If you are currently participating in an exercise class, you need to evaluate your instructor's ability to conform to standards set by exercise specialists like Dr. Cooper. By avoiding ballistic stretches (bouncing while stretching), kicking high in the air, hopping on the same foot repeatedly, and stretching with her body out of proper alignment, an instructor teaches class members to protect their bodies from harm. An aerobic instructor's training should include information about proper posture, range of motion, basic anatomy, and other factors related to exercise physiology. The only criteria that many certification programs require, however, is that candidates be able to perform the routines, attend a one or two-day workshop, pass an endurance test, and weigh in at a specified level.

Here are several things to look for as indications of a program's quality. These same criteria also apply to exercise records, videos, and audiocassettes.

The program should have been developed by a physician, a registered physical therapist, or someone with a master's or doctoral/degree in health or physical education; have a track record that is relatively injury free; be sponsored or endorsed by a university, hospital, or professional medical organization; and have a good reputation within your community.

The class environment should be well-lighted; have a wooden floor or protective covering such as gymnastic mats; provide good ventilation; be kept at a comfortable temperature; and have clearly posted charts so that participants may become familiar with their target heart rates.

The sessions should include five to ten minutes of warm-up and cool-down exercises, including numerous stretches held for ten to forty-five seconds each (no bouncing); stimulus periods combining fast and slow movements to maintain participant's heart rates within their target range for twenty to thirty minutes; heart rate checks near the beginning and end of the workout; frequent monitoring of heart rates during the stimulus periods; and emphasis on using arm movements to maintain heart rates rather than excessive jumping and kicking.

Instruction on warning signs should be included so that participants learn how to monitor themselves both during and after the workout for signs of overexertion. These signs include: nausea, vomiting, extreme breathlessness, side stitches, muscle cramps, prolonged fatigue lasting several hours after the session has ended, pain in the calf muscles, pain in the front of the shins (shin splints), abnormal heart action, dizziness, loss of coordination, confusion, light-headedness, blurred vision, flare-ups of gout or arthritis, sudden inability to sleep at night, cold sweats, pallor, blueness of the lips or fingertips, joint or muscle pain, or pressure in the chest, arm, or throat due to exercise.

The ultimate proof of a program's quality lies in the satisfaction of its participants. Do they feel refreshed and invigorated after exercising or are they too sore to move? Are injuries uncommon, or do many participants have to drop out due to strains and sprains? Do the majority of students keep coming back to the same program? Do they recommend it to others?

The individual's responsibility is to evaluate the level of one's personal involvement in a fitness program by answering these questions affirmatively:

1. Am I including adequate time for warm-up and cool-down periods?
2. Do I normally exercise at least three nonconsecutive days per week?
3. Do I spend at least twenty minutes in my target zone?
4. Do I avoid all warning signs?
5. Am I building up gradually to a pace that is right for me?

Choose an activity that *you* enjoy, and stay with it for at least six weeks before expecting to see a significant improvement in your fitness level. After two or three weeks, you should notice improved physical fitness, but after that time, you will be likely to sleep more soundly, feel less tired, and exercise more efficiently. As your fitness level improves, you will need to match your exertion with your heart rate to keep it in its target zone and may find that you will need to put more effort into exercising in order to challenge your heart and lungs sufficiently.

While a regular exercise program can't be the answer for all of our problems, it can produce a number of remarkable benefits that make spending time on physical activity a worthwhile investment. Reported benefits of effective exercise programs include:

- increased mental alertness

- improved memory

- self-discipline leading to a healthier lifestyle

- increased self-confidence

- improved sense of well-being

- decreased or eliminated periods of depression or anxiety

- improved coordination

- increased stamina

- improved eating habits

- increased ability to cope with stress

- decreased ratio of body fat in relation to muscle mass

- decrease in the severity, duration, and frequency of illness

- increased appreciation for others

- alleviation of menstrual discomfort

- decrease in the severity and duration of PMS

- increased sexual responsiveness

To sum it up, physical activity in daily life can be divided into occupational, household, sports, conditioning, or other categories. As a subset of physical activity, exercise is planned, structured, and repetitive. Its specific goal is to improve or maintain one's level of physical fitness. When our lifestyles do not adequately challenge our bodies, cardiovascular endurance, strength, and flexibility are lost. Incorporating the need for exercise into our lives plays a vital role in our ability to feel well. As wives and mothers, we can be more effective in promoting wellness within our families if we model the importance of maintaining physical fitness to our husbands and our children.

Pelvic Power

The places of the female body that are particularly vulnerable to stress are the muscles that lie in the pelvic region of our bodies. The muscles of the lower back, pelvic floor, and abdomen need to be kept strong by doing exercises that specifically are aimed at these areas. The benefits to be gained through such exercise are a reduction in discomfort during love-making, a reduction in the severity of premenstrual symptoms, decreased discomfort during menstruation, increased strength during childbirth, partial alleviation of the effects of aging, and increasing the strength of one's sexual response.

The exercises outlined here may be incorporated into your regular fitness routine or be done separately. They take about ten minutes to do and are easy to learn. Because poor condition of the pelvic muscles affect other parts of the body, it is not surprising that strengthening the pelvic floor can have dramatic results. Exercising this important area enables a woman to look and feel better about being a woman.

Strong abdominal muscles act like a natural corset by holding in the abdominal organs. They also prevent lower back pain by keeping the trunk of the body in proper alignment with the spine. Since muscles in this area put pressure on the intestines, constipation may be relieved by strengthening them. If surgery is ever necessary, these muscles will recover more quickly if they have been previously strengthened. The abdominal muscles also play an important role during childbirth by aiding the uterus in its expulsion of the baby through the birth canal.

The muscles of the lower back are responsible for our posture. By working in opposition to the muscles of the abdomen, they serve to stabilize the pelvis by keeping it in an upright position. Flexibility in the lower back helps to prevent stiffness and strain and promotes a woman's ability to relax during lovemaking.

The pelvic floor muscles are knit together in such a way that they form a muscular sling that supports the contents of the pelvic cavity and withstands the pressures that occur within it. The most distinctive part of this group is the pubococcygeus or P.C. muscle group. This dynamic, highly specialized portion of the pelvic floor lies directly over the midline of the pelvic outlet and contains the openings to the bladder, uterus, and rectum. It is attached to the pubic bones in front and the tailbone in back. The P.C. group controls the shape of the vagina and contracts forcibly during orgasm. During intercourse, the P.C. group determines the amount of contact that the vaginal wall has with the penis. Rich in nerve endings, it is the P.C. group that can be consciously relaxed and tightened to increase sexual enjoyment for both partners during lovemaking. Because it tends to sag and stretch over time, strengthening the P.C. group through exercise enhances sexual responsiveness during intercourse by allowing a woman to become vaginally expressive toward her husband.

The following routine should be done often (at least every other day for the rest of your life!) unless you have a condition that prohibits this type of exercise. If your back is weak, begin with just the pelvic tilts, forward curls, stretches, and pelvic lifts. As your back and abdominal muscles become stronger, slowly add the other exercises, gradually building up the number of repetitions of each, until you are able to do all ten exercises at a level that is comfortable to you.

1. *Pelvic tilts:* This exercise improves posture, relieves lower back stiffness, and strengthens muscles in the abdomen, buttocks, groin, and pelvic floor.
   a. Lie on your back, knees bent, feet on the floor about hip distance apart, with your toes turned slightly inward and hands palms down at your sides. Keep your head down on the floor with your chin down and close to your chest to lengthen your spine. Note the curve beneath your waist near the base of your back. Inhale.
   b. As you exhale slowly, pull in your stomach muscles as you erase the space beneath the waist by pressing your lower back firmly onto the floor. Your abdominal muscles will aid you by pulling upwards and inwards as your buttocks muscles tighten. Purposely squeeze your buttocks as you tilt. Your tailbone should be lifted one to two inches from the floor. Hold for five to eight seconds. Inhale as you relax, and return to your original position. Begin with five tilts, working up to ten as your goal.

2. *Forward curls:* This exercise tones and tightens the abdominal muscles.
   a. Begin in the same position as for the pelvic tilt but with your hands crossed over your chest, palms down. Inhale.
   b. Exhale slowly as you contract your abdominal muscles by using them to lift your head and shoulders up off the floor. Hold for two to three seconds. Be sure to keep your lower back pressed onto the floor in a modified pelvic tilt. Keep your stomach muscles tightened.
   c. Inhale as you lower your head and shoulders. By keeping them in an even line with your upper back, you need not lower your head all the way to the floor each time. Begin with eight curls, building up to between twelve and twenty as your goal.

3. *Knees to elbows:* You will strengthen lower back and abdominal muscles with this exercise.

a. Lie on your back, with your hands behind your head, knees slightly apart, feet flexed and in the air. Press your lower back onto the floor. Inhale.

b. As you exhale, contract your stomach muscles, lift your head, elbows forward, reaching toward your knees as you move them slightly toward your elbows. Hold for two to three seconds. Inhale as you resume your original position. Begin with four and build up to between eight and twelve repetitions.

4. *Elbow lifts:* Abdominal and thigh muscles will be strengthened by this exercise.

a. Begin in the same position as for knees to elbows, but cross your feet at the ankles. Inhale as you raise your feet up higher, keeping your knees slightly bent.

b. Exhale, contract your abdominals, keeping your knees bent and ankles crossed while bringing your chin toward your chest, elbows close together and to knees. Hold for two to three seconds. Inhale as you lower. Begin with four, building up to between eight and twelve as your goal.

5. *Criss-crosses:* This exercise strengthens the abdominal muscles with special attention to the oblique (side or waist) muscles.

a. Remain in the same position as for elbow lifts, but bend your knees and open them wide, keeping your feet crossed at the ankles. Inhale.

b. Exhale, contract stomach muscles, lift head tucking chin forward as you reach your right elbow toward your left knee. You will feel the muscles on your right side aid you as you lift. Inhale and lower. Repeat by touching your left elbow to your right knee.
Begin with four crosses on each side, working up to eight to twelve.

6. *Knee rolls:* This exercise also strengthens the oblique muscles as well as the lower back.

a. After finishing the criss-crosses, bring your knees together, uncross your ankles, and stretch your arms out to your sides at shoulder level, palms down on the floor. Inhale as your bring both knees as close to your chest as you can.

b. *Keeping your arms and shoulders on the floor,* exhale, rolling your knees as far to the right as possible. You may or may not be able to touch the floor. Inhale as you return your knees to the center, then repeat to the left side. Begin with four rolls to each side, working up to eight.

7. *Neck stretch:* The purpose of this stretch is to relieve stiffness in the neck and lower back.

Finish the knee rolls by bringing both knees to your chest and holding them with your arms. Slowly bring your head up to touch your knees, then lower. Repeat two more times.

8. *Back stretch:* To relieve lower back stiffness, do this stretch daily. Following the neck stretch, hold your left knee with both hands, pressing it toward your chest as you keep your right foot on the floor with knee bent. Hold for twenty to thirty seconds. Repeat with your right leg.

9. *Long stretch:* This stretch relieves tension in the back, neck, and shoulders.
   a. Now stretch both feet down by sliding your heels along the floor, feet flexed, arms stretched up over your head. Avoid arching your lower back. Inhale deeply as you stretch for six to eight seconds.
   b. Exhale, tighten buttocks, press back onto floor, count to four slowly. Repeat a. and b. two more times.

10. *Pelvic lifts (Kegels):* To strengthen the pelvic floor muscles, repeat this exercise four to eight times daily. No one will know you are doing pelvic lifts unless you raise and lower your eyebrows up and down! You can do them any time, anywhere, as long as your bladder is completely empty.
    a. You may remain on the floor after the long stretch to do this exercise. Simply relax your buttocks, abdomen, and thighs as you inhale.
    b. Now concentrate on lifting the sheet of muscles between your pubic bones and your tailbone as if it were an elevator moving up into your pelvis. You may place your hand over your pubic bone for a reference point as you try to lift the pelvic floor up to the level of your hand. Exhale as you lift—2-3-4, hold for two counts, then lower—2-3-4 as you inhale. Do not tense any other place in your body. Repeat twelve times, building up to twenty-five four to eight times daily. If your pelvic floor is weak, doing two hundred to three hundred pelvic lifts every day will greatly strengthen this important area of your body.

Nutrition, Food, and Weight Control

Health does not depend on nutrition alone. Food and nutritional supplements in and of themselves cannot make a person healthy, but good eating habits play an important role in promoting and maintaining our well-being, just as fitness does. Each of us needs about forty different nutrients to stay healthy. These include vitamins, minerals, proteins, carbohydrates, essential fatty acids, and water. By eating a variety of foods, all of the nutrients required by our bodies are supplied. Because most foods contain more than one nutrient, making wise food choices will provide us with many of the nutrients we need simply and economically.

The following list gives examples of highly nutritious foods that contain large amounts of major vitamins and minerals. Some of the foods appear in several categories. These foods are especially important to include as a regular part of our diets. For the sake of comparison, I have also included a nutritional analysis of the vitamin and mineral content of popular snack items, which tend to be high in calories and yet have little or no nutritional value. The foods at the bottom of the comparison chart are alternative snack foods that can replace junkie munchies when we feel like nibbling.

SUPER SOURCES OF NECESSARY NUTRIENTS

Figure 13-2

HIGH IN VITAMIN A: Needed for keeping eyes and skin healthy	HIGH IN VITAMIN C: Needed for keeping skin and gums healthy	HIGH IN VITAMIN E: Needed in formation of blood cells and muscles
apricots	broccoli	dried beans
asparagus	cabbage salads	green, leafy vegetables
broccoli	cranberry juice	liver
cabbage	grapefruit	margarine
carrots	green peppers	vegetable oils
eggs*	lemons	wheat germ
mangoes	oranges	whole grain cereals
milk, 1%	papayas	whole grain bread
nectarines	potatoes	
papayas	strawberries	
peaches	spinach	
red peppers	tangerines	
sweet potatoes	tomatoes	
tomatoes		
watermelon		
winter squash		

HIGH IN CALCIUM: Needed for bone strength and muscle function	HIGH IN POTASSIUM: Needed for nerve and muscle function	HIGH IN IRON: Needed to build oxygen-carrying capacity in blood and muscles
baked beans	baked beans	apricots
broccoli	bananas	avocadoes
cheese*	bran cereal	baked beans
cottage cheese	bran muffins	chili
custard*	dried apricots	eggs*
ice cream*	lean meats	liver

HIGH IN CALCIUM: Needed for bone strength and muscle function	HIGH IN POTASSIUM: Needed for nerve and muscle function	HIGH IN IRON: Needed to build oxygen- carrying capacity in blood and muscles

ice milk
milk,1%
refried beans
salmon (canned,
  with bones)
shrimp
tofu
yogurt
	orange juice
	parsnips
	peaches
	peanut butter
	potatoes
	prunes
	raisins
	rhubarb
		lean red meats
		nuts
		potatoes
		prunes
		raisins
		spinach
		sunflower seeds
		wheat germ
		whole grain breads &
		  cereals

*These foods are high in fat and cholesterol . . . go easy on them!

POPULAR SNACK FOODS COMPARISON CHART

Figure 13-3

Snack Item	Vitamin A	Vitamin C	Calcium	Iron	Potassium	Calories
Chocolate cupcake with chocolate icing	50 I.U.	trace	21 mg.	.5 mg.	46 mg.	120
Brownie with nuts, 1¾″ x 1¾″	40 I.U.	trace	8 mg.	.4 mg.	38 mg.	95
4 chocolate chip cookies, 2¼″ diameter	50 I.U.	trace	16 mg.	1.0 mg.	56 mg.	200
Glazed doughnut	25 I.U.	0	16 mg.	.6 mg.	34 mg.	205
Cola, 12 oz. can	0	0	0	0	0	145
10 potato chips	trace	3 mg.	8 mg.	.4 mg.	226 mg.	115

Compare these figures with those of more nutritious snacks:

1 carrot	7,930 I.U.	6 mg.	26 mg.	.5 mg.	246 mg.	30
8 oz. container of fruit-flavored yogurt	120 I.U.	1 mg.	269 mg.	.2 mg.	439 mg.	230
1 cup strawberries	90 I.U.	88 mg.	31 mg.	1.5 mg.	244 mg.	55
1 4″ x 8″ wedge of watermelon	2,510 I.U.	30 mg.	30 mg.	2.1 mg.	426 mg.	110

Snack Item	Vitamin A	Vitamin C	Calcium	Iron	Potassium	Calories
1 orange	260 I.U.	66 mg.	54 mg.	.5 mg.	263 mg.	86
8 oz. glass of 1% milk	500 I.U.	2 mg.	235 mg.	.1 mg.	381 mg.	90
1 oz. wedge of cheddar cheese	300 I.U.	0	204 mg.	.2 mg.	28 mg.	115
1 cup soft-serve ice milk (like D.Q.)	180 I.U.	1 mg.	274 mg.	.3 mg.	412 mg.	225

mg. = milligrams
I.U. = International Units

The dictum that "breakfast is the most important meal of the day" still holds true today. Eating a regular breakfast is an important component of one's total nutritional picture. If you tend to skip or minimize the importance of this meal, why not get into the good breakfast habit by eating a breakfast that will energize your entire morning? Each of the menu ideas that are listed below provide all the necessary nutrients you need to get your day off to a great start.

QUICK AND EASY BREAKFAST IDEAS

Figure 13-4

- Small glass of orange juice, slice of whole wheat toast with one tablespoon of peanut butter, and two tablespoons of raisins

- ½ cantaloupe, one cup of Special K, Total, or Product 19 cereal with ½ cup milk

- Small glass of grapefruit juice, a scrambled egg, and a slice of whole wheat raisin toast with a teaspoon of margarine

- Small glass of cranapple juice, two halves of a toasted bagel with two tablespoons of cream cheese, and one small orange

- A small tangerine, one slice of whole wheat toast with two teaspoons of low-sugar strawberry spread, and ½ cup cottage cheese

- Small glass of orange juice and a cup of vanilla yogurt mixed with chopped apple (skin left on) and sprinkled with cinnamon

- Banana milk shake: 12 oz. of low-fat milk whirled in the blender with one small ripe banana, one egg, one teaspoon of vanilla, a little nutmeg, and honey to taste.

- One cup of melon balls, four prunes, and a whole wheat English muffin spread with low-sugar orange marmalade with a glass of low-fat milk

- One cup of bran flakes with ½ cup of sliced strawberries and ½ cup of milk with a cup of herbal tea

- Small glass of pineapple juice, one cup of oatmeal with milk, and a pear (skin left on)

214

High Fiber Foods

It is important to include twenty to thirty-five grams of fiber in your daily diet because it can lower your blood cholesterol and reduce your risk of developing heart disease and cancer of the colon. Fiber also aids in weight loss. Pick eight to twelve servings from the following list to meet your fiber quota each day. Because these foods are loaded with complex carbohydrates, they are an excellent source of energy. Many of these foods are also on the Super Sources list, making them rich in vitamins and minerals that are essential to your health.

FIGURE 13-5

CATEGORY A: 8-12 GRAMS PER SERVING

Serving size is one ounce for cereals in all categories and ½ cup for beans and vegetables unless noted.

Kellogg's All Bran With
    Extra Fiber
General Mills' Fiber One
Kellogg's All Bran
Baked beans in tomato sauce

Nabisco 100% Bran
Kellogg's All Bran Fruit
    and Almond
Kellogg's Bran Buds

CATEGORY B: 4-7 GRAMS PER SERVING

Kidney beans
Split peas
Lentils
½ cup blackberries
1 medium pear
1 cup whole wheat spaghetti
Pinto beans
4 prunes
Lima beans
1 medium apple with skin

Quaker Corn Bran
Ralston Bran Chex
Ralston High Fiber Hot Cereal
Kellogg's Bran Flakes
Post Bran Flakes
Kellogg's Cracklin' Oat Bran
Kellogg's Raisin Bran
Post Raisin Bran
Nabisco Shredded What and Bran
Post Fruit and Fibre
Uhlmann's Wheatena
Weetabix

CATEGORY C: 2-3 GRAMS OF FIBER

Broccoli
4 brussel sprouts
Carrots
1 raw carrot
1 cup celery
Canned corn
Green beans
1 raw green pepper
½ cup blueberries
15 cherries
3 dates
1 cup melon balls
1 medium orange
1 large peach
3 small plums

2 cups raw lettuce
Parsnips
1 cup raw spinach
1 medium sweet potato
1 large tomato, raw
Zucchini
3 medium apricots, fresh
1 medium banana
1 bran muffin
1 slice cracked wheat bread
2 buckwheat pancakes
½ cup brown rice, cooked
3 2½" graham cracker squares
2 slices rye bread
2 slices whole wheat bread

¼ cup raisins
½ cup raspberries
1 cup strawberries
1 large tangerine

3 tablespoons of oatmeal, dry measure
1 whole wheat English muffin
1 whole wheat dinner roll
1 tablespoon of unprocessed bran
1 tablespoon of wheat germ
Crackers:
1 Fiber Rich Bran
2 Triple Ry Krisp
1 Wasa Fiber Plus
2 Fiber Crisp Bread
2 Finn Crisp

Eating a *variety* of foods makes it less likely that a person will develop either a deficiency or an excess of a particular nutrient. Selecting several foods each day from each of the major food groups is the key to good nutrition. These groups are: fruits and vegetables; breads, cereals, and grains; meats, poultry, eggs, and fish; dried beans and peas such as baked beans, refried beans, soybeans, kidney beans, and split-peas; and milk, cheese and yogurt.

Contrary to what the manufacturers of vitamin supplements say, there are no proven advantages to consuming excess amounts of any nutrient. A balanced diet provides all of the nutrients a healthy person needs. The exceptions to this are women during their fertile years, who may require iron supplements to replace the iron they use with menstrual bleeding, and women who are pregnant or breast-feeding. During pregnancy and lactation, a woman needs extra iron, folic acid, Vitamin A, calcium, and extra calories in the form of carbohydrates, proteins, and fats. Protein-rich foods are especially important to an expectant or nursing mother.

The Value of Weight Control

Being overweight increases the likelihood of developing chronic disorders such as high blood pressure and increased levels of cholesterol in the blood. These conditions are associated with an increased incidence of heart attacks and strokes. Maintaining one's ideal weight is a preventative measure to reduce these risks. The range of body weights suggested by the 1973 H.E.W. Conference on Obesity shows that there is an acceptable range for men and women that can be determined by one's height and frame size:

FIGURE 13-6

HEIGHT (feet, inches, without shoes or clothes)	MEN (pounds)	WOMEN (pounds)
4'10"		92-119
4'11"		94-122

HEIGHT (feet, inches, without shoes or clothes)	MEN (pounds)	WOMEN (pounds)
5'0"		96-125
5'1"		99-128
5'2"	112-141	102-131
5'3"	115-144	105-134
5'4"	118-148	108-138
5'5"	121-152	111-142
5'6"	124-156	114-146
5'7"	128-161	118-150
5'8"	132-166	122-154
5'9"	136-170	126-158
5'10"	140-174	130-163
5'11"	144-179	134-168
6'0"	148-184	138-173
6'1"	152-189	
6'2"	156-194	
6'3"	160-199	
6'4"	164-204	

If you have decided that it would be best for your health to weigh less, avoid crash dieting. Any diet containing less than one thousand calories per day is dangerous to your health and will not promote the long-term maintenance of whatever weight you do lose. In fact, the best diets are those that contain servings from all of the food groups and are based on a caloric intake of between one thousand two hundred and one thousand five hundred calories daily. All weight loss programs should include these important components:

- an increase in physical activity

- a reduction in fat and fatty foods

- a reduction in sugary and sweet foods

- a reduction in alcohol intake

- 20 to 35 milligrams of fiber daily

Although physical activity burns calories, its main role in weight loss and weight maintenance is that it changes the metabolic rate of the body to burn fuel (calories) more efficiently. By combining regular aerobic exercise with a reduction in caloric intake, the body not only burns fat but increases its percentage of lean tissue. This promotes a kind of redistribution of one's weight, from a soft, flabby appearance to a leaner, firmer look. Strain on the lower back is reduced with weight loss as well, because extra weight carried in the waist and abdominal areas increases the curve in the lower part of the spine.

217

It is not unusual for a woman to carry extra weight during pregnancy and breast-feeding. Weight reduction during pregnancy is contraindicated because it places an additional strain on the mother and may prevent the fetus from receiving vital nutrients necessary for proper growth. The solution? Eating a variety of foods, exercising in moderation, and making calories count instead of focusing on counting calories. It is also best to avoid severely restricting calories during lactation since an adequate number of calories (between five hundred to eight hundred and fifty extra calories per day) insures that the volume of milk being produced will be sufficient to nourish the baby.

For a woman who has struggled with feeling sexually desirable to men other than her husband, carrying extra weight may be a protection against being approached as an attractive woman, even if all this means is being flirted with or looked at while walking down the street. The fear of falling into a tempting situation may be great enough to make a woman *want* to look less desirable. Until this fear is confronted and dealt with, weight loss attempts will prove to be unsuccessful.

Even though our husbands have committed themselves to stay with us "for better or for worse," our love for them can motivate us to lose weight to promote our ability to feel attractive *just for them*. Few men would prefer to be married to a woman who does not care about her appearance or is threatened by feeling attractive. The same holds true for wives: we care enough about our husbands to want them to maintain their ideal weight so that they may lower their risks of heart disease as well as being more attractive to us.

As God heals our hearts, He desires to heal *all* our hurts. By accepting His forgiveness and facing the way we treat our bodies through the food we choose to eat, we can learn to accept our Heavenly Father's design for our lives. We can actually begin to believe that promoting our health and saying "I am worth caring for" is an appropriate response to the unconditional love of Jesus. Knowing we are loved makes us also feel less vulnerable to the sexual advances of men when they notice the radiant glow on our faces or the fitness of our bodies, because we no longer have to *prove* that we are lovable. A Christian woman can be a beautiful example of the power of Christ's love to bring health and wholeness, joy and strength into a person's life without making that person self-conscious and narcissistic.

If you have found attempts at losing weight or staying committed to an exercise program to be unsuccessful, consider strengthening your relationship with Jesus before making another vow to change your appearance. Take some time to get to know the Lord better before trying again. If your relationships within your family are hurting or you have found it difficult to find time to read the Bible and pray, your first priority is to develop your family's well-being and spiritual health first. Losing weight will make you feel healthier and will help you feel better about yourself, but it will not fill the emptiness you may have been trying to fill through overeating. That inner feeling will not go away until you tackle it head-on. Nutritionist Rebecca Cavnar recommends that before beginning a weight loss program, a person ask the following questions and "get their house in order" before devoting time and energy to losing weight:

- Do I pray regularly every day?

- Is my daily schedule organized?

- Are my relationships with those I live with going well?

- Am I able to follow through on the commitments I make?

Overeating may be a response to a lack of structure, hurtful relationships, or any number of things that require your attention before you are enough at peace with yourself to begin a weight loss program. Pray about whether the Lord would have you lose weight at this point in your life. Ask Him if this is a priority right now for you. Then discuss what you are thinking with someone whose opinion you value and respect. What is their advice to you? Because your friend will not have the bundle of emotions that you do regarding this area of your life, this person will be able to give you good counsel. Knowing that you "should" lose weight is not enough. It needs to be the right time first. Becoming thinner may actually be priority number ten on your list after you take a good look at what is going on in your life right now.

If you have gotten into a pattern of overeating and either inducing vomiting or using laxatives to flush the calories away afterwards, you need professional help that will enable you to understand why you are behaving this way. *Bulimia* is the term used to describe this eating disorder. Get help now. Do not attempt to rationalize your behavior to yourself or hide it from others. You are not "bad" for doing this to yourself, but you are trying to fill a need in your life with food that can only be met if you make a sincere effort to love and accept yourself. You will be able to eat normally and overcome this pattern if you ask the Lord to help you understand yourself.

When you are ready to begin a weight loss program, be sure to have a complete physical first. Discuss your plans with a health care provider who you feel comfortable talking to. If you have great difficulty controlling your appetite, ask your physician if there could be a physical disorder or biochemical imbalance that might lie at the root of your difficulty.

A pound of body fat contains about three thousand five hundred calories. For each pound of fat that you wish to lose, you will need to burn three thousand five hundred more calories than you eat. A weight loss in excess of two pounds per week is inadvisable because it will include the loss of body fluids and muscle tissue from your body in addition to fat. Reducing your caloric intake by five hundred to eight hundred calories daily and participating in an exercise program will enable you to lose weight safely and effectively.

20 WAYS TO BURN 100 CALORIES

Figure 13-7

	A	B	C
1. 30 minutes of easy walking (1-2 m.p.h.)	1	1	1
2. 22 minutes of light housework	1	2	2
3. 22 minutes of light gardening (pulling weeds, etc.)	1	2	2
4. 22 minutes of golf (flat course)	1	2	1
5. 20 minutes of brisk walking (3-3½ m.p.h.)	2	1	2
6. 17 minutes of badminton	2	3	2
7. 17 minutes of horseback riding (trotting)	2	3	2
8. 14 minutes of gymnastics	2	4	3
9. 14 minutes of fast walking (5 m.p.h.)	3	3	2
10. 14 minutes of aerobic dancing	3	3	2
11. 12½ minutes of jogging (5 m.p.h.)	3	1	2
12. 12½ minutes of bicycling (12 m.p.h.)	3	3	2
13. 12½ minutes of ice skating	3	3	2
14. 12½ minutes of downhill skiing	3	3	2
15. 11 minutes of cross-country skiing	4	4	4
16. 10 minutes of racquetball	3	3	3
17. 10 minutes of cycling (12 m.p.h.)	4	3	3
18. 9 minutes of running (5.5 m.p.h.)	4	2	3
19. 9 minutes of rapid cycling (13 m.p.h.)	4	3	3
20. 8 minutes of swimming (front crawl)*	4	4	4

KEY:
1. minimal   A. Value in improving heart & lung
2. fair   efficiency
3. good   B. Value in improving flexibility
4. excellent   C. Value in improving strength

*There is a wide caloric range for this activity depending on the swimmer's skill, stroke used, temperature of the water, current, body composition, and other factors. The rate given is based on very rapid swimming using the front crawl.

The following chart shows the amounts of various types of exercise that are needed to burn one hundred calories. Remember—the effects of aerobic exercise will keep your body's metabolism going faster for forty-eight hours, which will also enhance the quality of your weight loss program. Not all of the activities listed here are aerobic; so if you are seeking a metabolic change as an added benefit of exercise, choose an activity that is continuous and involves major muscle groups within your body. Aim for a total caloric expenditure of three hundred to four hundred calories for a minimum of three times per week.

Promoting Sexual Health

When a woman learns to accept and appreciate her body, she becomes more aware of the importance of developing skills that enable her to spot subtle changes in her body and early signs of problems that need to be brought to her physician's attention.

From the age of twenty, women should perform a breast self-exam (B.S.E.) on a monthly basis seven to ten days after their period begins. After menopause, this routine may be changed to the first day of the month. Breast cancer is the second cause of cancer deaths for women in the U.S., accounting for about forty thousand deaths per year. This disease is nearly 100 percent curable if detected and treated during its earliest stage. Becoming familiar with our own breasts is the best defensive strategy currently available, along with eating foods that are low in fat and high in fiber and by avoiding obesity.

To conduct a B.S.E., stand in front of a mirror undressed and inspect your breasts, keeping your arms at your sides. Raise your hands up over your head and look closely for any changes in the contour of each breast. Check visually for swellings, discoloration, dimpling of the skin, or changes in your nipples. Next, place your hand on your hips and press down firmly to flex the muscles in your chest. Do not be concerned if your right and left breasts are not identical—few women's are. But do compare their shape from month to month. Carefully look for any abnormalities. Examine your breasts while you are taking a shower, which will make it easier for your hands to glide over your skin. Use your left hand to examine your right breast and your right hand for the left breast. Move your hand over the surface of the skin to feel for any lumps or thickening within your breasts.

After you have taken your shower and dried off, lie down on your bed with a pillow under your right shoulder and your right hand behind your head. Using your left hand, with your fingers together and flat, press gently in small circular motions around your right breast. Start at the base of the breast. Move one inch closer to the nipple each time you make a circle until you have examined every part of your breast. When you have completed this step, gently squeeze the nipple between your thumb and index finger. If you notice any discharge, report this to your doctor, unless you are currently pregnant or breast-feeding. Repeat this same procedure on the left breast.

CANCER-RELATED CHECKUPS

Figure 13-8

Guidelines for the early detection of cancer in people without symptoms. Talk with your doctor—ask how these guidelines relate to you.

Age 20-40

CANCER-RELATED CHECKUP EVERY 3 YEARS
Should include the procedures listed below plus health counseling (such as tips on quitting cigarettes) and examinations for cancers of the thyroid, testes, prostate, mouth, ovaries, skin and lymph nodes. Some people are at higher risk for certain cancers and may need to have tests more frequently.

BREAST
- Exam by doctor every 3 years

- Self-exam every month

- One baseline breast X-ray between ages 35-40
    Higher Risk for Breast Cancer: Personal or family history of breast cancer, never had children, first child after 30

UTERUS
- Pelvic exam every 3 years

Cervix
- Pap test—*after 2 initial negative tests 1 year apart—at least* every 3 years, includes women under 20 if sexually active.
    Higher Risk for Cervical Cancer: Early age at first intercourse, multiple sex partners

Age 40 & Over

CANCER-RELATED CHECKUP EVERY YEAR
Should include the procedures listed below plus health counseling (such as tips on quitting cigarettes) and

examinations for cancers of the thyroid, testes, prostate, mouth, ovaries, skin and lymph nodes. Some people are at higher risk for certain cancers and may need to have tests more frequently.

BREAST
- Exam by doctor every year

- Self-exam every month

- Breast X-ray every year after 50; between ages 40-49, 1 every 1-2 years as recommended
    Higher Risk for Breast Cancer: Personal or family history of breast cancer, never had children, first child after 30

UTERUS
- Pelvic exam every year

Cervix
- Pap test—*after initial negative tests 1 year apart*—at *least* every 3 years
    Higher Risk for Cervical Cancer: Early age at first intercourse, multiple sex partners

Endometrium
- Endometrial tissue sample at menopause if at risk
    Higher Risk for Endometrial Cancer: Infertility, obesity, failure of ovulation, abnormal uterine bleeding, estrogen therapy

COLON & RECTUM
- Digital rectal exam every year

- Stool slide test every year after 50

- Procto exam—*after 2 initial negative tests 1 year apart*—every 3 to 5 years after 50
    Higher Risk for Colorectal Cancer: Personal or family history of colon or rectal cancer, personal or family history of polyps in the colon or rectum, ulcerative colitis

Remember, these guidelines are not rules and only apply to people without symptoms. If you have any of the *7 Warning Signals* listed, see your doctor or go to your clinic without delay.

Cancer's Seven Warning Signals

1. Change in bowel or bladder habits.
2. A sore that does not heal.
3. Unusual bleeding or discharge.
4. Thickening or lump in breast or elsewhere.
5. Indigestion or difficulty in swallowing.
6. Obvious change in wart or mole.
7. Nagging cough or hoarseness.

If you do happen to notice a new lump or a change in an existing lump, determine whether this may have been caused by a recent injury. If so, wait a few weeks to consult with your doctor. If it does not go away, have it checked by your physician. Although most breast lumps are not cancerous, see your doctor for any lumps that are unusual in your breast. Hormonal changes may be responsible. Your physician will discuss this with you and may ask you to monitor any changes in the size, texture, of frequency of occurrence. If you notice that the shape of your breasts ever becomes distorted or dimpled, see your doctor immediately to rule out breast cancer. Also, changes in the color of the skin on your breasts, discharge from a nipple, retraction of the nipple under the aereola, and a dry, scaly rash around the nipple are signs that warrant medical attention.

The American Cancer Society recommends that women have a baseline mammography to establish what the normal condition of their breasts is between the ages of thirty-five and forty. From age forty to fifty, having a mammogram every one to two years is advisable, and after the age of fifty a woman should have an annual mammogram. A mammogram is an X-ray exam of the breasts that is used to detect growths too small to be felt by a woman or her doctor. It is estimated that a mammogram test can detect cancer up to three years before it would be found during a breast exam. If found at this early stage, a cancerous tumor would be nearly 100 percent curable.

If a lump is discovered and found to be malignant, it must be surgically removed. Small lumps discovered in an early stage of growth may be treated by performing a lumpectomy in which the tumor and small portion of breast tissue are removed. Radiation treatment would be used as a follow-up procedure in this situation. Advanced tumors may require the entire removal of the breast, called a mastectomy. Breast-preservation surgery is being performed more often than ever before, however, and many women have been able to avoid having a mastectomy except when it is absolutely necessary. When a mastectomy is the only alternative, improved prosthetic devices and innovative reconstruction techniques are widely available to help women cope with the loss of a breast. Grief is a natural, normal part of the healing process in the aftermath of a mastectomy, regardless of the way a woman chooses to enhance her appearance.

Having a regular Pap smear done once a woman becomes sexually active is also a means of detecting cancer of the cervix in its early stages. For a woman who has had genital herpes, it is advisable to have a Pap smear done every six months or until her physician suggests that she return to an annual schedule. This has been medically questioned (vs. biannual).

Vaginal health is best maintained through the prevention of conditions that would encourage the growth of irritating organisms in this area of the body and lead to inflammation of the vagina, or vaginitis. Suggested measures include:

- avoiding wearing tight pants, panty hose with slacks, and any underwear or hosiery that does not have a cotton crotch

- sleeping without underwear at night

- limiting one's sugar intake

- avoiding lounging in a damp bathing suit

- washing or bathing every day, using nonperfumed soap and your own towel and wash cloth

- having your husband wash his genitals prior to lovemaking

- always wiping "from front to back" to avoid contaminating the vaginal area

- not using sprays, powders, or other irritating products near the vaginal area

- using panty liners that are "breathable"

- not taking antibiotics unnecessarily; eating yogurt if antibiotic therapy is unavoidable

Urinary tract infections are commonly associated with sexual activity and are a stubborn, chronic problem for many women. They are usually the result of bacterial colonization within the urinary tract, which is made up of the urethra, the bladder, the ureters, and the kidneys. The most common types of infection are urethritis, or inflammation of the urethra, and cystitis, involving inflammation of the bladder.

Normally bacteria are washed out with urination and do not have a chance to establish colonies in the urinary tract. These bacteria can multiply when something happens to interfere with this natural defense mechanism. Possible causes of this situation are irritation and swelling of the urethra or bladder as the result of lovemaking or pregnancy; vaginitis; exposure to chemical irritants such as feminine hygiene sprays, douches, bubble bath, or a diaphragm; and decreased resistance to infection due to stress, illness, or fatigue.

Women are more susceptible to U.T.I.'s than men because our urethras are only about one and a half inches long. This allows for bacteria to easily enter the urethral opening. Also, the urethra is close to the vagina and the anus, which can act as bacterial sources. The most common cause of U.T.I.'s is from bacteria from the intestinal tract that are transferred from the anus to the urethra inadvertently.

The following preventive measures may be helpful to you if you have had recurring problems with urinary tract infections:

- urinate frequently to rinse out the urinary tract

- drink plenty of liquids daily so that you feel the need to urinate at least every two hours during the day

- drink cranberry juice daily: 4 oz. four times a day if a U.T.I. seems to be developing or is already present (this makes the urine more acidic)

- always wipe front to back

- wash the genital and anal area often

- avoid using feminine hygiene products or bubble bath

- be sure to urinate before and after sexual sharing

The role that oral-genital sex plays in causing U.T.I.'s is not known, but if this has been a factor for you, washing the genital area and urinating before and after sexual activity should reduce your chances of developing an infection. Avoiding positions during intercourse that place pressure on the front wall of the vagina along the back of the bladder may also be useful. Soaking in a warm tub for ten to fifteen minutes after making love may be helpful as well.

The epidemic of sexually transmitted diseases in this country has reached such a significant level that millions of men and women are being affected every year. Sexual fidelity within a monogamous relationship is not only Scriptural, it is in the public health's best interest! Although it is highly unusual to contract an S.T.D. in a means other than sexual contact, it is possible with some organisms. For this reason, *always* wash your hands after using anyone's lavatory except your own (and even then it's not a bad idea). Never share someone else's bath towel. Do not frequent a health spa that is poorly sanitized or overused.

It is estimated that twenty million Americans harbor genital herpes infections. One million new cases or more occur annually. Called Herpes Simplex Virus II (HSVII), genital herpes involves blisterlike sores below the waist on or around the genital organs, including the cervix. After the first outbreak, the virus enters the spinal cord, where it is stored indefinitely. Seventy-five percent of recurrent herpes infections are triggered through trauma to the skin. Rubbing, kissing, shaving, menstruation, intercourse, fever, or emotional stress are examples of triggering factors. Using a lubricant to reduce friction during intercourse may help.

At this time, there is no known cure for genital herpes. A drug called acyclovir is often used to relieve symptoms and may actually prevent recurrence if used at an early stage during the first attack. Other helps include soaking in a salt solution, taking an analgesic, applying soothing ointments, and treating secondary infections with antibiotics. If a woman has herpes when she is due to have a baby, a cesarean birth will protect the baby from coming into contact with the virus. If a woman has a history of herpes infections, it is essential that she inform her health care provider of this during her pregnancy so that her condition can be closely monitored. It is important to remember that genital herpes is contagious for several weeks until the lesions heal.

If either you or your husband had genital herpes when you met, it was probably a difficult topic to discuss and may still be a source of tension in your relationship. Thankfully, we are forgiven in Christ of past sin. Having genital herpes need not be a stigma that causes guilt and continued heartache once a man or a woman has confessed and repented of sexual sin. Though the physical effects may linger, Jesus bids us to move on and sin no more.

Doing Our Part

Living a healthy lifestyle involves more than just being "whole" spiritually. It means doing our part in changing our habits and developing an awareness of the impact of our behavior on our bodies.

No matter what you have chosen to do in the past or will choose to do in the future, you can take one step at a time. Perhaps today it will mean going for a walk or refusing to take a second helping at dinner. Tomorrow it may be having a hot fudge sundae in the afternoon but saying no to chips and dip at a party later in the evening. Each of us must learn to form realistic expectations and reject the one-dimensional view of the perfect woman. We need to take our eyes off of our failures, deficiencies, and short comings and say yes to living God's way. In Christ, God will meet our every need. We are called to stand complete in Him.

> The Lord your God is with you,
>   he is mighty to save.
> He will take great delight in you,
>   he will quiet you with his love,
>   he will rejoice over you with singing.[3]

Attitudes of the Heart

"I am very tired of myself," said the princess, "But I can't rest till I try again."

"That is the only way to get rid of your weary, shadowy self, and find your strong true self. Come, my child; I will help you all I can, for now I can help you."

George MacDonald, The Lost Princess

If you could be any woman that you wanted to be, who would you choose? Recent lists of America's "Most Admired Women" include a strange assortment of female role models, from the Princess of Wales to Mother Teresa. Most of the women that we read about are those whose lives merit media attention. They are famous for having achieved status through political, powerful, glamorous, or spiritually significant positions. Presidents' wives and movie stars are photographed constantly and remind us of our relative insignificance as we read the coverage of their latest adventures. Of the women that we read about, only a very small number are dedicated women of God, and yet, to a degree, we are affected by the images of the women we read about and by the way they express their personalities.

Let's reflect for a moment on the women who have had the greatest impact on our lives. Are they famous? Rich? Dressed in the latest designer outfits? Probably not. Our mothers, our teachers, our sisters, and our friends are the ones we most often think of and are those who usually deserve the highest honors for what they have contributed to our lives. Women in our churches whom we've watched as they've served the Lord come to mind as well. We think of the nurses who attended us while we were giving birth and the neighbor who brought us cookies when we first arrived on the block. Our grandmother's steady hands, all wrinkled and so large as they guided our tiny fingers while we learned to knit or bake a pie, can be recalled as we think back over the years of our lives, picturing the women who have taught us what being a woman means. We wept when we moved away, when we looked in the casket, when other women wept. These are the ones we remember, the ones who have made a real impact on the way we live day to day. Our lives contain an endless list of women who have touched our lives, for better or worse. But who have we chosen to be our heroines? Which women do we think of when we want to get a new dress or change our hairstyle?

Attitude Shapers

Draw a line about five inches across. On one end of the line, write "least admired," in the center write "little effect," and on the right side "most admired." Add two midpoints on the scale on both sides of the middle. Fill in the names of five well-known women who you have been inspired, angered, or moved by.

Figure 14-1

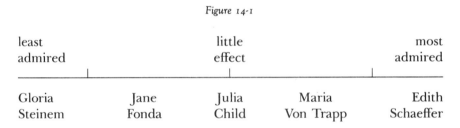

least admired		little effect		most admired
Gloria Steinem	Jane Fonda	Julia Child	Maria Von Trapp	Edith Schaeffer

Although I haven't met any of these women, I have been affected by their magazines, records, television shows, movies, and books. In a sense, I "know" them. My attitudes have been shaped by their values and outlooks on life. There are many more names that I could add to my line, as you probably could add to yours, because we live in a culture that carries the opinions of others into our homes and into places of learning. It is unavoidable, and we need to recognize the influence women such as these have upon our lives.

In thinking about the women I've listed and the things they represent to me (feminism, exercise fads, delicious food, joyous singing, and intelligent Christian womanhood), I realize that I actually have very few female role models and heroines who are being offered by our culture as examples of the kind of woman the Bible describes as "excellent." The hundreds of beautiful faces I have had a glimpse of over the years on television commercials and on magazine covers just can't compare to the real-life women who have touched my life on a personal level. When I think of who I would like to be like, however, it is often the image of a slender, attractive woman that comes to mind. If we are to avoid the trap of measuring ourselves against worldly standards, we must consciously develop alternative role models.

Excellent Womanhood

> An excellent wife who can find? For her worth is far above
> jewels. The heart of her husband trusts in her and he will
> have no lack of gain. . . . Charm is deceitful and beauty is
> vain, but a woman who fears the Lord, she shall be praised.[2]

> The fear of the Lord is a training in wisdom, and the way to
> honour is humility.[3]

Charm is deceitful and beauty is vain . . . If that's true, then Scarlett O'Hara was *way* off track! Do you remember her sister-in-law Melanie Wilkes? Plain, pale, and unable to believe that anything was wrong with Scarlett that love could not cure, Melanie was a shining example of true Christian charity in *Gone with the Wind.* But how often have any of us longed to be like Melanie rather than Scarlett? Scarlett wore beautiful gowns, fancy hats, and exquisite jewelry; she was a poor mother, a worse wife, and lusted after Melanie's husband constantly. Scarlett's flashing green eyes and eighteen-inch waist made her the belle of the county and the wealthiest woman in reconstructed Atlanta, but her heart was burning with envy and greed.

It is tempting to view Scarlett's "fire" as admirable and to see Melanie as a self-sacrificing wimp. Scarlett exemplifies everything worldly women want: beauty, power, and wealth. On the other hand, the world views women like Melanie with a mixture of pity and contempt because of their dedication to "outdated" concepts such as duty and honor.

Upon whom does the approval of the Lord rest? Which of these women would be acceptable to the Lord if they really existed?

> Who shall ascend to the hill of the Lord? Or who shall stand
> in his holy place? He that hath clean hands, and a pure heart;
> who hath not lifted his soul unto vanity, nor sworn
> deceitfully.[4]

Charm (deceit) and external beauty (vanity) have nothing to do with the qualities the Lord seeks to develop more fully in our hearts. Scarlett's life was devoid of Christ's love and light, and there is nothing about her that should cause us to admire her. Melanie exemplified what it means to be a woman of God. Who will we choose to be more like? Is it really possible to have it *all*, the best of both worlds, and still be devoted in our hearts to Christ?

231

Peter's first letter speaks of an "inner beauty" dwelling in the "inmost center" of a woman's being as the kind of beauty that will never develop wrinkles or gray hair.[5] He wrote about the "imperishable quality of a gentle and quiet spirit that is precious in the sight of God" and is to reside in the "hidden person of the heart."[6] It is a beauty that becomes more radiant over the years, even as the body ages. No amount of cosmetic surgery, dieting, expensive clothing, exercising, makeup, or hair coloring can create the kind of beauty Peter referred to. The external things will perish and are relatively worthless compared to the glory of God residing in the heart of a woman who has been transformed by the love of Jesus Christ.

It's so easy to forget this, isn't it? To spend more time worrying about our hair or weight than on bended knees in prayer. To think more often about our appearance than about living a life that is pleasing to the Lord. To devote ourselves to countless hours of study and work in pursuit of a career before we consider Jesus worthy enough to submit our lives and futures to.

Paul understood this struggle well and described it as a war that continually goes on between what he refers to as the "inner being" and the "flesh."[7] When we read his words, we can be comforted in knowing that God understands the battle we are engaged in and that He will stand with us in the fight. Paul asks, "Who will rescue me from this body of death?" and then replies, "Thanks be to God—through Jesus Christ our Lord!"[8]

Each and every one of us experiences the battle that Paul wrote about, from the youngest to the most mature in Christ. It's only natural to worry about what to wear and how to look more beautiful. In and of themselves, external things are neutral. It's when these things become too important, taking up more of our time or energy than they should, that we lose track of our priorities. To become beautiful in the *innermost* part of our beings is a much greater challenge than developing a perfect figure or a complex vocational skill. This can only result from submitting ourselves to the work of the Holy Spirit in our lives and committing ourselves to Christ completely, inwardly as well as outwardly. In order to do this God must bring us to a place of brokenness, where we realize, like George MacDonald's princess, that we have grown very tired of ourselves and long to be *truly* changed into His likeness.

External Appearances

Jesus really was quite a man. He could see right through the external appearances of things. He knew what was going on in people's hearts and minds even when they pretended to be something different than they actually were. The Gospels are full of examples of how Jesus confronted people about their internal attitudes. He did it pretty often, too—comparing what was going on externally with what was happening internally. In His time, as in ours today, there were lots of people who lived seemingly exemplary lives and yet were like Crabby Appleton on "Tom Terrific": they were "rotten to the core."

Our Lord could care less about the color of the lipstick we wear or how many miles we can run or how many solos we've performed at our church this year. That is because *the external things are irrelevant compared to the condition of our hearts!*

Don't get me wrong here. I'm not saying that Jesus forbids us to wear makeup or engage in aerobic exercise or express ourselves in song. *Looking pleasant, maintaining our health, and using our gifts are important ways of expressing ourselves and promoting our sense of well-being. It is just that these things are not nearly as important as what we are doing to promote our inner beauty, our spiritual health, and our use of talent on behalf of the gospel.* It is easy to become so absorbed in the external things that the internal aspects of our walk with the Lord develop a kind of spiritual malnutrition.

Two Examples

There were two women who had their priorities straight and were obedient to the Lord's command to seek His kingdom first in their lives. Their stories can have a powerful effect on us as we consider the depth of their commitment to God and the ways they chose to submit their lives to Him. They weren't afraid to act boldly as an expression of their faith in Jesus Christ.

Corrie Ten Boom was not an especially attractive woman. She never married. She wore clothing that many would consider to be old-fashioned, and her hair was usually piled up on top of her head in a rather large, thick bun. She lived well into her eighties, and the many wrinkles on her face were a testimony to the era that she had lived through, for Corrie had been a prisoner in a concentration camp under the Nazis for hiding Jewish people in the home of her family in Holland. All but her brother perished in the camp, and Corrie's release was apparently due to a "fluke." Corrie knew better: she realized that it was by the grace of God that she walked out of that nightmare alive. She was broken by the experience and began to live a life that was marked by her devotion, rather than anger, toward God.

Because Corrie dedicated her life to serving the Lord rather than blaming Him for what had happened in the camp, she was able to share Christ's love with a great many people. She traveled to countries all over the world and talked about God as if she knew Him. Corrie did know God! He was not only her Savior but her best friend, her Father, her mother, her *all*. She risked her life to spread the Good News of her Lord as she

233

smuggled Bibles behind the Iron Curtain and spoke of God without fear. She witnessed numerous miracles and saw how the Lord could meet her every need.

Corrie's eyes sparkled like the stars of the heavens, and her smile was brighter than that of the most glamorous women. Her incredible sweetness was the result of walking daily with the Lord, no matter what the circumstances, and knowing that she could trust Him completely. The simple wisdom that her writings and speeches revealed were the products of decades of obedience to the Lord. She loved Jesus and it showed.

Today we can safely say that Corrie Ten Boom is lovingly held in the hands of her Heavenly Father even while her body lies discarded in a grave far from the gates of heaven. Corrie *pressed on* and refused to look back at what was behind her, preferring to head toward the prize awaiting her as she moved in the direction of a heavenly call.

Mary of Bethany was probably considered by many in her community to be a fanatic. But Mary had good reason to love Jesus: she had witnessed the resurrection of her brother Lazarus from the dead. When Jesus had stood at the door of his tomb and spoken, her brother's body had walked out of the tomb, burial clothes and all, and had left that stony place *empty*.

Jesus had melted Mary's heart with a pure love that changed her life. The external things of the world mattered little to this woman, who Jesus said had "chosen what is better."[9] The holy love of her Lord was irresistible to her.

One night Jesus was visiting Simon's house six days before what was to be the Last Supper. Mary went into the gathering of Jesus and some of His followers as they were eating dinner. She took an alabaster box and broke it, then poured its costly contents over Jesus' head: a pound of spikenard oil. She knelt on the floor, and in full view of Simon's guests she leaned over and wiped the feet of her Master with her long, flowing hair. The room was filled with the fragrance of her offering, reminding all of the extravagance of her gesture and alarming those who could not understand the significance of her actions. What Mary gave to Jesus that day was not an obligatory tithe. The cost of her gifts in today's economy would be worth *thousands* of dollars.

What was the response? Judas, who soon would betray Jesus, asked, "Why this waste?"[10] He couldn't conceive of giving to Jesus, a "poor" man, something of that value in such a "casual" way, when there were many who could be clothed and fed by the sale of the nard. Today we might put it this way: "That's money down the drain for ya!"

The response of Jesus was much different though. He must have shocked everyone in that room as He praised Mary's gift and promised that what she had done would be spoken of in her memory "wherever this gospel is preached throughout the world."[11]

Like the alabaster box, Mary's heart had been broken of its hardness;

and like the oil, she sought to pour her life out to her Lord. Jesus kept His promise to Mary, and the story of her sacrifice has never been forgotten. Nearly two thousand years later, we recall that incredible moment and remember what it meant to our Lord to be anointed for His burial at a time when he had yet to face Pontius Pilate and the agony of the Cross. Our Lord wanted us to speak of Mary and consider the way she expressed her love to Him. We must not think like the others who were in the room that day, but aim to be more like Mary in the hidden person of our hearts.

Women such as these two are to be our role models! *These women loved God more than they loved the things of this world.* Let us remind ourselves of them, and of others like them, often. They represent the kind of excellent women who are "precious in the sight of God."

The Clothing of Christ

Television has become predictable in its evening programming these days. There are very few shows that have the capability of nourishing us. The number of shows revolving around the tangled love lives of fictitious characters is surprising. Their wealth is even more shocking, displayed in $300,000 furs, multiple Mercedes-Benzes, and mansions that require a full staff to keep them going. Inexpensive copies of the original designer clothes seen on these programs beckon to us from the racks of local department stores, even though they are still beyond the reach of the average woman's budget. Only a minority of women dress right for every occasion, and only the very wealthy can afford to wear a fox coat to the grocery store.

The clothing of Christ's design cannot be purchased with money. His garments are *truly* priceless. The kind of clothing that He offers cannot be put on casually; in fact, only *He* can dress us! In response to Christ's command, the Holy Spirit clothes us with garments that Jesus has purchased on our behalf, at a price that makes us feel ashamed of ourselves. Yet our Lord longs for us to wear His clothing, and He gives it freely to us as what He deems suitable for us to wear in His kingdom:

> . . . Put on the garments that suit God's chosen people, his
> own, his beloved: compassion, kindness, humility, gentleness,
> patience. Be forbearing with one another, and forgiving,
> where any of you has cause for complaint: you must forgive
> as the Lord forgave you. To crown all, there must be love, to
> bind all together and complete the whole.[12]

Wow! What an outfit! A crown of *love*. We are Christ's *own*, His *beloved*. It is His will that we put on this clothing . . . These are the things He wants us to wear. How very much our Savior loves us! Why do we make

235

things so difficult for Him, to the point where we even forget what He says?

We can only have the qualities of inner beauty if we stop resisting Jesus and let Him enter our lives more completely. The attitudes of our hearts are very important to the Lord. If we say we love Him but harden our hearts, we are deceiving ourselves. It may not make complete sense to us now, but understanding the fullness of His truth will come in time.

Solomon wrote that "humility comes before honor."[13] May the grace of God be with us as we seek to apply His truth to the hidden attitudes of our hearts.

> A heart at peace gives life to the body,
> but envy rots the bones.[14]

> Wisdom reposes in the heart of the discerning
> and even among fools she lets herself be known.[15]

> As water reflects a face,
> so a man's heart reflects the man.[16]

> Cleanse me with hyssop, and I will be clean;
> wash me, and I will be whiter than snow.
> Let me hear joy and gladness;
> let the bones you have crushed rejoice.
> Hide your face from my sins
> and blot out all my iniquity.
> Create in me a pure heart, O God,
> and renew a steadfast spirit within me.[17]

/ 15 /

The Law of Kindness

*One lesson I tried to teach my children from a very early age,
repeating over and over again the best explanation I could think
of, in different ways at different times, was the fact that some
things must never be said, no matter how hot the argument, no
matter how angry one becomes, no matter how far one goes in
feeling. . . . Some things are too much of a "luxury" ever to
say. . . . Saying certain things is an expense beyond reason.*[1]
Edith Schaeffer, *What Is a Family?*

Have you ever noticed how difficult it is to say kind and gentle things when your heart is piled high with feelings of resentment? Anger? Guilt? Have you ever been around someone who was so embittered by life that his or her entire personality turned sour? What was his or her speech like? How did that person look as the words were spoken? What was your immediate response?

We tend to avoid such people. They are unpleasant to be around and make us feel impatient as they recount the latest injustice they have suffered; they test our love for them as we listen to them tear down one person after another. We wonder what they must say about us when we aren't present. Some people have a way about them that makes us uncomfortable being with them.

Then there are the people we love to visit. We look forward to seeing them; they make us glad to be with them. Their words, demeanor, and ways of touching us enable us to relax. When we are with caring and loving people, we say that we can "just be ourselves" around them. It has very little to do with their occupation or social standing or I.Q. Through people like this, we feel blessed, welcomed, accepted . . . comfortable.

Words, and how they are spoken, are the vehicle the Lord has given to us to readily express the experiences and perceptions of our minds, hearts, and spirits. It is through words that we are able to build others up, to comfort, to share burdens, to instruct, to make covenants. Throughout Biblical history, God used both the spoken word and the written word to communicate with and through His people. Jesus Himself is referred to by the Apostle John as the Word with God from the beginning of time, who "became flesh and lived for a while among us."[2] What a beautiful and mysterious way to tell us about Christ's origin! Yet, we can all relate to words and their significance in our lives as we read John's account. Words have surrounded us from our own beginnings and have been a primary way for us to comprehend what goes on around us.

The Book of Proverbs has many verses that convey the importance of words. Solomon, who had been given wisdom and knowledge because he had asked the Lord for these qualities, was a man who understood the power of words. The idea that we can be destructive to those around us through the words we speak—or bring health and peace as we verbally express ourselves to others—is a theme that Solomon emphasized. He especially made the point that we are actually *hurting ourselves the most* when we speak harshly or unkindly to others. David's son tells us that a "wise woman builds her house, but with her own hands the foolish one tears hers down"[3] and that "a fool's talk brings a rod to his back, but the lips of the wise protect them."[4] In this way, speech becomes a circular process. When we seek to harm another, we are harmed; when we seek to bless another, we are blessed. In James we read that ". . . the wisdom that comes from heaven is first of all pure; then peace loving, considerate, submissive, full of mercy and good fruit, impartial and sincere. Peacemakers who sow in peace raise a harvest of righteousness."[5]

Jesus spoke of the harvest time that awaits us when He related our hearts to a picture of a tree and our words with the kind of fruit the tree produces. He underscored the relationship of our words to the condition of our hearts in using this illustration, to emphasize that we are known by the words we speak, in addition to our actions. After saying that we speak out of the treasure we have stored up within our hearts, Jesus warned His followers that they would have to give account of every careless word they had uttered.[6]

When I read this I find myself asking God, rather incredulously, "*Every* word, Lord?" As I look at His words, their meaning is unmistakable. In silence, I swallow hard. (Am I trying to swish the evidence away?) "I know that I am guilty, Jesus," comes my reply, "but what can I possibly do about it? Controlling what I say is *so hard!* I fall short every single day." After thinking about the implications of the things I say, and how easy it is to say the wrong things, I am reminded that *nothing* is impossible with God. In my weakness He can become strong, if I continue to look to Him for strength and direction.

I also know that I am not alone: controlling what we say is a challenge for every believer. When a thought pops into our heads, our lips move to

238

express what we are thinking; when a feeling arises in our hearts, our mouths give shape to the emotion we are experiencing. Staying silent at key moments can only be accomplished if we surrender our thoughts and feelings to the Lord through prayer. Otherwise, words will gush forth before we even realize what the impact of what we're saying might be on those around us. James wrote that "out of the same mouth come praise and cursing."[7] And it all takes place so fast! In the blink of an eye, out comes the biting remark of sarcasm, the mumbled bit of profanity, the critical put-down. We feel helpless to control the words that seem to fly about so effortlessly!

Contemporary psychotherapists urge people to just "let it all hang out," to "vent your anger before it destroys you," and to "express yourself completely," without inhibition, as a means of avoiding mental illness. But Solomon wrote that there is a season, a time, and a purpose to everything, ". . . a time to be silent and a time to speak."[8] The Bible encourages self-control, not full self-expression, because the condition of our hearts must be transformed by God and cleansed from sin. It is usually more appropriate to ask God to change our hearts and to cooperate with Him in that process, to let Him help us deal with the situations we are faced with. We need to give Him time to work upon our hearts, through His Holy Spirit, rather than blurt out what we're bugged about. "A man finds *joy* in giving an apt reply," Solomon said, "and how good is a timely word."[9] The Lord has promised that we will find joy, not despair, if we choose to express ourselves wisely.

Self-Talk Is Telling

Have you ever noticed how you tend to have a running conversation with yourself throughout the day? This silent conversation has a tone that changes often as it is affected by external circumstances, your mood, other people, things you're doing, and how you feel physically. Each of us tends to reflect on all of these things as they are happening within and around us, as a way of "processing" what is taking place in our environment.

A typical day might begin something like this: "Is that the alarm? It seems too early . . . I better get up. This bed feels so good. I really don't feel like moving. I'll just close my eyes for a couple of minutes more . . . What? It's 7:45? I can't believe it! I just closed my eyes! Now I've *really* got to get up." (After a big yawn and a good stretch, legs swing out of bed, feet are on the floor, and with a wince you push yourself out of bed.)

Throughout each day, similar thoughts drift in and out of our heads, structured in phrases that define how we are responding to our experiences. This type of inner conversation is referred to as "self-talk." Self-talk gives us clues about the state of our hearts; it is merely a way of gauging what kind of "treasure" we have stored up within our minds. The

Lord tunes His ear to our self-talk, listening to our words and searching our hearts and minds, and we are conducting this conversation within His range of hearing. We may be able to hide ourselves from those around us, but we don't fool the Lord one bit! David put it this way:

> O Lord, you have searched me and you know me. You know when I sit and when I rise; you perceive my thoughts from afar. You discern my going out and my lying down; you are familiar with all my ways. Before a word is on my tongue you know it completely, O Lord. You hem me in—behind and before; you have laid your hand upon me. Such knowledge is too wonderful for me, too lofty for me to attain.[10]

David continued by saying that God is with us wherever we are and he prayed that God would search his heart and test him. He asked the living God to know his anxious thoughts, to see "if there is any offensive way" in him, and to lead him in "the way everlasting."[11] This should be our own prayer as well, our hope, and our encouragement. Like David, let us ask that the words of our mouths and the meditations of our hearts be pleasing in God's sight.[12] "In quietness and trust is your strength," said the prophet Isaiah.[13] *We can ask the Lord to provide these things for us.* We cannot manufacture the kind of peace the Lord alone provides.

Things to Think About

Paul's letter to the Phillipians takes us another step toward being able to understand the interrelationship of thoughts and words as he instructed the church to "think about . . . things" that are true, noble, right, pure, lovely, admirable, excellent and praiseworthy.[14] Of himself, Paul wrote that he took "captive every thought to make it obedient to Christ.[15] He spoke in terms of waging war in a spiritual sense in regard to his thinking. Our struggle today is no less difficult. We need to realize that we have a tendency to be lazy. The Lord calls us to be diligent and urges us to change the ways we tend to think and feel in favor of becoming obedient to Him.

If we dwell on our losses, disappointments, hurts, and fears, it doesn't take very long to lose our sense of who we are in Christ. When we choose to "set our minds on things above, not on earthly things,"[16] we discover we can view our circumstances from a broader perspective that allows us to see our position in Christ with greater clarity.

I am not suggesting that we totally deny what is going on around us at any given moment or pretend that our feelings don't exist. The Word of God calls us to acknowledge where we stand before our Maker, so we can honestly share our concerns with Him. There is no need to think that our needs will go unnoticed; God knows our *every* need. Sharing our hearts and minds openly with the Lord is so important—anything else is hypocrisy.

Openly acknowledging our thoughts and feelings before God and baring our souls to another person are two very different things. We need to pray continually, not talk continually; and when we talk to others we must weigh the effects that our words might have *before* we speak them. Learning to trust the Lord to minister to us will replace much of the need that we feel for others to help us cope. Fretting, nagging, complaining, gossiping, and worrying out loud are all ways of showing to others that we lack faith. God's Word exhorts us to avoid *all* of these things.[17] We are to "put on the new self, which is being renewed in knowledge in the image of its Creator."[18] We can praise God for this process and rejoice that even now we are becoming the women that He desires us to be!

Speaking with Wisdom

> A wife of noble character who can find? . . .
> She is clothed with strength and dignity;
> she can laugh at days to come.
> She speaks with wisdom,
> and faithful instruction is on her tongue.[19]

We honor God when we honor our husbands. In guarding our tongues, we protect our marriages. When we wear the clothing of Christ's design, we live in a position of strength and dignity; and the love we express through the words we speak generates respect and esteem. Solomon was perfectly right when he described the wise woman as one who builds her house with her own words. Word by word, we construct the relationships we have within our families. It takes years to build trust, commitment, and refuge within our homes; it takes only a few moments to tear down large chunks of the structure we have painstakingly constructed.

Marriage affords us the luxury of intimacy unlike any other relationship. Intimacy, in turn, produces vulnerability. We know one another's weaknesses and tender places, and we know how to really hurt one another as a result. If we struggle over issues, we must "fight fairly," never allowing ourselves to say things that must *never* be said. Think for a few moments about the areas of your husband's life that involve the deepest hurts, inadequacies, or problems. The longer you are married, the more you realize what these things are, just as he knows these things about you. These are the things that Edith Schaeffer said would be too costly to ever speak unkindly about. Resolve to never say hurtful things about these areas, no matter how angry or hurt you might feel.

"The law of kindness" is upon the tongue of the virtuous woman.[20] A law is a "binding rule of action established by authority,"[21] and in this case the authority we are referring to is the Word of God. *Kindness is to govern our tongues.* Ranier Maria Rilke summed it up this way: "Love consists in this, that two solitudes protect and touch and greet each other." Love really does cover a "multitude of sins," keeping no record of wrongs suffered. It isn't humanly possible to love this way. We can't love perfectly, but we can choose to give up whatever at any given time is causing us to stumble in our attitude. It is our responsibility as Christians to persevere, keep moving on, and press toward our heavenly calling in Jesus.

So what does all of this have to do with our sexuality? *Everything!* When our hearts have been cleansed by God and our mouths are able to speak well of others, we become a blessing to our husbands. Our husbands are not drawn to our physical bodies alone, but to the beauty that resides in "the hidden person of the heart." Solomon wrote that "a quarrelsome wife is like a constant dripping on a rainy day"[22] and that it is "better to live on a corner of a roof than share a house with a quarrelsome wife."[23] What man in his right mind would *choose* to spend much time with a woman who made him miserable? Our speech is as much a part of our sex lives as how we look, how our skin feels, and how our reproductive organs function. The act of making love takes place within the overall framework of our total relationship. How we feel about ourselves as lovers cannot be isolated to the relatively brief span of time we spend in sexual interaction each day.

"The tongue that brings healing is a tree of life," wrote Solomon.[24] "A gentle answer turns away wrath."[25] As wives and as mothers, we can resolve to practice these principles more fully in our lives and make our homes a haven from the craziness and hectic pace of modern life. The words we use will make up large pieces of the "houses" we build, displaying the qualities we are developing in our lives as we surrender them with increasing obedience to Christ.

Love-Talk Is Giving

Come, my lover, let us go to the countryside,
let us spend the night in the villages.
Let us go early to the vineyards
to see if the vines have budded,
if their blossoms have opened,
and if the pomegranates are in full bloom—
there I will give you my love.
The mandrakes send out their fragrance,
and at our door is every delicacy,

both new and old,
that I have stored up for you, my lover.[26]

What an invitation! What sexy talk! Here is a Biblical example of love-talk that is rich and meaningful, laden with the promise of things to come. It isn't shameful at all to talk about such things! In fact, words create an atmosphere for lovemaking that prepares our bodies and our feelings for sexual expression. Words arouse us deeply and profoundly as we whisper private references to our sexuality in our husbands' ears.

Developing this language of love is as important as learning how our bodies respond to sexual stimulation. Loving words spoken at different times during the day, in different settings, remind our husbands that we enjoy participating in this aspect of our relationship with them. Love-talk is the exclusive domain of sexual conversation between a wife and her husband; it is a kind of language they alone can understand, enjoy, and benefit from.

It isn't necessary to call the various phases of sexual activity by their proper terms or use anatomically correct words to refer to specific body parts when using love-talk. Since no one else will be listening, you can be quite creative with the language you use. The words we associate with pornographic sex are restrictive in their meanings, in addition to being cruel in intent; but not all slang terms are ugly or debasing. You may even invent some words or expressions of your own that might have a special meaning to you. If we appreciate our sexuality as being the gift of God that it is, and see the Song of Songs as the type of eroticism that pleases the Lord, we are free to have fun with our husbands rather than worrying about whether we sound silly or stupid.

Some suggestions: use terms that seem friendly to you, not clinical or disgusting. Avoid the temptation to manipulate your husband, as if he were a sex machine that you have the power to turn on and off, as you talk to him in sexual terms. Go slowly if this is new to you, and abandon anything that feels uncomfortable. The point of love-talk is to help you relax and become sexually aroused, not guilty or frustrated! Be yourself and use words that seem natural to you. If you're still unsure if love-talk is okay, reread Song of Songs several times and think about what some of the words might mean. During lovemaking, don't be afraid to verbally express what you are feeling and experiencing to your husband. Be bold enough to talk about specific sensations. He'll love it! Keep in mind that the way you are communicating your experience to your husband helps him to realize what his embraces and touches mean to you, as well as affirming his ability to be sexually satisfying to you.

It is truly a joy to integrate our sexuality with our spirituality, to recognize that any dividing lines we impose between the two are artificial. The freedom we have to live lives pleasing to God in *all* that we do and say is based upon the amazing fact of His love for us. Through the spoken word, we are able to share the love the Lord has bestowed upon us. When we are motivated by love, we can rest securely under the shadow of His wings.

Filling Up Your Well

By this point in this chapter you must be wondering if I'll come back down to earth and say something about what happens when there is nothing nice you can think of to say to your husband. Since few of us are capable of minding the dictum "if you can't think of something nice to say, then don't say anything at all," we tend to heap hot coals of self-condemnation on our heads when, at the end of a long, tiring day, we can't talk sexy and we can't talk nicely to our bed partner.

The scenario goes something like this: Your husband has had little to say all day that was caring or supportive, and the kids have been in one fight after another all day. Everyone has been snappy toward one another—cross, irritable, and unfriendly. The weather had been dreary, and you had all looked forward to spending the day at the park since Saturday is really the only day you have that isn't filled up with school, work, and church activities. You have honestly tried to keep things going smoothly, but everyone has been critical of your efforts. You have been tempted to explode several times, but went in your bedroom and calmed yourself down instead. Now it's time to get in bed for the night. You feel totally drained. Your husband suddenly turns toward you with this big grin on his face and all you can think of is, "How can that man expect me to make love to him when he's ignored me all day?" You turn away, hoping he'll get the message that you aren't the least interested in cuddling (or anything else for that matter), which he certainly does after getting the cold-shoulder treatment. Before you know it, you're silently crying tears of exhaustion. All you can think of now is that you wish *he would just hold you without expecting anything in return.*

This is what I call the empty-well syndrome. People have been dipping into the "well" of your resources all day long while you have been supplying *their* needs. . . . but the well eventually runs dry. This partly has to do with the way the human body is structured: we need calories, nutrients and rest to build energy. But we need to have some basic emotional needs met as well. The Lord created us to have these various needs, and if our needs go unmet for too long a time, we feel the effects. There is nothing we can do to change the way we are. It is a fact of our existence!

Beyond food, shelter, and rest, we also need loving touch that is nonsexual and nurturing; we need to feel a sense of identity and a sense of belonging to another, as well as to a group of others; we need to love and be loved in return. We expect family and friends to meet many of our needs. When they don't, we wind up hoping that they will eventually as we keep trying to meet their needs until our wells run dry. It's a wonderful feeling to be able to meet the needs of others with joy; it's a lonely, empty feeling when we realize that we can't.

Jesus understood the empty-well phenomenon during the days of His ministry, and He took steps in His own life to make sure that His well was kept full. The Gospels contain numerous references to times when the Lord Jesus left the multitudes that often gathered around Him so He could spend time with His Father. Presumably the Lord prayed, reflected, rested, and shared what was on His mind and heart with God during such times. His physical body could only endure so much at a time, and the fact that He was the Son of God did not exempt Him from feeling what it was like to live in human flesh.

We need to be careful that we don't expect more of ourselves than Jesus expected of Himself. We can't outdo Jesus! At those moments when we feel our body send out its signals for rest or touch or wholesome food, we must stop and figure out how best to take care of ourselves. Sometimes it means being really honest with one's husband: "Honey, this has been a tiring, difficult day for me, and I need a back rub every bit as much as you need to make love." Wives need to teach their husbands how to respond to tears and wifely exhaustion. The alternative is to "suffer in silence" as a dried-up well and to become resentful and bitter about meeting one's husband's needs when one's own needs go unmet. We need to understand that our own needs are just as important as everyone else's.

Each one of us has a kind of set-point that determines the amount and types of stress we can handle. If we compare ourselves too closely with others, we are likely to feel disappointed at our inadequacy to cope with certain things as well as our acquaintances can. Some women seem to be able to do everything they set out to do and then some. Organization is their forté, and their efficiency is a testimony to their seemingly endless zest and energy. Let's face it—none of us actually knows what goes on "behind the scenes" at such a woman's house. If we did, we would all breathe a sigh of relief, because we would finally know the truth: *No one is perfectly composed 100 percent of the time! We need to accept our own limitations as well as thank God for the abilities He has given to each and every one of us.* At times we'll be stretched by the kinds of projects and relationships we're involved in. We'll always need to keep growing in respect to our relationship to the Lord, but He doesn't ask us to do things He doesn't think we can handle (for example, read 1 Corinthians 10:13).

In Hebrews we are reminded that we have a High Priest who can sympathize with our weaknesses, One who has been tempted in all things as we are, yet is without sin.[27] We are encouraged to "approach the throne of grace with confidence, so that we may receive mercy and find grace to help us in our time of need." God has promised us mercy and the grace that will help us! The Lord understands, because He became one of us! This is good news. We aren't alone in our times of frustration, depression, fatigue, or exasperation. The Lord is our Shepherd, and with such a One as Him, we shall not want.

The Rock That Is Higher Than I

> One thing I have asked from the Lord, that I shall seek: That I may dwell in the house of the Lord all the days of my life, to behold the beauty of the Lord, and to meditate in His temple. For in the day of trouble He will conceal me in His tabernacle; in the secret place of His tent He will hide me; He will lift me up on a rock. And now my head will be lifted up above my enemies around me; and I will offer in His tent sacrifices with shouts of joy; I will sing, yes, I will sing praises to the Lord . . . Wait for the Lord; be strong, and let your heart take courage; yes, wait for the Lord.[28]

> From the ends of the earth I call to you, I call as my heart grows faint; lead me to the rock that is higher than I.[29]

Seeking, beholding, meditating, joyfully shouting, singing, and waiting . . . calling upon the living God for help, sustenance, and courage. What happens when our needs aren't met by those we love? When we're tempted to explode? What can we do if we feel that no one really can relate to what we're going through? When we find that attempts at talking keep dissolving into a rehashing of the same old "I would if you would" song and dance routine? We come to the end of ourselves, the place where real faith begins.

There must be a balance between communicating our needs to others, in order to help them better understand how to love us, and communicating our needs to our Heavenly Father, who loves us in spite of our needs. If we're constantly telling others how to love us, we won't have the time or energy left to love *them!* We must go to "the rock that is higher than" our individual "I's." It is there that we learn about the love of God for us, the love with which we are to love others. As God imparts His truth to us, as His ways become more familiar to us as we read His Word and spend time alone with Him, we find that He fills our wells with *living* water. The love of God *never* fails us. There is no equivalent to what the Lord alone can supply His people with.

So in the middle of the night when tears are flowing because of difficulties you're experiencing, in the middle of dinner when your husband criticizes your latest attempt at gourmet cooking, or in the middle of your Bible study when you'd like to unload your burdens publicly rather than ask God to share them with you, wait . . . be strong . . . take courage. Ask the Lord to lead you to His Rock, for Jesus is our true foundation. Everything else amounts to slipping sand. Give God time to heal your wounds and mend your heart. Then the words will come that will bind the wounds of others and bring the healing for their hearts that is so desperately needed. Go boldly, with confidence, to the throne of grace. It is there that you will find rest and the energy to start anew.

> The tongue has the power of life and death; make friends
> with it and enjoy its fruits.[30]

/16/

Questions Anyone?

Be like the bird
That, pausing in her flight
A while on boughs too slight,
Feels them give way
Beneath her and yet sings,
Knowing that she hath wings.

Victor Hugo

This book was born out of my reflections on the many conversations I have had with women about female sexuality, this chapter out of actual counseling with women who have asked for help. Although each individual's experiences are unique, I have found that many of the concerns I have addressed are similar. Little has been written by women from a Christian perspective on this area of our lives, leaving a limited number of resources that include a Biblical view of female sexuality. Although a one question—single answer format is not encountered in reality, I hope that the ideas generated here by these ten questions will enable you to seek solutions to concerns you may be facing in this area of your life.

Why is it easier for some women to have greater sexual satisfaction than others?

It is important to remember that no two women are exactly alike. The ability to respond to the God-given design of one's sexuality depends primarily on a woman's willingness to open up to the strong feelings and sensations her body is capable of producing. A woman is more likely to value the sexual relationship she shares with her husband when she views her sexualtiy as a gift of God that can be received with thanksgiving. When she gets rid of any fear and guilt that may be associated with how she looks at lovemaking, she will find herself able to be truly comfortable with her body. Orgasmic response is especially dependent on a woman's decision to let go of controlling her body as she accepts the pleasure that is meant to accompany sexual arousal.

Why is it so easy for my husband to become sexually stimulated? It often seems to take me forever!

To a certain degree, the ability to become sexually aroused is learned. Although women usually require a longer period of caressing and skin contact before becoming aroused enough to experience orgasm, this need not always be the case. Making mental preparations beforehand can greatly reduce the amount of time it takes to become sexually excited.

Thinking of sex as an activity that is separate from the context of one's daily life is a setup for disappointment. The Lord has created us to be *whole persons* in body, mind, and spirit. Good sex is the result of weaving the physical dimension of our sexuality into the fabric of our everyday lives. Sexual fulfillment is much more than what we see charted on a graph of what constitutes the four phases of sexual response. It starts with a time of embracing before getting up in the morning, in riding to work together, or sharing conversation over breakfast. It continues later in the day when an "I love you" is expressed over the phone or during a prayer sent heavenward as one's spouse is remembered in the afternoon. A warm hug in the kitchen before dinner, a time of hand holding while reading the newspaper, and a walk alone around the block together while discussing one another's impressions of the day can all be part of a prelude to physical sharing later in the evening.

Nourishing expressions of intimacy and learning to cherish our husbands plays a big part in keeping the excitement of marriage alive. Sexual arousal is not simply something that is "worked up." Marital relationships are enlivened in many ways outside the bedroom.

When two people are courting and anticipating getting married, do they require any kind of fancy maneuvering to produce sexual desire for one another? Not at all! Over time, it is all too easy to lose that sense of urgency and just take one another for granted. Some of that change is a relief! But we need to realize and accept the fact that we will never outgrow the things that sustain and empower the bond that is shared between two married lovers.

Evaluate your level of intimacy, and determine whether you have been neglecting meeting one another's needs for affection. Find ways to share what is on your mind, and daily communicate your experiences to one another. Think about the times when your arousal was totally unplanned and spontaneous—what made the difference? Do you think you may be somewhat unrealistic about lovemaking and are waiting for it to become more romantic and less routine? What *do* you expect? Is sex disappointing compared to what you think it should be? Why?

Rather than dwell on what you think you may have been missing, why not take some positive steps to enrich this aspect of your marriage, starting today? When is the last time you splurged on a new nightgown that made you feel irresistible? Have you had a night away from your children in the past year? What about the possibility of setting up regularly scheduled dates so you can spend time giving your husband undivided attention? Use your imagination to plan ways of building the anticipation of lovemaking right into your day. In this way, your ability to be sexually responsive will become the natural expression of the closeness you have felt with your husband all day long.

It really bothers me when the first thing that happens after I get into bed is that my husband starts initiating lovemaking and expects me to feel the same way. I don't know how to deal with the negative reaction I have toward his attitude.

Instead of viewing your husband's arousal as an instinctive drive for sexual satisfaction, stop and think for a moment about your body from your husband's point of view. Lying next to you is likely to make your husband yearn to be physically close to you. The closer he gets, the more his body will respond. Sexual sharing is the way he feels closest to you.

If you have not discussed your feelings before going to bed, he may automatically assume you want the same thing he wants: the union of your two bodies, followed by the pleasant release of sexual tension and a sound night's sleep. Unless you share your feelings in a more neutral setting, you are both going to end up feeling frustrated.

What is it that you feel uncomfortable about? What could you both do differently? How might the two of you work out a way to communicate your desire for lovemaking? Do you feel that your husband is neglecting your need for hugging and kissing without intercourse? For emotional intimacy? Does he touch you in ways that irritate you rather than excite you? What might he do differently?

Frequently resentment is the result of mixed communication about sexual sharing. The way out of this trap is to identify what is bothering you and find ways to alleviate the source of your anxiety or frustration through being able to talk with your husband about how you feel. Using "I" messages will help you to emphasize your point of view and may help you to avoid having your statements viewed as an attack or a criticism, such as:

> "I would really like it if you would touch me like this rather
> than being so direct, honey. There . . . that's great! That's
> much better."

"I get pretty tense when you do that. Let's try this instead."

"I can see that you're ready to make love right now, but I'm feeling kind of uptight. I think a quick back rub would help me to unwind from the crazy day I've had."

There will be times when your husband will need to make love and you won't want to. At other times you may want to be sexually expressive and *he* will be too tired. A close friend of mine worked this out with her husband in a unique way: whenever *either* of them wants to make love, the other partner makes time to make love. What an incredible gift this is!

Before we got married, my husband and I had quite a bit of sexual contact. Now that we are husband and wife, we seem to be too busy for lovemaking during the week. On the weekends, all my husband seems interested in is sex. It really bothers me. What can I do to feel more accepting of his needs?

First of all, it is important for you to think about how you used to view sex before you were married. In the back of your mind, you may still be associating sex with sneaking behind your parents' backs or parking along a deserted road. Sexual activity that takes place outside the covering of marriage may be exciting physically, but produces a separation between a woman's body and her spiritual identity because it takes place outside the protection of marriage. It is almost as if her body is like a tool that she uses to attract and arouse a lover rather than as the means of fulfilling her deepest needs for complete trust and openness during lovemaking.

What you are feeling is something that many women encounter after getting married. Now everyone knows that you are a sexual person. When you were dating, you could still be your father's daughter, a "good" girl who did not express her sexuality openly. Perhaps your parents often warned you that having sex before marriage could cause you to become pregnant or expose you to V.D. You may not have heard an authentically Biblical view of sexuality before. Under these circumstances, it should not be surprising that it would feel unnatural for a woman to feel responsive with her body. In your mind, you may still see sex as being dirty or dangerous or disgusting. God's view of sexuality, as you have seen in this book, is quite the opposite of what it is often interpreted to be. Now that you know this, you will need to transfer this "head knowledge" into your heart. Because your body responds to your deepest feelings and inner emotions, you will need to ask God to enable you to see your husband's sexual desire toward you as a lovely gift.

Through lovemaking, your husband's feelings of attachment toward you are solidified. God has created him to want to be inside you, to be one with you. When you open yourself up to really accept the way your husband's sexuality was designed to be expressed, you will find yourself welcoming his touches instead of being repelled by them.

Now that you are married, sex *will* seem different. The tingling excitement that you used to feel is gone because your husband's body has become familiar to you. Now your love has a chance to deepen as you learn to give yourself to your husband *because you love him.* Not because you want to win him. Not to entrap him. Not to get him to love you. Not even to prove that you are attractive. But because the love you are able to express to him through your body strengthens the bond that brings unity to your marriage. Making love is not a frivolous act that is disconnected with the rest of your lives. As your husband's wife, your invitation to share sexually signifies far more because you embrace him for what he is. It is just the two of you now, with all of your strengths *and* all of your weaknesses.

Sexual expression, after all, is not meant to be the fitting together of two identical halves into a neat package marked "one flesh." It is the merging of two entirely different personalities as they learn how to say, "I love you even though I am not like you. You have become a part of me. I accept you as you are. I love you." This involves giving one's body out of joy for our beloved. It means that my body is no longer my own, but my husband's, and that my husband's body belongs to me. This is a radical departure from the mind-set of our culture. I urge you to consider the beauty of your sexuality from a Biblical point of view rather than from a worldly perspective.

The practical side of this is that you need to begin making love more often. Don't wait for weekends to express your love to one another. Cut back on outside activities. For the time being, start to look at your bed as the most important place for the two of you to spend time together. Learn to speak with your body. Use it to comfort your husband as well as arouse him. Plan your time together creatively.

Perhaps it's time for you to invest in a tape player for your bedroom and get some tapes that you would enjoy listening to together. Or you could get some massage oil and spend an hour caressing your husband in a way you would like to be caressed. Maybe this weekend would be a great time to just stay at home and turn the phone off. Let down the walls you have placed between yourself and the powerful sensations your body is capable of feeling. Accept the pleasure of your husband's touch and the peaceful feeling between the two of you that is produced in the afterglow of lovemaking.

You have nothing to hide. God has covered your past in Jesus and now invites you to celebrate your marriage by affirming the beauty of your sexuality as you freely give yourself to your husband.

Before our baby was born, my husband and I made love practically every day, but now we're lucky if it's once a week. It has been six months since our daughter was born, and I still don't feel back to normal. Is something the matter with me?

It sounds like you and your husband have enjoyed having an intimate relationship that provided the two of you with a strong bond to see you through this period of transition in your lives. Now that you are parents, your focus cannot be on just the two of you. Your love is expanding to include a new person in your lives who has a personality and temperament that is unique and different from each of your own. Your daughter has many needs that can be exhausting at times to meet. What you are experiencing is a normal reaction to learning how to balance your personal needs with the needs of your husband and child. All of this takes time. In a society that often expects instant relief from distressing symptoms, we often wish God could grant us instant maturity as well.

Even though your baby is almost completely dependent on you, it is important to remember that she is growing less so each day. The goal of all of your efforts as her mother is to raise her to eventually be able to leave your home and have a full, productive life of her own. On the other hand, the bond that you and your husband share is one that will need to be nurtured and closely tended for life.

I once had a couple in one of the childbirth classes I teach who were in their forties and expecting their eighth child. Out of the thousands of men and women I have had the privilege to work with, this particular couple stands out as a shining example of devotion and caring for one another. They were like a couple of teenagers. They would laugh and tickle one another during the exercises, hold hands during breaks, and acted just as interested in learning about giving birth for the eighth time as they probably were for the first. Here was this couple with a daughter who was a sophmore in college, expecting a baby young enough to have been their grandchild, who acted like the entire process was completely brand new. Finally, on the fourth night of class, I asked them what their secret was. The wife smiled as she glanced over at her husband, and they both began to give me the same answer simultaneously. It turned out that ever since they had dated before getting married, they had spent Friday nights out together. "Even if it's just to go for a half-hour walk, Bob and I make sure we have time alone. He's made me feel just like I used to before I married him by *always* taking that time out for me."

You see, this couple had learned an important lesson early in their marriage: marriage is the most important human relationship a man and woman have. It was designed to survive raising kids to adulthood and all of the stresses and strains involved in family life. This relationship does not automatically outlast all of these things. It must be carefully and lovingly nourished if it is to survive the demands that are placed upon it.

I think that if you talk to your husband and encourage him to plan times for just the two of you, that would be a good start. Cultivate the art of dating. I have included a list here that my husband and I compiled from an assignment we gave to participants in the marriage enrichment class we teach. Your own community probably has a wide variety of things unique to your own locale that you could add to the list. Whether it is a special night out that involves dressing up and making reservations at an exclusive restaurant or an evening of fishing in a canoe, it's spending time alone together that counts. Getting away from the dishes, the laundry, and the baby will do each of you good.

The other thing I would like to encourage you to do is to pay attention to what you are eating, how much rest you are getting, and whether you are getting the exercise you need. (Review the chapters on stress management and choosing a healthy lifestyle for specific information on these topics.) Caring for an infant is a demanding job.

Every child deserves to have parents who love each other enough to value the importance of promoting one another's physical, emotional, and spiritual health.

These things will give you a place to start. It may seem like a big effort at first, but you will begin to reap the benefits immediately. As your bond is renewed and enlivened by your commitment to spend time together and promote one another's health, your sexual relationship will be refreshed as well.

70 Activities for Enlivening Your Marriage

1. Go for a ride and a talk in the country.
2. Work together outdoors, planting trees or gardening.
3. Sit outside in the moonlight, and share goals and dreams.
4. Go to a rodeo.
5. Offer to give your spouse a body massage with a vibrator.
6. Get up early together and have coffee or tea out on the patio.
7. Go for a walk in the woods.
8. Go horseback riding and picnic on the trail.
9. Bathe together by candlelight.
10. Go out for dessert.
11. Rent a VCR and a good movie (like *It's a Wonderful Life*) and eat popcorn together.
12. Take a bicycle ride together. (You could even rent a tandem bike!)

13. Share a meal at a nice restaurant and go to a play afterwards.
14. Visit a planetarium.
15. Take a dinner train ride.
16. Go sledding or ice skating. (Take hot cocoa along.)
17. Go to a small town with lots of history for a walk and a talk.
18. Go down waterslides or to a pool for a swim.
19. Get up and watch the sun rise together. (Someone suggested that playing golf at this time of day can be fun, too.)
20. Take a buggy ride together at Christmastime.
21. Take dancing lessons together.
22. Go to the State Capitol building for a tour, but get lost in an abandoned hallway.
23. Attend a high school or college football game (or volleyball, basketball . . .)
24. Enroll in an adult ed class together.
25. Go to a hospital nursery and reflect on the wonder of your child(ren)'s birth(s).
26. Go miniature golfing.
27. Go to a motel for the evening, but return home by midnight.
28. Build sand castles at area beaches.
29. Rent a sailboat or paddleboat at a nearby lake.
30. Sit on a blanket at the park, fly a kite, read.
31. Arrange for a hot air balloon ride.
32. Go for a paddleboat cruise on the Missouri River. (Oh, the joys of living in Nebraska!)
33. Go out and do some photography together at a local nature center.
34. Attend a concert, especially one held outdoors so you can curl up and look at the stars while listening to the music.
35. Go bowling.
36. Go on a walk through an area of town with old, interesting homes.
37. Get your hair cut at the same time and place. (One woman in a recent class privately confided that she found that her husband enjoys having her cut his hair . . . with her topless!)
38. Get all dressed up and go to an exotic restaurant.
39. Go shopping together: groceries, gifts, or plants.
40. Spend time at a mountain cabin together.

41. Plan and work on a creative project building something together.
42. Attend a wedding and reminisce.
43. Rent a canoe and go on a canoe ride.
44. Go to an auction and purchase something funny.
45. Visit antique shops and learn about old furniture.
46. Go for a drive and look at Christmas decorations while sharing memories.
47. Go to the drive-in.
48. Plan a surprise date: Blindfold your spouse and take her (him) to someplace unusual.
49. Shoot an entire roll of film of one another outdoors.
50. Go on a hayride.
51. Take a walk in the rain under an umbrella.
52. Go to a department store and buy each other some sexy underwear. (No peeking until you get home!)
53. Go to an art gallery and browse.
54. Share a plate of nachos at your favorite Mexican restaurant.
55. Set aside an evening for making photo albums or looking at slides.
56. Meet each other for lunch in the middle of a workday.
57. Go to the library and find a new subject to explore together.
58. Get season tickets for the symphony (or travel series or theatre . . .).
59. Play tennis at a local park.
60. Go Christmas caroling with other couples.
61. Drive out to the country to see Halley's comet. (Never mind if it's already gone—none of us could ever see it anyway!)
62. Go for a hike along trails in a nearby park.
63. Browse in a Christian bookstore and listen to demo tapes.
64. Go to a park and swing on the swings while holding hands.
65. Share a sundae or a soda at a local ice cream parlor.
66. Stroll along the main street in your town and go window shopping after all the stores have closed (assuming the streets are safe at night).
67. Take a ride to see the colors change in the autumn or spring.
68. Have someone babysit your child at *their* house, then go back home and spend the evening in bed.

69. Attend an art, antique, recreation, or craft show.
70. Go fishing by moonlight. Forget about the fish. Gaze at the moon and stars instead.

My husband often seems to be more interested in masturbating by himself than he is in making love to me. When we do make love, there have been several times that he has been really rough with me. Is this normal?

If your husband has spent or is currently spending time in looking at erotic or pornographic magazines, he is likely to have developed a view of female sexuality that does not line up with a Biblical perspective of love-making. All too often, sexually explicit materials depict violent themes, creating a desire to dominate or exploit one's sexual partner in an effort to gain a sense of power through sex. The view of women presented in such materials promotes lust and destroys the purity that is to be maintained within marriage:

> Marriage should be honored by all, and the marriage bed
> kept pure, for God will judge the adulterer and all the
> sexually immoral.[1]

We live in a society that uses sex to sell everything from deodorant soap to vodka. A man in Des Moines made the paper this week because he had opened up a jiffy lube business serviced by topless female employees. He claimed that his income jumped from twenty to two hundred fifty dollars per day when he tried this new marketing technique. Males are instructed to remain in the car. Employees will wear a bikini or tight sweater upon request.

From an early age, males are confronted with visual images of women who are paid large sums of money to seduce the photographer's camera. Hoping to sell more of their products, companies hire advertisers who attempt to create an association between what they are selling and the physical and emotional reactions induced by their ads. These images seduce men in subtle ways, not the least of which is to think that there is nothing wrong with "admiring" a large pair of breasts as they are casually exposed in the latest diet soda commercial.

Gradually, our sensivity to nudity and sexual themes has been eroded through our constant exposure to sexual images. An era of unprecedented acceptance of pornography has been the result. A weekly newsmagazine noted this trend and pointed out, "After a decade of not-so-benign-neglect, virtually any adult American has a license that the Lord never allowed Sodom and Gomorrah."[2]

Your husband's behavior is not an unusual occurrence. His private

258

involvement in sexual fantasy is nurtured by a culture that has devalued the sanctity of sexuality and the human body. Jesus clearly spoke to the issue of sexual fantasy and its effects on marriage when He said:

> You have heard it said, "Do not commit adultery." But I tell you that anyone who looks at a woman lustfully has already committed adultery with her in his heart.[3]

Adultery is the ultimate betrayal of the marriage bond. When Jesus compared visually-oriented lust to extramarital intercourse, He was teaching about the spiritual and emotional impact of one's thought life upon one's beliefs and attitudes about sexuality. Looking at another woman's breasts and genitalia violates her privacy and constructs a way of seeing her as an object rather than as a person. This attitude denies women their dignity as having been created in the image of God. Whether the women themselves give their consent to be used in this way is irrelevant. As Christians, we recognize the importance of each individual to God. To look at another person's body and deny this truth violates the basic principles that underlie the meaning of human sexuality.

Erotica and pornography, then, depersonalize sex by removing it from the purpose for which it was created, treating people as sexual objects that emphasize parts of the body over the worth and value of the individual. Women and men who participate in displaying their bodies for profit are *real* people, with feelings of emptiness, alienation, and guilt before a holy and righteous God. We are called to reject treating other human beings as objects and to love them compassionately. We are also to wage war upon the powers of darkness that seek to debase and dehumanize sexuality through sexual sin.

You are not in *any* way obligated to act out sexual situations with your husband that are derived from a fantasy life fed by pornography. By just saying no, you can enable your husband to grow closer to the Lord as you pray for healing in this area of his life. You are not merely a body for your husband to have sex with in whatever way he pleases. Your husband is called by God to love your body as he loves his own.[4] When your husband forcefully dominates you during intercourse without considering how it is affecting you, he is not loving you according to God's plan for your marriage.

You may or may not feel comfortable confronting him about this aspect of his life. There may not be anyone that you feel you can discuss this situation with. Begin by praying. Ask the Lord to forgive you for anything you may have done to hurt your husband. Forgive your husband for hurting you. With a loving attitude, encourage your husband to talk to your pastor or to a Christian counselor. If you attend a church that defends erotica as an acceptable means of enhancing sexual pleasure, look elsewhere for help. Until he is willing to accept his share of the responsibility for damaging the sanctity of your bond, your husband will prevent both of you from living in sexual harmony with one another.

More than anything else, your husband needs you to love him enough to refuse to downplay the significance of his sexual behavior. While you are not to act the part of the Holy Spirit in his life, you are called to purity. As you demonstrate your love through caring for him as a woman of God, the Holy Spirit will do the rest. I know that this is not going to be easy for you, but as you strengthen yourself through prayer and study of the Word, God will give you what you will need to be a comfort and a witness to your mate. You may also find it very helpful to receive counseling as you walk through this time in your life. God knows your heart. He will meet your needs. He will never forsake you.

After divorcing my first husband, I became a Christian and am now married to a man who I dearly love. I find myself at times, however, remembering what it was like in bed with Brad, and feel terrible about having ever been with anyone but Mike.

We have already discussed the spiritual reality of what it means to have sexual intercourse in terms of the bond that is created between a man and a woman. However much we would like things to be different at times, we cannot change the past. The truth is that you and Brad were husband and wife. Your marriage did take place. You had a relationship that included intimate sexual sharing. You have experienced the shattering of that bond through the breakup of your marriage. It is a part of your history that is a part of who you are today.

Divorce is a tragic event in the lives of two people. Sexual sharing was created by God to produce emotional, physical, and spiritual intimacy within marriage. The memory of that intimacy reminds you of the destruction of a relationship that exposed the deepest parts of you to another person. Remembering the things that you shared together reminds you that sexual openness is not something that can be taken back once it has been shared. Wishing that you had not had sexual experiences with anyone but Mike is a natural response to the love you feel for him.

As memories from your past surface, try to view this recall as part of a cleansing process. Through your faith in Jesus Christ, God has forgiven you for "missing the mark" when you were living in ignorance of His design for your life. Do not let the Devil accuse you of sin that has been covered over in Christ. Commit passages of Scripture to memory, such as 1 John 1:9, to use against the enemy whenever you feel burdened with sin from the past. When you think of something painful, use it to remind you to grow closer to Jesus. There is no need to pretend it did not happen. With the passing of time and the commitment you have made to making your marriage to Mike succeed, you are walking away from the wounds that were left after your first marriage. You are right in viewing this as a less than ideal situation, but now that you know Jesus, the Lord has made you a new creation.[5]

It is now your responsibility to see to it that no one robs you of the reality of your reconciliation to God and the joy of your salvation. Stand firm in the knowledge that your debts are canceled. You no longer have to keep paying interest on debts you no longer owe through fearing memories of your first marriage or regretting your past. We have been called to "live a new life" as we glorify God for enabling us to make peace with the past through the free gift of life He has bestowed upon us through Jesus Christ our Lord.[6] I pray that this truth will saturate your mind and heart as you continue to learn what it means to love your husband as you open yourself up to receive the love he has for you.

My 16-year-old daughter has asked me to help her obtain a prescription for birth control pills. She knows that I am against her having intercourse outside marriage, but I am convinced that she will be sexually active whether I like it or not and I don't want her to get pregnant.

It sounds like you have already made it clear to your daughter that you do not want her engaging in premarital sexual activity, but have you shared why? Simply saying that it is wrong is not enough. Expressing the reasons extramarital sex is not in your daughter's best interest is essential. Avoid using S.T.D.'s and pregnancy as scare tactics and stick to the heart of this issue: sexual openness produces emotional as well as physical vulnerability, joining two people together in such a way that a unique bond is produced between the two of them. In serial relationships, this bond is repeatedly fractured and lessens the possibility that a lifelong commitment to one person can be sustained. God has designed marriage to protect our hearts and minds and bodies. When His covering is missing, deep wounds result.

In asking for your help, your daughter is seeking your approval for something that you believe would injure her emotionally and spiritually. As her mother, you have always wanted to keep her from harm. An unwanted pregnancy would be a difficult situation to have to face. But what about having to deal with the fruit of a relationship that will produce long-term memories that will affect how your daughter views her sexuality?

You have always sought your daughter's best interest and are trying to do so now. Consider the responsibility you have in showing your daughter God's truth in a loving way, and know that you have a right to act according to your values even though other moms may think you're crazy. Until your daughter is an adult and on her own, your values and decisions will

261

continue to influence and guide her life. Sit down and explain how you feel about sexuality and the role it has played in your own life. Pray that the Lord will help you to know what to say. Even though your daughter is sixteen, she is still watching you as she learns about what it means to be a woman. If you humbly represent God's love to her in a way she can understand, she cannot help but be touched by your example.

I haven't been interested in sex at all lately. It seems like whenever we finally get the chance to be alone at the end of the day, there is something going on that prevents me from becoming aroused.

The most common excuses for avoiding lovemaking have deeper reasons behind them. If a woman tells her husband that it's too cold, too hot, too late, or too early, something more important must be going on. Look at the list below and check off any of the *real* reasons you may have had for not making love during the past few months:

_____ I felt neglected by my husband.

_____ I felt resentful that he expected sex but had not related to me in a loving way.

_____ I felt unattractive.

_____ I have had difficulty feeling sexually fulfilled during lovemaking.

_____ I just wanted to be held or have a back rub without my husband expecting sex afterwards.

_____ I was sick and had no interest in sex.

_____ I felt like my husband just takes me for granted.

_____ My sex drive was low so I couldn't get excited about lovemaking.

_____ I resent his enjoying sex while ignoring my needs.

_____ I don't know how to tell him how to "pleasure" me or touch me.

_____ I have difficulty expressing my needs and end up feeling depressed or resentful.

_____ I expect my husband to take responsibility for my sexual pleasure instead of taking responsibility for myself.

_____ Sex just isn't fun anymore.

_____ I expect my husband to take the lead in lovemaking. I am unable to be the "aggressive partner" in our relationship.

_____ I often feel bored or disinterested in lovemaking and participate only to please my husband.

Once you have completed this list, look back over your replies and think about the times that lovemaking has been satisfying to you. What do you think made the difference? Have you seen any connection between your active participation in sexual sharing and your husband's ability to enjoy it? The Lord has designed a reciprocal principle into this dimension of your life so that as you give pleasure, you open up your ability to receive pleasure. Have you structured your lives together to fully accommodate this principle and to nourish this part of your relationship?

In several chapters of this book, I have outlined ways that can help you cultivate your marriage garden. A summary of some of the most important are listed below. Check off the steps you will take *this week* to become more comfortable with your body as you seek to enliven your marriage through your ability to be sexually responsive.

_____ Bathe or shower *before* going to bed in order to relax, feel fresh, and smell yummy.

_____ Take a nap before dinner to have more energy for lovemaking.

_____ Stop complaining, and start receiving the gift of your sexual design (and his!).

_____ Try something new: Be open to enjoying your body and being more expressive with it during lovemaking. Ask your husband what would please him and try it!

_____ Reduce daily stress by taking two concrete steps to manage it (exercise, time by yourself for at least thirty minutes daily, long bath, listening to music, etc.).

_____ Give each other a massage. Do not combine this with making love. The night afterwards, spend an hour touching before making love.

_____ Go away for the weekend alone together. Use room service for meals. Take along a tape player with your favorite music, and surprise your husband with new underwear or a silky nightgown.

When I am angry at my husband, the last thing in the world I feel like doing is making love to him. Any suggestions?

It's funny you should ask . . . I just happen to have heard of a way of solving this predicament and although it might not apply to all couples, this particular husband and wife team told me that it has worked for them every time:

It seems that whenever they reach an impasse in an argument, they retreat to their bedroom, take off all their clothing, and sit on their bed directly facing one another. They have never been able to stay mad at each other by using this method.

The happiness of life is made up of minute fractions—the little soon forgotten charities of a kiss or smile, a kind look, a heartfelt compliment, and the countless infinitesimals of pleasurable and genial feeling.

(Samuel Taylor Coleridge, *The Improvisatore*)

/**17**/

Closing Thoughts

The bed is the heart of the home, the arena of love, the seedbed of life, and the one constant point of meeting. It is the place where, night by night, forgiveness and fair speech return that the sun may not go down on our wrath; where the perfunctory kiss and the entirely ceremonial pat on the backside become unction and grace. It is the oldest, friendliest thing in anybody's marriage, the first used and the last left, and no one can praise it enough.[1]

Robert Farrar Capon,
Bed and Board: Plain Talk About Marriage

After teaching a Sunday adult education class with my husband called "Enlivening Your Marriage," one of the members stayed to help put away chairs, lingering behind the rest of the group as they left the classroom. This particular young man has been married less than a year. We could tell that he wanted to share something, but sensed his reluctance to begin talking until others were out of hearing distance. Once he saw that he could speak freely, he confided that during the past week he and his wife were "finally" beginning to enjoy the sexual aspect of their relationship. Just spending more time together in bed seemed to have helped, as well as having taken the time to talk about one another's needs. It was especially rewarding to see the joy on his face as he spoke about his wife. The class assignment given the first week of class seemed to have had a positive effect on this young couple's marriage because they had mutually agreed to take their homework seriously!

In this book, a personal and intimate view of a Biblical perspective of female sexuality has been presented. I hope that it has touched your heart in reading it. It has certainly done so for me as I have written it. There have probably been parts that you did not agree with, but if you have opened up to receive the gift of your sexuality more fully as a result of thinking about this area of your life, that is what is most important. Like the newlyweds in the marriage class, I know that you will be blessed as you commit yourself to enlivening the sexual relationship you share with your husband, believing that God will honor your desire to make your marriage bed "the place where, night by night, forgiveness and fair speech return that the sun may not go down" on your wrath. Do not be surprised that this does not always happen smoothly. As Father Capon has said, people mistakenly think it's easy to make love, but that it's hard to pray.[2] If lovemaking is depicted as an automatic, desire-driven process by the media, then why should anyone expect it to be any different than that?

The willingness to share one's body openly in marriage needs to be developed, nurtured, and encouraged over the span of a lifetime. Each day will bring its own unique challenges and opportunities for us to learn about the wonder of God's plan for our lives. As the time we share with our husbands unfolds, our ability to care for and about them will be refreshed and renewed on a continuing basis if we commit ourselves to loving God. When we find the true source of our identity in our Creator, as well as the strength to follow Him in this present age, we will find our attitudes and outlooks transformed. In Christ we are complete. If we dedicate ourselves to loving our husbands and our children, God will honor us for making choices that conform to Biblical truth rather than the expectations of our culture.

I hope that you have been inspired to embrace the fullness of your sexuality anew as you have considered its many facets and expressions. Through the chapters presented here, it has been my intent to share a truly feminine view of what it means to be sexual in the *complete* sense of the word. The rest is up to you.

It is customary to close in prayer at the end of a class or a time of fellowship. As you reflect on what you have read in this book, I would like to offer a prayer just as if we were sitting in the same room having talked about its contents together. Let us praise God for what He is teaching us and for the bond we share through Jesus as sisters in the Lord:

> Dear Heavenly Father, thank You for creating us in Your image! We praise You that we are fearfully and wonderfully made. We also praise You for the many diverse dimensions of our sexuality as women. We pray that You will enable us to glorify You through our marriages as we open up our hearts to receive the gift of our sexuality in all of its fullness. We thank You for joining us together with our husbands as one in You, Lord God. In Your strength, we ask that You would help us to be a source of love in our husbands' lives. Through the power of Your Holy Spirit, grant us wisdom to know when to speak and when to listen. Lead us, O God, with your strong steady hand in an era that we often find confusing and frustrating, so that we may abide in You more

completely. Make Your truth clear to us as we follow You, so that we may live our lives in a way that is pleasing in Your sight. We ask these things in the name of Your precious Son, Jesus Christ. Amen.

We are not alone. One by one, marriage by marriage, there are homes all over America that are standing firm in the midst of a crumbling revolution that has attempted to prove that promiscuity liberates people from the bonds of oppression. Women who have walked away wounded from the "freedom" of fornication are finding themselves set free by Christ's love as they discover the joy and beauty of marital sexuality. Let us stand together with one voice to proclaim the source of our healing and tell others of His love!

> I will exalt you, O Lord,
>   for you lifted me out of the depths
>   and did not let my enemies gloat over me.
> O Lord my God, I called to you for help
>   and you healed me.
> O Lord you brought me up from the grave;
>   you spared me from going down into the pit.
> Sing to the Lord, you saints of his;
>   praise his holy name.
> For his anger lasts only for a moment,
>   but his favor lasts a lifetime;
> weeping may remain for a night,
>   but rejoicing comes in the morning. . . .
> You turned my wailing into dancing;
>   you removed my sackcloth and clothed me with joy,
> that my heart may sing to you and not be silent.
>   O Lord my God, I will give you thanks forever.[3]

Appendix:
A Comparison of Three
Views of Human Sexuality

I. HUMANISTIC

Origin of human life:

Humans evolved from apes and "lower" life-forms; are characterized by higher brain functions.

Purpose of sex:

Sex is viewed as a means to an end:
1. Attainment of mutual satisfaction.
2. A way to give and receive love.
3. Erotic pleasure seen as a symbol of achievement.

Acceptable forms of sexual expression:

Any form of sexual activity is okay if it occurs between consenting partners.

View of sex as it relates to the family:

Sex may be unrelated to producing children, to marriage, or to an absolute value system.

Individual rights:

An individual has the right to choose how to express his or her sexuality based upon considering one's self and the dignity of one's sex partner(s).

Belief in an afterlife:

Beyond death lies endless peace, bright white light . . . or nothing at all.

Accountability:

An individual is accountable to the rest of humanity for his or her actions.

269

Summary of goals:
1. Mutual satisfaction.
2. Self-determination.
3. The "best for the most" or for the collective good.

Consequences:
Serial relationships leading to:
1. Fragmentation of self.
2. Divided allegiances.
3. Adulteration of pair-bonding through the formation of multiple bonds.

Social results:
- Unwanted children disposed of through abortion.
- Cohabitation viewed as normal.
- Divorce viewed as normal.
- Pornography widely distributed.
- Prostitution and hustling common.
- Greater acceptance of "alternative lifestyles: group marriage, homosexuality, "swinging sex."
- Sexually transmitted diseases now epidemic.
- Greater tolerance for the sexual victimization of others.
- Increase in the incidence of sexual assault and abuse.

II. HEDONISTIC

Origin of human life:
Not concerned with own origin; humans viewed as sophisticated animals.

Purpose of sex:
Sex is viewed as an end in itself:
1. Pleasure for pleasure's sake.
2. Anything goes.
3. Focus on self-gratification.

Acceptable forms of sexual expression:
Any form of sexual activity is okay if it occurs between consenting persons.

View of sex as it relates to the family:
Sex is unrelated to producing children, to marriage, or to an absolute value system.

Individual rights:
An individual has the right to choose how to express his or her sexuality based upon one's physical desires.

Belief in an afterlife:
What may happen after death makes no difference—live for today.

Accountability:
An individual is accountable to no one for his or her actions.

Summary of goals:
1. Satisfaction of one's sex drive.
2. Sex as an expression of self.
3. Seeking one's own good above that of others.

Consequences:
Sexual addiction leading to:
1. Enslavement to physical desires.
2. Diffusion of identity.
3. Fornication; approaching others as sexual objects.

Social results:
- Unwanted children disposed of through abortion.
- Cohabitation viewed as normal.
- Divorce viewed as normal.
- Pornography widely distributed.
- Prostitution and hustling common.
- Greater acceptance of "alternative lifestyles: group marriage, homosexuality, "swinging sex."
- Sexually transmitted diseases now epidemic.
- Greater tolerance for the sexual victimization of others.
- Increase in the incidence of sexual assault and abuse.

III. JUDEO-CHRISTIAN

Origin of human life:
Humans were created in the image of their Creator God (Gen. 2:18, 23-25).

Purpose of sex:
Sex is viewed as a means to an end:
1. The means through which "two become one flesh."

2. To make the earth fruitful for God.
3. An end to "aloneness" and emotional isolation.

Acceptable forms of sexual expression:
Sexual activity between a man and a woman within marriage only.

View of sex as it relates to the family:
Sex is a gift of God that strengthens the marriage bond; children are viewed as a blessing, and certain forms of sexuality are viewed as destructive to sexual identity in *all* situations:

- adultery	- prostitution	- rape
- promiscuity	- incest	- bestiality
- homosexuality	- pornography	- exhibitionism

Individual rights:
An individual expresses his or her sexuality in accordance with the will of God as it is expressed within the Bible because "I belong to God."

Belief in an afterlife:
Beyond death lies heaven or hell, eternal life or eternal damnation.

Accountability:
Each individual is accountable to a personal Creator for his or her life choices, words, and actions.

Summary of goals:
1. Mutual belonging.
2. Self-control.
3. Seeking the good of one's partner above oneself.

Consequences:
Lifetime bonding leading to:
1. Liberation from sin.
2. Living in harmony with self and others.
3. Living in harmony with God.

Social results:
- The continuation of family heritage: children, grandchildren and great-grandchildren.
- Respect for the dignity and worth of each person as having been created in the image of God.
- Rejection of sexual sin in all forms contributing to the health and stability of one's culture.

Glossary

Abdomen: The portion of the body containing the stomach, intestines, bowels, bladder, and reproductive organs.

Abdominal wall: The muscles that form a corsetlike structure between the pubic bone and the ribs and from side to side across the abdomen.

Abortifacient: Any drug or substance that is capable of inducing abortion.

Abortion: The spontaneous or deliberate ending of a pregnancy before an unborn child can survive independently of the mother.

Adultery: Sexual intercourse in which at least one partner is married to another person.

Acquired immune deficiency syndrome (AIDS): A disease affecting the system of the body that fights infection which currently has a 100 percent mortality rate.

Adrenaline: A naturally secreted substance that stimulates the adrenal glands and narrows blood vessels. Also called epinephrine.

Aerobic exercise: Any type of physical exercise that causes the heart and lungs to work harder through the repetitive movement of large muscle groups for a sufficient length of time.

Alveoli: Milk glands in the breast that secrete milk when stimulated by prolactin.

Amenorrhea: The absence of menstruation. Primary amenorrhea is the term meaning that menstruation has never begun; secondary amenorrhea refers to cases in which the menstrual cycle has either temporarily or permanently stopped.

Amniocentesis: The removal of a small amount of amniotic fluid for diagnostic or therapeutic purposes.

Androgens: Any steroid hormone that produces the growth of male features.

Androgynous: Bearing both anthers and pollen (plants) or having both male and female qualities.

Anemia: A reduction of the number of red blood cells resulting in reduced ability of the blood to carry oxygen.

Anorexia nervosa: A potentially fatal psychological disorder resulting in severe weight loss, amenorrhea, and emaciation.

273

Anovulation: The absence of ovulation.

Antepartum: Around the time of birth.

Anus: The opening of the rectum between the buttocks.

Areola: The pigmented ring of skin around the nipple.

Autonomic nervous system: The division of the nervous system that regulates vital functions of the body that are not consciously controlled, including the activity of the heart, smooth muscles, and glands.

Bartholin's glands: Two small glands found at either side of the vaginal entrance that secrete a lubricative substance during sexual arousal.

Basal body temperature: The temperature of the body, taken orally, rectally, or vaginally after at least three hours of sleep. It is taken before doing anything else.

Basal body temperature method of family planning: A method of family planning that relies on identifying the fertile period of a woman's menstrual cycle by taking and observing the basal body temperature each morning.

Battered woman syndrome (B.W.S.): The repeated episodes of physical assault on a woman committed by the man with whom she lives, often resulting in serious physical and psychological damage.

Bidet: A plumbing fixture designed to cleanse the female genitals and rectal area.

Billings method: See *Ovulation Method of Family Planning.*

Biopsy: The surgical removal of body tissue for diagnostic purposes.

Birth: The process by which a new human being enters the world and begins life outside the mother.

Birth canal: Passage formed by the vagina and the uterus when the cervix has completely opened up during labor.

Birth control: The prevention of birth.

Birth rate: The number of births during a specific period of time in relation to the total population of a certain area.

Blastocyst: The fertilized ovum during its second week of development when it is a hollow ball of cells.

Bulbourethral glands: Two small glands located on each side of the prostate that secrete into the male urethra.

Breast self-examination: A method in which a woman may routinely check her breasts and surrounding areas for signs of change that could indicate cancer.

Cardiovascular fitness: Well-being of the heart and circulatory system promoted through diet, weight management, and aerobic exercise; enhances the oxygen level in the blood.

Celibacy: A way of life that involves commitment to sexual abstinence.

Central nervous system: One of two main divisions of the nervous system made up of the brain and spinal cord, the main network of control and coordination for the body.

Cervical canal: The opening within the uterine cervix which protrudes into the vagina.

Cervical crypts: Indentations within the lining of the cervical canal that act as storage compartments for sperm.

Cervix: The lower necklike segment of the uterus that forms the passageway into the vagina.

Chromosomes: Threadlike bodies within the nucleus of a cell that make up strands of DNA (deoxyribonucleic acid). Chromosomes contain the genetic material that is passed on from parents to their children. Each normal cell in humans contains forty-six chromosomes arranged in twenty-three pairs from the time of conception.

Cilia: Small hairlike projections that line the surface of the fallopian tubes which create motion to direct the ova to the uterus.

Circumcision: Surgical removal of the foreskin of the penis or the hood of the clitoris.

Clitoris: The female organ devoted entirely to increasing sexual tension and providing pleasurable sensations when stimulated. It is the structure that corresponds to the glans penis in males and plays a key role in sexual response.

Coccyx: The tailbone or small bone located at the tip of the spine.

Coitus: The sexual union of two people of the opposite sex during which the penis is inserted into the vagina.

Coitus interruptus: See *Withdrawal Method.*

Colostrum: The substance that precedes the production of milk which is rich in protein and high in antibodies.

Conception: The physiological union of a sperm and an egg that initiates the growth of a new person and triggers the onset of pregnancy.

Conception control: The prevention of fertilization.

Condom: A soft, flexible sheath worn over an erect penis during lovemaking to prevent sperm from entering the vagina.

Contraception: Any drug, device, surgery, or method of family planning that prevents conception.

Contraction: A unit of work performed by a muscle over a period of time, including the rhythmic tightening of muscles during orgasm and the uterine muscles during childbirth.

Copulation: Sexual intercourse.

Corpus luteum: A term meaning "yellow body" that describes a small secretory structure that develops within an ovarian follicle after an egg is released.

Cystitis: Inflammation of the bladder and urinary tract. See *Urinary Tract Infection.*

Cystocele: The bulging of the bladder and the front wall into the vagina as the result of giving birth, advanced age, or surgery.

Deoxyribonucelic acid: (DNA) A large molecule carrying the genetic information within the chromosomes of a cell.

DES (diethystilbestrol): A synthetic estrogen used during the 1950s and 1960s to prevent miscarriage. In 1971, it was found to cause a rare form of vaginal cancer, and vaginal changes were discovered in a significant number of the daughters who were born to women who had taken DES during pregnancy.

Diaphragm: A dome-shaped latex device worn over the cervix during sexual intercourse to prevent sperm from entering the uterus.

Dilation: The normal increase in the size of a tube, blood vessel, or body opening.

Dilation and curettage (D & C): A surgical procedure in which the cervix is opened and the uterus is scraped with a small spoonlike instrument called a curette. Used to remove polyps or an overgrowth of uterine tissue, as a way of diagnosing cancer, and after childbirth to remove tissue retained by the uterus. Also a method of abortion involving the crushing of the unborn child and its extraction from the uterus.

Diuretic: Any drug which increases the passage of urine from the body. Used to prevent the excessive accumulation of fluid and commonly used as a treatment for high blood pressure.

Divorce: The separation of a married couple through legal means.

Douche: The cleansing of the vagina with fluid.

Dysmenorrhea: Painful menstruation resulting from the shape of the uterus and/or the process of menstruation. Prostaglandins have been linked to menstrual pain and antiprostaglandin medication such as ibuprofen often greatly relieves the pelvic discomfort associated with menstrual cramps.

Dyspareunia: Painful or difficult sexual intercourse.

Ectopic pregnancy: A pregnancy ocurring outside the uterus, usually in an oviduct.

Edema: The presence of an excessive amount of fluid in body tissues. Also referred to as fluid retention.

Ejaculation: The sudden release of semen from the male urethra. The feeling of ejaculation is called orgasm. It is a reflex action that occurs in two phases. First, sperm fluid and secretions from the prostate and bulbourethral gland are moved into the urethra. Second, strong muscular contractions force ejaculation. 200-300 million sperm are the average number of male sex cells contained in a single ejaculation.

Ejaculatory duct: The passage through which semen enters the urethra.

Embryo: In humans, an unborn child between the second and eighth week of pregnancy, a period that involves rapid growth, initial development of the major organ systems, and early formation of the main external features.

Emotion: The feeling part of human awareness. Physical changes often come with changes in emotion, whether the feelings are conscious or not.

Emotional response: A response to a specific feeling, occurring with physical changes that may or may not be obvious.

Empathy: The ability to know and share the emotions of another person and to understand the meaning of that person's behavior.

Endocervix: The membrane which lines the inner canal of the cervix.

Endocrine system: A system of ductless glands that secrete hormones into the bloodstream. These glands are the adrenals, ovaries, pancreas, pituitary, parathyroid, testicles, thymus, and thyroid.

Endometriosis: A growth of endometrial tissue outside of the uterus, thought to occur in about 15 percent of women. Women who do not get pregnant until later in life are more likely to get this disease, with the average age at diagnosis being thirty-seven. Pregnancy seems to prevent or correct this problem in some women. The most common symptoms of endometriosis are severe menstrual cramps and painful intercourse, painful bowel movements, and soreness above the pubic bones.

Endometrium: The lining of the inner surface of the uterus, consisting of three layers, with two of the layers being shed during each menstrual flow. The third layer provides the surface that theeaplacenta attaches to during pregnancy.

Endorphin: Any one of the substances of the nervous system made by the pituitary gland producing effects like that of morphine as a way of reducing pain within the body.

Engagement: The descent of the fetus into the pelvic cavity, occurring during late pregnancy or at some point in labor.

Engorgement: Swelling of the breasts with milk.

Epidemic: A disease that spreads rapidly through a part of the population.

Epididymis: A long, tightly coiled tube that carries sperm from the testicles to the vas deferens. Each testes has an epididymis attached to it that is approximately twenty feet in length.

Episiotomy: A surgical procedure performed during the second stage of childbirth in which the opening of the vagina is enlarged with a cut.

Erectile: A term used to describe tissue that is capable of being raised to an erect position as it fills with blood.

Erection: The condition of hardness, swelling, and raising of the penis or clitoris.

Estrogen: A hormone secreted by the ovaries that regulates the development of secondary sexual characteristics in women. Estrogen is also produced by the adrenal glands, testicles, and both the fetus and the placenta.

Fallopian tube: One of a pair of funnel-shaped tubes opening at one end into the uterus and at the other end into the pelvic cavity over the ovary. Ova pass through these tubes and are carried to the uterus by muscular contractions and the beating of hairlike structures called cilia. Fertilization of an egg usually takes place at the far end of the tube. Also called oviducts.

Female sexual dysfunction: The inability of a woman to enjoy participating in lovemaking or the inability to have an orgasm. Characteristics include pain, vaginal spasms, lack of sexual arousal, anxiety, fear, and negative feelings about sexual response.

Ferning test: A test for the presence of estrogen in cervical mucus which is an indication of fertility.

Fertile: Having the ability to reproduce offspring; fruitful; not sterile.

Fertile mucus: Cervical mucus that is capable of facilitating the transport of sperm through the female reproductive tract.

Fertile period: The time during the menstrual cycle during which fertilization may take place, beginning three to six days before ovulation and lasting for two to three days afterward.

Fetus: An unborn child after the eighth week of pregnancy.

Fibroid: A noncancerous tumor of the uterus, usually occurring in women between thirty and fifty years of age.

Fimbria: The fringelike borders of the open ends of the fallopian tubes.

Folic acid: A form of Vitamin B that is water soluble and is vital to the production of blood cells and hemoglobin, especially during pregnancy.

Follicle: A pouchlike recessed spot in the ovary, the place in which the ovum matures.

Follicle stimulating hormone (FSH): A pituitary gland hormone that stimulates the growth of graafian follicles in females and the production and maturation of sperm in males.

Foreskin: The loose fold of skin covering the end of the penis or clitoris.

Freudian: Referring to the concepts of Sigmund Freud (1856-1939), who stressed that the early years of childhood form the basis for later neurotic disorders.

Frigidity: The inability to respond to sexual stimulation.

FSH: The abbreviation for follicle stimulating hormone.

Fundus: The rounded portion of the uterus from which contractions originate during labor.

Gender: The specific sex of a person; male or female.

Gene: The basic unit of heredity in a chromosome that carries characteristics from parents to their child.

Generation: The act or process of reproduction; procreation.

Genesis: Origin; generation; the act of producing or procreating.

Genetic code: A code that fixes patterns of amino acids that are the building-blocks of body tissue proteins, determining the physical traits of an offspring.

Genetic engineering: The process of creating new DNA molecules.

Genitals: External sex organs.

Gestation: The period between conception and birth.

Gland: An organ of highly specialized cells capable of releasing material not related to its normal metabolism.

Glans: The sensitive tissue lying on the end of the penis and clitoris that is capable of swelling and hardening when filled with blood during sexual arousal.

Gonad: A primary sex organ; an ovary or a testis.

Gonorrhea: A common sexually transmitted disease that has few early symptoms in women and is capable of producing sterility if not treated early.

Graafian follicle: A mature ovarian sac that ruptures during ovulation to release a mature egg.

G-spot: A small spongelike structure lying on the front wall of the vagina behind the bladder that is responsive to sexual stimulation in some women.

Gynecology: The branch of medicine dealing with diseases of the female reproductive tract.

Healing: The process or act in which health is restored to the mind or body.

Health: A state of mental, physical, emotional, and spiritual well-being.

Health care provider: A person who provides health services to health care consumers.

Herpes genitalis: An infection caused by the herpes simplex II virus that is usually transmitted sexually and causes painful blisters on the skin and mucous membranes of the male and female genitals.

Homeostasis: A relatively steady state maintained by the body.

Hormone: Chemical substances produced by ductless glands in one part of the body that starts or runs the activity of an organ or a group of cells in another part of the body.

Hymen: The fold of mucous membrane, fibrous tissue, and skin that partially covers the vaginal entrance. When broken, small rounded elevations remain. These are referred to as hymenal tags.

Hypertension: High blood pressure.
Hysterectomy: The surgical removal of the uterus.

Implantation: Embedding of the developing baby in the lining of the uterus.
Incest: Sexual relations between family members.
Induced abortion: An intentional termination of a pregnancy before an unborn child has developed enough to survive outside of the uterus.
Infertile: The inability to produce offspring.
Intrauterine device: A form of contraception consisting of a bent strip of plastic or other material that is inserted into the uterus to prevent pregnancy; does not prevent ovulation or fertilization.
In vitro fertilization: Conception ocurring in laboratory apparatus.

Labia: The fleshy, liplike folds of skin at the opening of the vagina; the labia majora, forming the border of the vulva; and the labia minora, which extend from the clitoris backward on both sides of the vagina.
Labor: The series of stages during the process of childbirth through which the baby is born and the uterus returns to a normal state.
Lactation: The process of the production and secretion of milk from the breasts for the nourishment of an infant.
Let-down reflex: The ejection of breast milk from the milk glands resulting in the flow of milk from the nipple.
Levator ani: One of a pair of muscles lying at the base of the pelvis that stretches across the bottom of the pelvic cavity like a hammock as a support for the pelvic organs.
Lochia: The discharge from the uterus that flows from the vagina after a baby is born.
Luteal: Referring to the corpus luteum, its functions or its effects.
Luteinizing hormone: A hormone produced by the pituitary gland in both males and females. It stimulates the production of testosterone in men and the secretion of estrogen in women.

Male sexual dysfunction: An impaired or inadequate ability to participate in lovemaking which is usually psychological in origin.
Mammary gland: See *Breast.*
Mammogram: X-ray of the soft tissue of the breast used to identify various cysts or tumors.
Massage: The manipulation of the soft tissue of the body through stroking, kneading, rubbing, or tapping for the purpose of increasing circulation, improving muscle tone, and relaxation.
Mastectomy: The surgical removal of the breast.
Mastitis: Inflammation of the breast.

Masturbation: Sexual activity in which the penis or clitoris is stimulated by a means other than sexual intercourse.

Maternity cycle: The cycle that lasts from conception until six weeks after birth.

Menarche: The onset of menstruation and the beginning of the first menstrual cycle.

Menopause: The end of menstruation when the menses stop as a normal result of the decline of monthly hormonal cycles.

Menorrhea: Same as *Menstruation.*

Menses: The normal flow of blood and discarded uterine cells that takes place during menstruation.

Menstrual cycle: The cycle of hormonal changes that begins at puberty and repeats itself on a monthly basis unless interrupted by pregnancy, lactation, medication, or metabolic disorders.

Menstruation: The casting off of the lining of the nonpregnant uterus resulting in the periodic discharge of blood and mucosal tissue through the vagina.

Metabolism: The sum of all the chemical processes that take place in the body.

Miscarriage: The loss of a baby before the twenty-eighth week of pregnancy.

Mittelschmerz: The painful sensation that occurs in one side of the lower abdomen during ovulation.

Morning-after pill: A very large dose of estrogen taken orally within twenty-four to seventy-two hours after intercourse.

Mucus: The slippery, sticky secretion released by mucous membranes and glands.

Natal: Referring to birth.

Natural family planning: Any method of family planning that does not use drugs or devices to avoid pregnancy.

Nipple: A small cylindric bump positioned just below the center of each breast and containing fourteen to twenty openings to the milk ducts.

Noninvasive: Referring to any test, treatment, or procedure that does not invade the boundaries of the body.

Obstetrics: The branch of medicine dealing with pregnancy and childbirth.

Oogenesis: The growth of female eggs or ova.

Oral contraceptive: A steroid drug taken orally to produce infertility.

Orgasm: A series of strong, pleasurable, muscular contractions within the genitals that are triggered by intense sexual excitement and cannot be controlled once initiated.

Orgasmic platform: The tightening of the lower vagina during sexual arousal.

Osteoporosis: The loss of normal bone density marked by a thinning of bone tissue and the growth of small openings in the bone.

Ovary: One of the pair of primary sexual organs in females located on each side of the lower abdomen beside the uterus.

Oviduct: See *Fallopian Tube.*

Ovulation: The release of an egg, or ovum, from the ovary after the breaking of a follicle.

Ovulation method of family planning: A method of family planning that relies on the observation of the type and amount of cervical mucus secreted during the menstrual cycle as a means of predicting fertility.

Ova: Human eggs (singular: ovum).

Pap smear: A method of examining tissue cells shed by the cervix taken by collecting cells in the vagina and at the opening of the cervix.

Parasympathetic nervous system: The division of the autonomic nervous system that produces muscular relaxation and causes blood vessels to widen in the clitoris and the penis.

Peak mucus: A cloudy to clear white mucus coating the vaginal area during times of high estrogen levels at the most fertile point in the menstrual cycle.

Pelvic floor: The muscles and tissues that form the base of the pelvis.

Pelvic inflammatory disease: Inflammation of the female reproductive organs in the pelvis, often resulting in scarring, blocked fallopian tubes, and sterility.

Pelvic lifts: Conscious contractions of the pelvic floor muscles done for the purpose of improving muscle tone and sexual response. Also referred to as Kegels, after Dr. Arnold Kegel, a physician whose research proved the value of exercise to this area of the body.

Pelvic tilt: An exercise designed to strengthen the lower back and abdomen.

Pelvis: The bowl-shaped lower portion of the trunk of the body.

Penis: The male organ of urination and sexual intercourse made up of three circular masses of spongy tissue covered with skin.

Perineum: The part of the body lying between the inner thighs, with the buttocks to the rear and the sex organs to the front.

Petting: Sexual touching and fondling that does not include intercourse.

P.I.D.: See *Pelvic Inflammatory Disease.*

Pituitary gland: A small gland lying at the base of the brain that supplies many hormones to regulate a variety of processes within the body, including growth, reproduction, and lactation.

Pornography: Obscene materials that portray the sexual degradation and humiliation of women.

Polyp: A small, tumorlike growth that protrudes from a mucous membrane surface.

Postpartum: After childbirth.

Potent: The ability to have an erection or perform sexual intercourse.

Pregnancy: The growth and development of a new individual within a woman's uterus.

Premenstrual syndrome: The presence of a set of interrelated symptoms which recur regularly at the same phase of each menstrual cycle.

Premenstrual tension: The presence of emotional symptoms which recur regularly at the same phase of each menstrual cycle.

Prenatal: The period before birth.

Progesterone: The hormone secreted by the corpus luteum each month to prepare the sexual organs for pregnancy.

Progestin: Any one of a group of hormones, natural or synthetic, that have progesterone-like effects on the uterus.

Progestogen: See *Progestin.*

Prolactin: The hormone which is responsible for milk secretion that is released in response to the suckling of an infant at the breast.

Proliferative phase: The portion of the menstrual cycle between menstruation and ovulation.

Prostaglandins: A group of strong hormonelike fatty acids that act on certain organs. Used as a method of terminating pregnancy.

Prostate gland: A structure that surrounds the neck of the bladder and the beginning of the male urethra.

Psychosexual dysfunction: Any problem or disorder related to sexual responsiveness that is emotional in origin.

Pubic bone: One of the two bones that form the front part of the pelvis.

Rape: Sexual assault without consent.

Rectocele: The bulging of the rectum and the back wall of the vagina into the vagina occurring as the result of giving birth, advanced age, or surgery.

Rectum: The lower part of the large intestine lying above the anal canal.

Scrotum: The pouch of skin that holds the testicles.

Semen: The thick white-colored fluid released by the male sex organs for the purpose of transporting sperm.

Seminal fluid: See *Semen.*

Seminal vesicles: The saclike glands lying behind the bladder in the male that release fluid that forms part of the semen.

Sex: A division of male or female that is based on many characteristics, including body parts and genetic differences.

Sexual: Of or relating to sex.

Sexual abuse: Sexual contact without consent.

Sexual dysfunction: Difficulty related to sexual expression or experience due to a physical or emotional problem.

Sexual intercourse: See *Coitus.*

Sexual identity: How a person views their sexuality.

Sexuality: The sum total of the physical, functional, emotional, intellectual, and spiritual traits that are shown through a person's identity and behavior, whether related to the reproductive organs or to procreation.

Sexual role: The expression of a person's sexual identity.

Sexually transmitted disease (S.T.D.): A contagious disease that is spread through intimate sexual contact.

Side effect: A reaction resulting from medical treatment or therapy.

Slough: To cast off or shed dead cells from living tissue.

Smegma: A substance secreted by glands under the foreskin and at the base of the labia minora near the glans of the clitoris.

Spasm: A sudden, unconscious tightening of muscle.

Sperm: The male sex cell contained in semen that fertilizes the female sex cell, or ovum, in order to create a new human being.

Spermatogenesis: The process of sperm production.

Spermatic cord: A stringlike structure by which each testicle is attached to the body.

Spermicide: Any chemical substance that kills sperm cells.

Sphincter: A strong circular band of muscle that narrows a passage or closes off a natural opening in the body.

Staphylococcus aureus: A type of bacteria that produces a poison causing toxic shock syndrome.

Sterile: The condition of barrenness; the inability to produce children.

Sterilization: An act or process that renders a person incapable of reproduction.

Stress: Any factor that requires response or change on the part of an organism or an individual.

Stressor: Anything capable of causing wear and tear on the body's mental, physical, emotional, or spiritual resources.

Striae: Streaks or narrow furrows in the skin resulting from stretching. Also called stretch marks.

Sympathetic nervous system: A division of the autonomic nervous system that triggers the release of substances that speed up the heart, narrow blood vessels, and raise blood pressure.

Symptom: Something felt or noticed by an individual that can be used to detect what is going on within the body.

Sympto-thermal method of family planning: A method of family planning requiring fertility awareness that is based on the ovulation and basal body temperature methods of family planning.

Syphilis: A sexually transmitted disease caused by a type of bacteria called a spirochete.

Tactile: Of or relating to the sense of touch.
Tampon: A compact pack of absorbent material designed to soak up the menstrual flow within the vagina.
Tension: The condition of feeling strained or under pressure.
Testicle: See *Testis.*
Testis: One of the pair of primary sex organs, or gonads, that produce semen and testosterone.
Testosterone: A naturally secreted hormone in both males and females that is capable of producing masculine characteristics.
Therapy: The treatment of an abnormal condition.
Thromboembolism: A condition in which a blood vessel is blocked by a clot.
Toxic shock syndrome: A potentially fatal sudden disease associated with the use of tampons during menstruation caused by staphylococcus aureus.
Trimester: Period of three months; one of the three phases of pregnancy.
Tubal ligation: One of several sterilization procedures in which both fallopian tubes are sealed to prevent conception from taking place.
Tubal pregnancy: A pregnancy in which the fertilized ovum implants within the fallopian tube and cannot develop normally.
Tubercles of montgomery: Small glands that resemble pimples on the surface of the areola that release a fatty lubricative substance.

Urethra: The canal that carries urine from the bladder.
Urinary stress incontinence: The involuntary passage of urine when coughing, sneezing, or laughing resulting from poor sphincter control of the urethra.
Urinary tract: All of the structures involved in the release and elimination of urine from the body.
Urinary tract infection (U.T.I.): An infection of the urinary tract marked by frequency of urination, a painful burning sensation while voiding, and possibly pus in the urine.
Urogenital: Of or relating to the urinary and the reproductive systems.
Urology: The division of medicine concerned with the care of the urinary tract in men and women and of the male genital tract.
Use-effectiveness: The actual level of effectiveness of a contraceptive method.
Uterus: The thick-walled, hollow, muscular female organ of reproduction in which the fertilized ovum imbeds and an unborn child develops during pregnancy.

Vacuum aspiration: A method of abortion in which an unborn child and placenta are removed from the uterus by suction to end a pregnancy.

Vagina: The muscular tubelike membrane which forms the passageway between the uterus and the entrance between the external genitals. It receives the penis during intercourse and becomes the canal through which the baby passes during birth.

Vaginal discharge: Any discharge from the vagina.

Vaginismus: An involuntary tightening of the muscles surrounding the vagina caused by fear of painful intercourse or a pelvic examination.

Vaginitis: Inflammation and swelling of the vaginal tissues.

Vas deferens: One of a pair of tubes within the male reproductive tract through which sperm pass.

Vasectomy: A procedure which produces sterility by cutting a section out of each vas deferens.

Vasocongestion: The state in which blood vessels become overfull, causing tissue to swell during sexual arousal.

Virgin: A person who has never had sexual intercourse.

Virginity: The state of being a virgin.

Virile: A term used to describe one's masculine characteristics or fertility.

Virilism: The masculinization of a female.

Voyeur: A person who receives pleasure from observing the sexual anatomy or behavior of others.

Vulva: The external female genitals, including the labia majora, labia minora, and the clitoris.

Withdrawal method: A technique of conception control in which the penis is withdrawn from the vagina prior to ejaculation. Highly unreliable since the pre-ejaculatory fluid released through the urethra contains sperm. Also called coitus interruptus.

Woman-year: One year in the life of a fertile woman who is sexually active. Used to represent a unit of twelve months of exposure to the risk of pregnancy.

Womb: See *Uterus*

Wrongful life action: A lawsuit brought against a physician or health facility because an unwanted child was born.

X chromosome: The sex-determining chromosome carried by all ova and approximately one-half of the sperm. Its presence as a pair produces a female child.

Y chromosome: The sex-determining chromosome carried by about one-half of all sperm, never by an egg, that produces a male child.

Yeast infection: A fungal infection resulting in itching and inflammation of the vagina that is characterized by a thick white discharge and caused by the growth of candida albicans.

Zygote: The developing egg between the time of fertilization and its implantation in the wall of the uterus.

Notes

CHAPTER ONE

1. Smedes, Lewis B., *Sex for Christians* (Grand Rapids, MI: Eerdmans, 1976), p. 29.
2. Genesis 2:23.
3. Romans 1:23, 25.
4. 1 John 1:8.
5. Genesis 2:20-22 (NASB).
6. Genesis 1:27.
7. MacDonald, George, *Unspoken Sermons,* second series, Self-denial, 1885, in C. S. Lewis, *George MacDonald: An Anthology* (New York: Macmillan, 1947), p. 68.

CHAPTER TWO

1. Chambers, Oswald, *My Utmost for His Highest* (New York: Dodd, Mead and Co., 1935), p. 52.
2. Genesis 2:25.
3. 1 John 1:9.
4. 1 John 1:7.
5. 1 John 1:9.
6. Colossians 3:3.
7. Philippians 3:12-15.
8. Song of Songs 2:8-13.
9. Romans 8:1, 2.
10. Song of Songs 1:2, 13; 2:3, 4, 16a; 3:1.
11. Song of Songs 6:3; 8:6, 7.
12. 1 Corinthians 6:18.
13. Deuteronomy 5:18.
14. Psalm 100:3, 5 (NASB).
15. 1 Corinthians 6:16.
16. 1 Corinthians 7:4.
17. Ephesians 5:25.
18. Psalm 18:30-32.

CHAPTER THREE

1. Deutsch, Ronald M., *The Key to Feminine Response in Marriage* (New York: Ballantine, 1968), p. 137.
2. Wheelis, Alan, *The Quest for Identity* (New York: Norton, 1958), p. 174.
3. Romans 12:2, italics mine.

4. 1 Peter 1:3-6.
5. Matthew 20:28; Titus 3:7.
6. James 1:8.
7. 1 Peter 2:1, 2.
8. *Strong's Concordance.*
9. 1 Timothy 4:1-3.
10. 1 Timothy 4:7.
11. Jude 4, 8.
12. Jude 10.
13. Jude 12b, 13a.
14. James 3:17 (KJV), italics mine.
15. Proverbs 10:29.
16. 1 Corinthians 2:12, 14.
17. 1 Corinthians 3:18, 19.
18. 1 John 4:4.
19. 1 John 2:15-17.
20. Matthew 6:21.
21. Psalm 127:3, KJV; Gen. 49:25.
22. Keyes, Dick, *Beyond Identity; Finding Your Self in the Character and Image of God* (Ann Arbor, MI: Servant, 1984), pp. 216, 217.
23. Deuteronomy 30:15, 16, 19, 20a.

CHAPTER FOUR

1. Henry, Matthew, *Matthew Henry's Commentary,* Vol. 1 (Old Tappan, NJ: Revell), p. 20.
2. 1 Corinthians 3:16.
3. Romans 8:11.
4. 1 Corinthians 7:5.
5. Ephesians 4:25.
6. Ephesians 4:31.
7. Ephesians 4:29.
8. Ephesians 4:32; 5:1, 2.
9. Romans 12:9, 10, 16, 21.
10. Proverbs 18:16.
11. Luke 9:48.
12. Matthew 23:11.
13. 1 Corinthians 7:3.
14. Psalm 139:14.
15. Psalm 139:13-16.
16. Proverbs 18:22.

CHAPTER FIVE

1. Sidney, Algernon, in Tasha Tudor, *All for Love* (New York: Philomel, 1984), p. 17.
2. 1 Corinthians 7:4.
3. Song of Songs 2:16.
4. Psalm 95:1-7.
5. Psalm 107:22.
6. Psalm 22:3 (KJV).
7. Jeremiah 33:10, 11.
8. 1 Corinthians 6:20.
9. Song of Songs 2:3; 8:10.

CHAPTER SIX

1. Alcorn, Randy, *Christians in the Wake of the Sexual Revolution* (Portland, OR: Multnomah, 1985), pp. 177, 178.
2. See Song of Songs 1:9-15; 2:10-14; 4:1-15.
3. Song of Songs 5:1.
4. Song of Songs 5:2, 3.
5. Song of Songs 4:16; 5:1.
6. Song of Songs 7:7, 9; 6:2; 7:6.
7. James 1:17.
8. Psalm 85:8, 9.

CHAPTER SEVEN

1. Genesis 2:24.
2. Psalm 85:10-12.
3. Proverbs 5:18, 19 (NEB).
4. 1 Corinthians 7:5.
5. Galatians 5:22, 23.
6. Song of Songs 7:10-13 (NEB).

CHAPTER EIGHT

1. Stott, John, *Involvement, Vol. II: Social and Sexual Relationships in the Modern World* (Old Tappan, NJ: Revell, 1985), p. 140.
2. Psalm 139:23.
3. John 13:25.
4. Mark 10:16.
5. Psalm 143:8-10.

CHAPTER NINE

1. Trobisch, Ingrid, *The Joy of Being a Woman* (New York: Harper & Row, 1975).
2. Leviticus 15:19-21, 24, 31.

CHAPTER TEN

1. Pride, Mary, *The Way Home* (Westchester, IL: Crossway, 1985), p. 20.
2. Genesis 1:28; 9:1; 17:2, 20; 28:3.
3. Deuteronomy 1:10, 11.
4. Genesis 17:16; 20:18; 30:22; 1 Samuel 1:5, 19, 20; Isaiah 66:9; Job 33:4; Ruth 4:13; Isaiah 44:2; Psalm 139:13-16; Job 10:8, 9.
5. Genesis 3:16 (KJV).
6. Genesis 1:28.
7. Schaeffer, Francis A., *The Great Evangelical Disaster.* (Westchester, IL: Crossway, 1984), pp. 149, 150.
8. Revelation 7:17.
9. Proverbs 16:9.
10. 1 Corinthians 7:28.
11. Romans 12:1, 2 (NEB).
12. Wolfensberger, Wolf, Training Institute Publication Series, Syracuse, NY: Syracuse University, Vol. 5, No. 2, August 1985, p. 20.
13. Gibling, M. et al, "From Fantasy to Reality—An Interview with Malcolm Muggeridge," *Christianity Today*, April 21, 1978, p. 10.

14. Toufexis, A., "Birth Control: Vanishing Options," *Time,* September 1, 1986, p. 78.
15. Brown, H. "Not Enough Children," *Christianity Today*, October 18, 1985, p. 10.
16. Bonhoeffer, Dietrich, *Ethics* (New York: Macmillan, 1955 [1975]), pp. 180, 181.
17. Hosea 9:11, 14.
18. Luke 23:28, 29.
19. Luke 21:10-27.
20. Hilgers, T. W., *Fertility Appreciation: The Ovulation Method of Natural Family Planning* (Omaha, NE: Creighton University Natural Family Planning Education and Research Center, 1983), p. 45.
21. Hatcher, R., et al. *Contraceptive Technology 1984-1985* (New York: Irvington).
22. Isaiah 12:2.

CHAPTER ELEVEN

1. Peterson, Eugene H., *Earth and Altar* (Downers Grove, IL: InterVarsity Press, 1985), p. 163.
2. 2 Peter 1:3-8.
3. Sarrel, Lorna and Philip, "Sexual Passages—Pregnancy and Becoming Parents," *Redbook,* July 1979, p. 69.
4. Psalm 36:5-9 (NASB).

CHAPTER TWELVE

1. Lewis, C. S., *George MacDonald: An Anthology* (New York: Macmillan, 1947), pp. 100, 121.
2. Romans 8:6, 11.
3. Proverbs 31:25-30.
4. American Medical Association, *Health and Well-Being After 50* (New York: Random House, 1984), p. 74.
5. Acts 9:36.
6. Proverbs 3:5-8.

CHAPTER THIRTEEN

1. Shedd, Charlie W., *The Fat Is in Your Head* (Waco, TX: Word, 1972), p. 106.
2. Colossians 3:10.
3. Zephaniah 3:17.

CHAPTER FOURTEEN

1. MacDonald, George, *The Lost Princess* (orig. 1875).
2. Proverbs 31:10, 11, 30 (NASB).
3. Proverbs 15:33 (NEB).
4. Psalm 24:34 (KJV).
5. 1 Peter 3:4 (NEB).
6. 1 Peter 3:4 (NASB).
7. Romans 7:14-25.
8. Romans 7:24, 25.
9. Luke 10:42.
10. Matthew 26:8.
11. Matthew 26:13.
12. Colossians 3:12-14 (NEB).
13. Proverbs 18:12.

14. Proverbs 14:30.
15. Proverbs 14:33.
16. Proverbs 27:19.
17. Psalm 51:7-12.

CHAPTER FIFTEEN

1. Schaeffer, Edith, *What Is a Family?* (Old Tappan, NJ: Revell, 1975), p. 80.
2. John 1:14.
3. Proverbs 14:1.
4. Proverbs 14:3.
5. James 3:17, 18.
6. Matthew 12:33-37.
7. James 3:10.
8. Ecclesiastes 3:7.
9. Proverbs 15:23, italics mine.
10. Psalm 139:1-6.
11. Psalm 139:24.
12. Psalm 19:14.
13. Isaiah 30:15.
14. Philippians 4:8.
15. 2 Corinthians 10:5.
16. Colossians 3:2.
17. Matthew 6:24-34; Colossians 3:13; Philippians 2:14; Colossians 3:8.
18. Colossians 3:10.
19. Proverbs 31:10, 25, 26.
20. Proverbs 31:26 (KJV).
21. *Scribner-Bantam English Dictionary,* 1979.
22. Proverbs 27:15.
23. Proverbs 25:24.
24. Proverbs 15:4.
25. Proverbs 15:1.
26. Song of Songs 7:11-13.
27. Hebrews 4:15, 16.
28. Psalm 27:4-6, 14 (NASB).
29. Psalm 61:2.
30. Proverbs 18:21 (NEB).

CHAPTER SIXTEEN

1. Hebrews 13:4.
2. Press, Aric, "The War Against Pornography," *Newsweek,* March 18, 1985, p. 58.
3. Matthew 5:27, 28.
4. Ephesians 5:28.
5. 2 Corinthians 5:17.
6. Romans 6:4.

CHAPTER SEVENTEEN

1. Capon, Robert Farrar, *Bed and Board: Plain Talk About Marriage* (New York: Fireside, 1965), pp. 70, 71.
2. *Ibid.,* p. 76.
3. Psalm 30:1-5, 11, 12.

Bibliography

*Books expanding on themes presented in *The Mystery of Womanhood* that would be useful as additional reading. Check your local library or Christian bookstore for these titles.

Books

Adams, J. *Understanding and Managing Stress.* San Francisco, CA: University Association, 1980.

Ahlem, L. *Living with Stress.* Ventura, CA: Regal Books, 1978.

Alcorn, R. *Christians in the Wake of the Sexual Revolution.* Portland, OR: Multnomah, 1985.

*Aguilar, N. *The New No-Pill, No-Risk Birth Control.* New York: Rawson, 1986.

American Medical Association. *Health and Well-Being After 50.* New York: Random House, 1984.

American Medical Association. *Women: How to Understand Your Symptoms.* New York: Random House, 1986.

Beals, P. *Parent's Guide to the Childbearing Year.* Minneapolis: International Childbirth Education Association, 1975.

Bennet, J. P. *Chemical Contraception.* New York: Columbia University Press, 1974.

Benson, H. *The Relaxation Response.* New York: Avon, 1975.

Billings, E. and Westmore, A. *The Billings Method—Controlling Fertility Without Drugs or Devices.* New York: Random House, 1980.

Bing, E. and Colman, L. *Making Love During Pregnancy.* New York: Bantam, 1977.

Blitchington, W. P. *Sex Roles and the Christian Family.* Wheaton, IL: Tyndale, 1981.

*Bloesch, D. G. *Is the Bible Sexist? Beyond Feminism and Patriarchalism.* Westchester, IL: Crossway, 1982.

Blumenfeld, S. L. *The Retreat from Motherhood.* New Rochelle, NY: Arlington House, 1975.

Bonhoeffer, D. *Ethics.* New York: Macmillan, 1965.

*Brand, P. and Yancey, P. *Fearfully and Wonderfully Made.* Grand Rapids, MI: Zondervan, 1980.

*Brand, P. and Yancey, P. *In His Image.* Grand Rapids, MI: Zondervan, 1984.

Brazelton, T. B. *On Becoming a Family: The Growth of Attachment.* New York: Delacorte Press/Seymour Lawrence, 1981.

Brestin, S. and Brestin, D. *Building Your House on the Lord: Marriage and Parenthood.* Wheaton, IL: Harold Shaw, 1980.

Budoff, P. W. *No More Menstrual Cramps and Other Good News.* New York: G. P. Putnam's Sons, 1980.

Burt, J. and Meeks, L. *Education for Sexuality,* 3rd ed. New York: Holt, Rinehart and Winston, 1985.

Calderone, M. S. and Johnson, E. *The Family Book About Sexuality.* New York: Bantam, 1981.

Capon, R. F. *Bed and Board: Plain Talk About Marriage.* New York: Simon and Schuster, 1965.

Carlson, C. *Corrie Ten Boom: Her Life and Faith.* Old Tappan, NJ: Revell, 1983.

*Cavnar, R. *Winning at Losing.* Ann Arbor, MI: Servant, 1983.

Chambers, O. *My Utmost for His Highest.* New York: Dodd and Mead, 1935.

Clarke, J. I. *Self-Esteem: A Family Affair.* Minneapolis: Winston, 1978.

*Cole, C. D. *Basic Christian Faith.* Westchester, IL: Crossway, 1985.

Colman, A. D. and Colman, L. *Pregnancy—The Psychological Experience.* New York: Herder and Herder, 1972.

*Colson, Charles. *Loving God.* Grand Rapids, MI: Zondervan, 1983.

*Cooper, K. *The Aerobics Program for Total Well-Being.* New York: M. Evans, 1982.

Dalton, K. *The Premenstrual Syndrome.* Springfield, IL: Charles C. Thomas, 1964.

Davis, B. and Wright, G. *Hugs and Kisses.* New York: Workman, 1977.

Delitzsch, F. *Commentary on the Song of Songs and Ecclesiastes.* Grand Rapids, MI: Eerdman's, n.d.

Deutsch, H. *The Psychology of Women,* Vol. II. New York: Grune and Stratton, 1945.

*Deutsch, R. *Realities of Nutrition.* Palo Alto, CA: Bull Publishing, 1976.

*_____. *The Key to Feminine Response in Marriage.* New York: Ballantine, 1968.

Dillow, J. *Solomon on Sex.* Nashville: Thomas Nelson, 1977.

Douglas, J. D. *The New Bible Dictionary*. Grand Rapids, MI: Eerdman's, 1962.

Eheart, B. K. and Martel, S. K. *The Fourth Trimester: On Becoming a Mother*. New York: Ballantine, 1984.

*Evans, D. *The Complete Book on Childbirth*. Wheaton, IL: Tyndale, 1986.

Everly, G. and Girdano, D. *Controlling Stress and Tension*. Englewood Cliffs, NJ: Prentice-Hall, 1979.

Ewy, D. *Preparation for Parenthood: How to Create a Nurturing Family*. New York: Plume, 1985.

Finch, B. E. and Green, H. *Contraception Through the Ages*. London: Peter Owen, 1963.

Fraiberg, S. *Every Child's Birthright: In Defense of Mothering*. New York: Bantam, 1977.

Friedman, R. C. *Behavior and the Menstrual Cycle*. New York: Marcel Dekker, 1982.

Gannon, L. R. *Menstrual Disorders and Menopause: Biological, Psychological and Cultural Research*. New York: Praeger, 1985.

*Guilder, George. *Sexual Suicide*. New York: Quadrangle, 1973.

Hafen, B. *Nutrition, Food and Weight Control*. Boston: Allyn and Bacon, 1981.

Hatcher, R., et al. *Contraceptive Technology, 1984-1985*. New York: Irvington, 1984.

Henry, C. F. H. *Baker's Dictionary of Christian Ethics*. Grand Rapids, MI: Baker, 1973.

Henry, M. *Matthew Henry's Commentary*, Vol 1. Grand Rapids, MI: Baker, 1983.

Hilgers, T. W. *Fertility Appreciation: The Ovulation Method of Natural Family Planning*. Omaha, NE: Creighton University Natural Family Planning Education and Research Center, 1983.

Hotchner, T. *Pregnancy and Childbirth*. New York: Avon, 1976.

Howard, J. G. *The Trauma of Transparency*. Portland: Multnomah, 1979.

Huggins, K. *The Nursing Mother's Companion*. Cambridge, MA: Harvard Press, 1986.

Hurley, James B. *Man and Woman in Biblical Perspective*. Grand Rapids, MI: Zondervan, 1981.

Jelliffe, D. and Jelliffe, E. F. P. *Human Milk in the Modern World*. Oxford: Oxford University Press, 1978.

Jones, J. M., et al. *Women's Health Management: Guidelines for Nurse Practitioners*. Reston, VA: Reston, 1984.

Jones, K. L., et al. *Health Science*, 5th ed. New York: Harper and Row, 1985.

Joy, D. M. *Re-bonding: Preventing and Restoring Damaged Relationships.* Waco, TX: Word, 1986.

Kaplan, H. S. *The New Sex Therapy.* New York: Brunner/Mazel, 1974.

Keirsey, D. and Bates, M. *Please Understand Me.* Del Mar, CA: Prometheus Nemesis, 1984.

Keith, L. G. *The Safety of Fertility Control.* New York: Springer, 1980.

*Keyes, D. *Beyond Identity: Finding Your Self in the Character and Image of God.* Ann Arbor, MI: Servant, 1984.

Keyser, H. H. *Women Under the Knife.* Philadelphia: George F. Stickley, 1984.

Kippley, J. and Kippley, S. *The Art of Natural Family Planning,* 3rd ed. Cincinnati: Couple-to-Couple League, 1984.

Kippley, S. *Breastfeeding and Natural Child Spacing.* New York: Penguin, 1975.

Ladas, A. K. and Whipple, B. *The G-Spot.* New York: Holt, Rinehart and Winston, 1982.

LaHaye, T. and LaHaye, B. *The Act of Marriage.* Grand Rapids, MI: Zondervan, 1976.

Lance, K. and Agardy, M. *Total Sexual Fitness for Women.* New York: Rawson and Wade, 1981.

Lauersen, N. and Whitney, S. *It's Your Body: A Woman's Guide to Gynecology.* New York: Grossett and Dunlap, 1977.

Lawrence, R. *Breastfeeding—A Guide for the Medical Profession.* St. Louis: C. V. Mosby, 1980.

Leifer, M. *Psychological Effects of Motherhood—A Study of First Pregnancy.* New York: Praeger, 1980.

Lewis, C. S. *George MacDonald: An Anthology.* New York: Macmillan, 1946.

———. *The Four Loves.* London: Fontana, 1963.

———. *Mere Christianity.* New York: Macmillan, 1943.

Linn, D. and Linn, M. *Healing Life's Hurts.* New York: Paulist Press, 1978.

Lynch, J. J. *The Broken Heart: The Medical Consequences of Loneliness.* New York: Basic Books, 1977.

*Macaulay, Susan Schaeffer. *Something Beautiful from God.* Westchester, IL: Crossway, 1980.

*———. *How to Be Your Own Selfish Pig.* Elgin, IL: David C. Cook, 1982.

Masters, W. H. and Johnson, V. E. *Human Sexual Response.* Boston: Little, Brown and Co., 1966.

———. *Human Sexual Inadequacy.* Boston: Little, Brown and Co., 1970.

———. *Masters and Johnson on Sex and Human Loving.* Boston: Little, Brown and Co., 1986.

Montagu, A. *Touching: The Human Significance of the Skin.* New York: Harper and Row, 1978.

McCary, J. L. *Human Sexuality*, 2nd edition. New York: D. Van Nostrand, 1973.

The Mosby Medical Encyclopedia. New York: New American Library, 1985.

Moulton, R. G. *Lyric Idyl: Solomon's Song in the Literary Study of the Bible.* London: Isbiter, 1903.

Narramore, B. *You're Someone Special.* Grand Rapids, MI: Zondervan, 1978.

Navigator Studies. *God's Design for the Family,* Books 1-4. Colorado Springs: Navpress, 1980.

Nelson, E. C., et al. *Medical and Health Guide for People Over 50.* Washington, DC: American Association of Retired Persons, 1986.

Newton, N. *Maternal Emotions: A Study of Women's Feelings About Menstruation, Pregnancy, Childbirth, Infant Care and Other Aspects of Their Femininity.* New York: Harper and Brothers (Paul B. Hoeber Medical Book Dept.), 1955.

_____. *The Family Book of Child Care.* New York: Harper and Row, 1957.

Nilssen, L. *A Child Is Born.* New York: Dell, 1978.

Notman, M. T. and Natelson, C. C. *Sexual and Reproductive Aspects of Women's Health Care.* New York: Plenum, 1978.

*Nystrom, Carolyn. *Before I Was Born.* Westchester, IL: Crossway, 1984.

Paul, B. *Health, Culture, and Community.* New York: Russell Sage, 1955.

Penner, C. and Penner, J. *The Gift of Sex.* Waco, TX: Word, 1981.

Peterson, E. H. *A Long Obedience in the Same Direction: Discipleship in an Instant Society.* Downer's Grove, IL: InterVarsity, 1980.

_____. *Earth and Altar: The Community of Prayer in a Self-Bound Society.* Downer's Grove, IL: InterVarsity, 1985.

Pocs, Ollie. *Human Sexuality 84/85.* Guilford, CT: Dushkin, 1984.

Powell, J. *The Secret of Staying in Love.* Allen, TX: Argus, 1974.

_____. *Why Am I Afraid to Love?* Allen, TX: Argus, 1972.

_____. *Why Am I Afraid to Tell You Who I Am?* Allen, TX: Argus, 1969.

Pride, M. *The Way Home: Beyond Feminism, Back To Reality.* Westchester, IL: Crossway, 1985.

Pryor, K. *Nursing Your Baby.* New York: Pocket Books, 1973.

Rakowitz, E. and Rubin, G. S. *Living with Your New Baby.* New York: Berkley, 1980.

Raphael, D. *The Tender Gift: Breastfeeding.* New York: Schocken, 1978.

Redford, M. H., et al. *The Condom: Increasing Utilization in the United States.* San Francisco: San Francisco Press, 1974.

Roetzer, J. *Family Planning the Natural Way.* Old Tappan, NJ: Revell, 1981.

Schaeffer, E. *Common Sense Christian Living*. Nashville: Thomas Nelson, 1983.

*_____. *Lifelines: The Ten Commandments for Today*. Westchester, IL: Crossway, 1983.

_____. *What Is a Family?* Old Tappan, NJ: Revell, 1975.

Schaeffer, F. *Genesis in Space and Time*. Downers Grove, IL: InterVarsity, 1972.

*_____. *Letters of Francis A. Schaeffer*. Lane T. Dennis, ed. Westchester, IL: Crossway, 1985.

*_____. and Koop, C. E. *Whatever Happened to the Human Race?* Old Tappan, NJ: Revell, 1979.

Schrotenboer, K. and Subak-Sharpe, G. *Freedom from Menstrual Cramps*. New York: Pocket, 1981.

Seaman, B. *The Doctor's Case Against the Pill*. Garden City, NY: Doubleday, 1980.

Selye, H. *Stress: General Adaptation Syndrome and the Disease of Adaptation*. Montreal: ACTA, 1950.

Shedd, C. *The Fat Is in Your Head*. Waco, TX: Word, 1972.

*Shettles, L. and Rorvik, D. *Rites of Life: The Scientific Evidence of Life Before Birth*. Grand Rapids, MI: Zondervan, 1984.

Simon, S. *Caring, Feeling, Touching*. Allen, TX: Argus, 1976.

*Smedes, L. *Sex for Christians*. Grand Rapids, MI: Eerdmans, 1976.

_____. *Forgive and Forget*. New York: Harper & Row, 1984.

*Sproul, R. C. *Ethics and the Christian*. Wheaton, IL: Tyndale, 1983.

_____. *The Holiness of God*. Wheaton, IL: Tyndale, 1985.

Stoppard, M. *Being a Well Woman*. New York: Holt, Rinehart and Winston, 1982.

Storch, M. *How to Relieve Menstrual Cramps and Other Menstrual Problems*. New York: Workman, 1982.

Stott, J. *Involvement: Social and Sexual Relationships in the Modern World*. Old Tappan, NJ: Revell, 1984.

Stuart, R. B. and Davis, B. *Slim Chance in a Fat World*. Champaign, IL: Research Press, 1978.

Thielicke, H. *The Ethics of Sex*. Grand Rapids, MI: Baker, 1975.

Trobisch, I. and Roetzer, E. *An Experience of Love—Understanding Natural Family Planning*. Old Tappan, NJ: Revell, 1982.

Trobisch, I. *The Joy of Being a Woman*. New York: Harper and Row, 1975.

Trobisch, W. *A Baby Just Now?* Downer's Grove, IL: InterVarsity, 1978.

*_____. *I Married You*. New York: Harper and Row, 1971.

*_____. *I Loved a Girl*. London: Lutterworth, 1970.

_____. *Love Yourself: Self-Acceptance and Depression*. Downer's Grove, IL: InterVarsity, 1976.

Vitz, P. C. *Psychology As Religion: The Cult of Self-Worship.* Grand Rapids, MI: Eerdmans, 1977.

Voda, A. M., et al. *Changing Perspectives on Menopause.* Austin, TX: University of Texas, n.d.

Wangerin, W. *Ragman and Other Cries of Faith.* New York: Harper and Row, 1984.

Ward, T. *Values Begin at Home.* Wheaton, IL: Victor, 1979.

Weideger, P. *Menstruation and Menopause: The Physiology and Psychology, The Myth and the Reality.* New York: Knopf, 1976.

Whelan, E. M. *A Baby? . . . Maybe.* New York: Bobbs-Merrill, 1975.

Wright, N. H. *Communication: The Key to Your Marriage.* Ventura, CA: Regal, 1974.

_____. *The Pillars of Marriage.* Ventura, CA: Regal, 1979.

*Young, C. *The Least of These: What Everyone Should Know About Abortion.* Chicago, IL: Moody Press, 1983.

Zatuchni, G. I., et al. *Vaginal Contraception: New Developments.* Hagerstown, MD: Harper and Row, 1979.

Articles

Abplanalp, J. M. et al. "Psychoendocrinology of the Menstrual Cycle: I. Enjoyment of Everyday Activities and Mood." *Psychosomatic Medicine,* 41 (1979), pp. 587-604.

_____. "Psychoendocrinology of the Menstrual Cycle: II. The Relationship Between Enjoyment of Activities, Moods, and Reproductive Hormones." *Psychosomatic Medicine,* 41 (1979), pp. 605-615.

Abramson, M. and Torghele, J. R. "Weight, Temperature Changes and Psychosomatic Symptomatology in Relation to the Menstrual Cycle." *American Journal of Obstetrics and Gynecology,* 81 (1961), pp. 223-232.

Ager, J. W. et al. "Vasectomy: Who Gets One and Why?" *American Journal of Public Health,* 640 (1974), p. 680.

Akiksal, H. S. "A Biochemical Approach to Depression." In R. A. Depue, *The Psychology of the Depressive Disorders: Implications for the Effects of Stress.* New York: Academic Press, 1979.

Allen, F. D. "Menopause: Crisis or Opportunity? *The Female Patient,*" 6 (1981), pp. 72-74.

Anthanasion, R. et al. "Sex." *Psychology Today,* 4 (1970), pp. 37-52.

Askel, S. "Luteinizing Hormone—Releasing Hormone and the Human Menstrual Cycle. *American Journal of Obstetrics and Gynecology,* 135(1) (1979), pp. 96-100.

Aslan, S. et al. "Stress and Age Effects on Catecholamines in Normal Subjects." *Journal of Psychosomatic Research,* 25 (1981), pp. 33-41.

Barone, M. "Era of Sexual Restraint Returns as Social History Repeats Itself." *Washington Post,* August 1986.

Berger, L. R. "Factors Influencing Breast-feeding." *JCE Family Medicine,* October 1978, pp. 11-27.

Bernstein, G. S. "Conventional Methods of Contraception:" Condom, Diaphragm, and Vaginal Foam." *Clinical Obstetrics and Gynecology,* 17 (1974), p. 21.

———. "Physiological Aspects of Vaginal Contraception." *Contraception,* 9 (1974), p. 333.

Brooks-Gunn, J. and Ruble, D. "The Menstrual Attitude Questionnaire." *Psychosomatic Medicine,* 42 (1980), pp. 503-512.

Brown, H. "Not Enough Children." *Christianity Today,* October 18, 1985, p. 10.

Brown, M. A. "Social Support, Stress and Health: A Comparison of Expectant Mothers and Fathers." *Nursing Research,* 35 (2) (1986), pp. 72-76.

Budoff, P. W. "The Use of Prostaglandin Inhibitors for the Premenstrual Syndrome." *Journal of Reproductive Medicine,* 28 (1983), pp. 469-478.

———. "Use of Mefenamic Acid in the Treatment of Primary Dysmenorhea." *JAMA,* 241 (25) (1979), pp. 2713-2716.

Burchfield, S. R. "The Stress Response: A New Perspective." *Psychosomatic Medicine,* 41 (1979), pp. 661-672.

Carey, J. "The Message About Massage." *Newsweek,* October 15, 1984, p. 110.

Chan, W. Y. et al. "Prostaglandins in Primary Dysmenorhea." *American Journal of Medicine,* 70 (1981), pp. 535-541.

Clark, A. "Sex During and After Pregnancy." *American Journal of Nursing,* 74 (1974), p. 1430.

Connell, E. "The Risk of Being Female." In *The Safety of Fertility Control,* L. Keith, ed. New York: Springer, 1980.

Copeland, J. "Are Health Clubs Risky?" *Newsweek,* February 17, 1986, p. 62.

Cooke, D. J. and Greene, J. G. "Types of Life Events in Relation to Symptoms of the Climactericum." *Journal of Psychosomatic Research,* 25 (1981), pp. 5-11.

Coulam, C. B. "Age, Estrogen and the Psyche." *Clinical Obstetrics and Gynecology,* 24 (1981), pp. 219-229.

Curtis, P. et al, "Uterine Responses to Three Techniques of Breast Stimulation." *Obstetrics and Gynecology,* 67 (1986), pp. 25-27.

Dalton, K. "Cyclical Criminal Acts in the Premenstrual Syndrome." *Lancet,* ii (1980), pp. 1070ff.

Dalton, K. "Premenstrual Tension: An Overview. In *Behavior and the*

Menstrual Cycle, R. C. Friedman, ed. New York: Marcel Dekker, 1982.

Davis, J. E. "Risks and Benefits of Vasectomy." In *The Safety of Fertility Control,* L. Keith, ed. New York: Springer, 1980.

Debrovner, C. H. "Medical, Psychological and Social Aspects of Contraceptive Choice." *Medical Aspects of Human Sexuality,* July 1976, p. 33.

Dimsdale, J. E. and Moss, J. "Short-term Catecholamine Response to Psychological Stress." *Psychosomatic Medicine,* 42 (1980), pp. 493-497.

d'Orban, P. T. and Dalton, K. "Violent Crime and the Menstrual Cycle." *Psychological Medicine,* 10 (1980), pp. 353-359.

Duin, J. "We Must Learn to Celebrate Celibacy." *Christianity Today,* March 21, 1986, p. 13.

Edmondson, D. "Birth Control: What You Need to Know." *Parent's,* October 1986, pp. 156-162.

Ellis, D. "Sexual Needs and Concerns of Expectant Parents." *JOGN Nursing,* September/October 1980, pp. 306-308.

Falicov, C. J. "Sexual Adjustment During Pregnancy and Postpartum." *American Journal of Obstetrics and Gynecology,* 117 (1973), p. 991.

Flint, M. "The Menopause: Reward or Punishment?" *Psychosomatic Medicine,* 16 (1975), pp. 161-163.

Ford, C. S. "A Comparative Study of Human Reproduction." *Anthropology,* 32 (1964), pp. 1-111.

_____. "Psychological Factors Influencing the Choice of Contraceptive Method." *Medical Aspects of Human Sexuality,* January 1978, p. 91.

Frank, E., et al. "Frequency of Sexual Dysfunction in 'Normal' Couples." *New England Journal of Medicine,* 299(3) (1978), p. 115.

Frank, E. P. "What Are Nurses Doing to Help PMS Patients?" *American Nursing,* February 1986, pp. 137-140.

Frank, R. T. "The Hormonal Causes of Premenstrual Tension." *Archives Neurological Psychiatry,* 26 p. 2053.

Friedrich, E. G. et al. "Tampon Associated Vaginal Ulcerations." *Obstetrics and Gynecology,* 55(2) (1980), pp. 149-156.

Frey, K. A. "Middle-aged Women's Experience and Perception of Menopause." *Women and Health,* 6 (1982), pp. 25-36.

George Washington University Medical Center. "Condom: An Old Method Meets a New Social Need. Barrier Methods." Population Reports, Series H, No. 1.

_____. "The Diaphragm and Other Intravaginal Barriers: A Review. Barrier Methods." Population Reports, Series H, No. 4.

Gibling, M. et al. "From Fantasy to Reality—An Interview with Malcolm Muggeridge." *Christianity Today,* April 21, 1978, pp. 6-10.

Glass, R. et al. "Use-effectiveness of the Condom in a Selected Family

Planning Clinic Population in the United Kingdom." *Contraception,* 10 (1974), p. 591.

Goldsmith, M. F. "Sexually Transmitted Diseases May Reverse the 'Revolution.'" *JAMA,* 255 (13) (1986), pp. 1665-1672.

Green, J. "Recent Trends in the Treatment of Premenstrual Syndrome: A Critical Review." In *Behavior and the Menstrual Cycle,* Friedman, R. C., ed. New York: Springer, 1982.

Greene, R. and Dalton, K. "The Premenstrual Syndrome." *British Medical Journal,* May 1953, pp. 1007-1014.

Halbreich, U. and Endicott, J. "Classification of Premenstrual Syndromes." In *Behavior and the Menstrual Cycle,* R. C. Friedman, ed. New York: Marcel Dekker, 1982.

Hames, C. T. "Sexual Needs and Interests of Postpartum Couples." *JOGN Nursing,* September/October 1980, pp. 312-315.

Harrison, B. G. "Does Sex Appeal to Women?" *Mademoiselle,* June 1985, p. 102.

Helsing, E. "Women's Liberation and Breastfeeding. Symposium on Breast-feeding." *Environment and Child Health,* Monograph No. 43, October 1975, pp. 34-36.

Heneson, N. "The Selling of PMS." *Science '84,* May 1984, pp. 66-71.

Hill, E. C. "Your Morality or Mine? An Inquiry into the Ethics of Human Reproduction." *American Journal of Obstetrics and Gynecology,* 154(6) (1986), pp. 1173-1180.

Holmes, T. H. and Rahe, R. "Stress Rating Scale." *Journal of Psychosomatic Research,* 2 (1967), p. 216.

Hopson, J. and Rosenfeld, A. "PMS: Puzzling Monthly Symptoms." *Psychology Today,* August 1984, pp. 30-35.

Huffman, S. L. "Determinants of Breast-feeding in Developing Countries: Overview and Policy Implications." *Studies in Family Planning,* 15(4) (1984), pp. 170-183.

Hurt, S. W. et al. "Psychopathology and the Menstrual Cycle." In *Behavior and the Menstrual Cycle,* R. C. Friedman, ed. New York: Springer, 1982.

Jelliffe, D. B. and Jelliffe, E. F. P. "Breast Is Best: Modern Meanings." *New England Journal of Medicine,* 259 (1977), pp. 912-915.

Jones, E. "Vasectomy Sequelae: Empirical Studies." *Journal of Reproductive Medicine,* 19 (1977), p. 254.

Kantrowitz, B. "More Bad News About Sex." *Newsweek,* April 21, 1986, pp. 70, 71.

Kemmann, E. "The Female Climacteric." *American Family Physician,* 20(5) (1979), pp. 14-151.

Kenny, J. A. "Sexuality of Pregnant and Breast-feeding Women." *Archives Sexual Behavior,* 2(3) (1973), pp. 215-229.

Kitzinger, S. "Sex After the Baby Comes. *The Pennypress* (1980).

Knable, J. "Hand Holding: One Means of Transcending Barriers of Communication." *Heart and Lung*, 10(6) (1981), pp. 1106-1110.

Klebanoff, M. A. et al. "Epidemiology of Vomiting in Early Pregnancy." *Obstetrics and Gynecology*, 66(5) (1985), pp. 612-616.

Konner, M. and Worthman, C. "Nursing Frequency, Gonadal Function and Birth Spacing Among !Kung Hunter-gatherers." *Science*, 207 (1980), pp. 788-791.

Krantz, K. E. "The Innervation of the Human Vulva and Vagina, A Microscopic Study." *Obstetrics and Gynecology*, 12 (1958), pp. 363, 364.

Lahmeyer, H. W. et al. "Anxiety and Mood Fluctuation in the Normal Menstrual Cycle." *Psychosomatic Medicine*, 44 (1982), pp. 183-194.

Lane, M. E. "Benefits and Risks of the Diaphragm and Condom Use." In *Risks, Benefits and Controversies of Fertility Control*, J. J. Sciarra, Zatuchni, G. I., and Speidel, J. J., eds. New York: Harper and Row, 1978.

Larkin, R. M. et al. "Dysmenorrhea: Treatment with an Antiprostaglandin." *Obstetrics and Gynecology*, 54 (1979), pp. 456-460.

Larsson-Cohn, V. "Oral Contraceptives and Vitamins: A Review." *American Journal of Obstetrics and Gynecology*, 121 (1975), pp. 84-90.

Larwin, R. B. "The Song of Songs and Its Modern Usage." *Christianity Today*, August 3, 1962.

Leander, K. and Grassley, J. "Making Love After Birth." *Birth and the Family Journal*, 7(3) (1980), pp. 181-185.

Leff, J. and Israel, M. "The Relationship Between Mode of Masturbation and Achievement of Orgasm in Coitus." *Archives of Sexual Behavior*, 12 (3) (1983), pp. 227-236.

Lo Piccolo, J. and Lobitz, W. "The Role of Masturbation in the Treatment of Orgasmic Dysfunction." *Archives of Sexual Behavior*, 2 (1972), pp. 163-171.

Lyon, K. E. and Lyon, M. A. "The Premenstrual Syndrome: A Survey of Current Treatment Practices." *Journal of Reproductive Medicine*, 29 (1984), pp. 705-711.

Majewski, J. L. "Conflicts, Satisfactions and Attitudes During Transition to the Maternal Role." *Nursing Research*, 35(1) (1986), pp. 10-14.

Mandell, A. J. and Mandell, A. P. "Suicide and the Menstrual Cycle." *American Medical Association Journal*, 200 (1967), pp. 792, 793.

Marshall, J. "Thermal Changes in the Normal Menstrual Cycle." *British Medical Journal*, January 1963, pp. 102-104.

Matthews, K. A. and Carra, J. "Suppression of Menstrual Distress Symptoms: A Study of Type A Behavior." *Personal Social Psychological Bulletin*, 8 (1982), pp. 146-151.

May, R. R. "Mood Shifts and the Menstrual Cycle." *Journal of Psychosomatic Research*, 20 (1976), pp. 125-130.

McClintock, M. K. "Major Gaps in Menstrual Cycle Research: Behavioral and Psychological Controls in a Biological Context." In *The Menstrual Cycle, Vol. 2: Research and Implications for Women's Health,* Komneinich, P. et al., eds. New York: Springer, 1981.

Mead, M. and Newton, N. "The Cultural Patterning of Perinatal Behavior." In *Childbearing: Its Social and Psychological Aspects,* Richardson, S. and Guttmacher, A., eds. Baltimore, MD: Williams and Wilkins, 1967.

Moawad, A. H. "The Sympathetic Nervous System and the Uterus." In *Uterine Contraction—Side Effects of Steroidal Contraceptives,* Josimovich, J. B., ed. New York: Wiley, 1973.

Moos, R. H. "Typology of Menstrual Cycle Symptoms." *American Journal of Obstetrics and Gynecology,* 103 (1968), pp. 390-402.

Morse, J. M. et al. "Minimal Breast-feeding." *JOGN Nursing,* July/August 1986, pp. 333-338.

National Dairy Council. "Diet and Bone Health." *Dairy Council Digest,* 53 (1982), pp. 25-30.

Newton, N. R. and Newton, M. "Relationship of Ability to Breast-feed and Maternal Attitudes Toward Breast-feeding." *Pediatrics,* 5 (1950), pp. 869-875.

Newton, N. "Trebly Sensuous Woman." *Psychology Today,* July 5, 1971, pp. 68-71, 98, 99.

Norris, R. V. "Progesterone for Premenstrual Tension." *Journal of Reproductive Medicine,* 28 (1983), pp. 509-516.

O'Brien et al. "Treatment of Premenstrual Syndrome with Spironolactone." *British Journal of Obstetrics and Gynecology* 86 (1979), pp. 142-147.

O'Brien, Shaugh-, P. M. "The Premenstrual Syndrome." *Journal of Reproductive Medicine,* 30 (1985), pp. 113-126.

Peyser, M. R. et al. "Stress Induced Delay of Ovulation." *Obstetrics and Gynecology,* 42 (1973), pp. 667-671.

Posner, N. A. et al. "Changes in Carbohydrate Tolerance During Long-term Oral Contraception." *American Journal of Obstetrics and Gynecology,* 123 (1975), p. 119-127.

Potts, M. and McDevitt, J. "A Use-effectiveness Study of Spermicidally Lubricated Condoms." *Contraception,* 11(6) (1975), p. 702.

Press, A. "The War Against Pornography." *Newsweek,* March 18, 1985, pp. 58-66.

Preston, S. N. "Oral Contraceptive Controversy." *American Journal of Obstetrics and Gynecology,* 111 (1971), pp. 994-1007.

Rausch, J. and Janowsky, S. "Premenstrual Tension: Etiology." In *Behavior and the Menstrual Cycle,* Friedman, R. C., ed. New York: Marcel Dekker, 1982.

Reid, R. L. and Yen, S. S. C. "Premenstrual Syndrome." *American Journal of Obstetrics and Gynecology,* 139 (1981), pp. 85-104.

Riordan, J. and Rapp, E. "Pleasure and Purpose: The Sensuousness of Breast-feeding." *JOGN Nursing,* March/April 1980, pp. 109-112.

Rubin, R. "Body Image and Self-esteem." *Nursing Outlook,* 16 (1968), pp. 20-23.

Salmon, Y. et al. "Cervical Ripening by Breast Stimulation." *Obstetrics and Gynecology,* 67 (1986), p. 21.

Ruble, D. N. "Premenstrual Syndrome: An Interpretation." *Science,* 197 (1977), pp. 291, 292.

Sarrel, L. and Sarrel, P. "How to Have Great Sex with Your Same Old Spouse." *Redbook,* March 1983, pp. 75-77.

_____. "Sexual Passages—Pregnancy and Becoming Parents." *Redbook,* July 1979, pp. 66-69.

Seligman, J. "American Abortion Dilemma." *Newsweek,* January 14, 1985, pp. 20-27.

Semmen, J. P. et al. "Effects of Estrogen Therapy on Vaginal Physiology in Menopause." *Obstetrics and Gynecology,* 66 (1985), pp. 15-18.

____. "Sexual Function and the Menopause." *Clinical Obstetrics and Gynecology* 27(3) (1984), pp. 697-705.

Shands, K. N., et al. "Toxic Shock Syndrome in Menstruating Women." *New England Journal of Medicine,* 303(25) (1980), pp. 1426-1432.

Short, R.V. "Breast-feeding." *Scientific American,* 250(4) (1984), pp. 35-41.

Smith, S. L. and Sander, C. "Food Cravings, Depression and Premenstrual Problems." *Psychosomatic Medicine,* 31 (1969), pp. 281-287.

Solberg, D. A. et al. "Sexual Behavior in Pregnancy." *New England Journal of Medicine* 288: (1973), pp. 1098-1103.

Sommer, B. "PMS in the Courts: Are All Women on Trial?" *Psychology Today,* August (1984), pp. 36-38.

____. "Stress and Menstrual Distress." *Journal of Human Stress,* 4 (1978), pp. 5-10, 41-47.

Speroff, L. and Ramwell, P. W. "Prostaglandins in Reproductive Physiology." *American Journal of Gynecology,* 107 (1970), pp. 1111-1130.

Steinman, D. et al. "Comparison of Male and Female Patterns of Sexual Arousal." *Archives of Sexual Behavior,* 10 (1981), pp. 529-547.

Steptoe, A. "Stress and Medical Disorders." In *Contributions to Medical Psychology,* Rachman, S., ed. New York: Pergamon, 1980.

Stone, K. M. et al. "Primary Prevention of Sexually Transmitted Diseases." *JAMA,* 255 (1986), pp. 1763-1766.

Stone, S. C. and Cardinale, F. "Evaluation of a New Vaginal Contraceptive." *American Journal of Obstetrics and Gynecology,* 133 (1979), p. 635.

Swanson, J. "The Marital Sexual Relationship During Pregnancy." *JOGN Nursing,* September/October 1980, pp. 267-270.

Sweet, E. and Korpivaara, A. "Is There Sex After Children? Yes . . . And It May Be Better Than Ever." *Redbook,* January 1983, pp. 106-109.

Tauber, A. S. "A Long-term Experience with Vasectomy." *Journal of Reproductive Medicine,* 10 (1973), p. 147.

Thompson, M. "The Convenience of Breast-feeding." *American Journal of Clinical Nutrition,* 24 (1971), pp. 990-992.

Toufexis, A. "Birth Control: Vanishing Options." *Time,* September 1, 1986, p. 78.

Tyndall, K. "Contraception to a Natural Rhythm." *Insight,* April 14, 1986, pp. 56-58.

Udry, R. "Changes in Frequency of Marital Intercourse from Panel Data." *Archives of Sexual Behavior,* 9(4) (1980), pp. 319-325.

U.S. Dept. of Health and Human Services. "Morbidity and Mortality Report (Center for Disease Control). Toxic Shock Syndrome. United States, 1970-1980" (1981).

Walker, L. O. et al. "Maternal Role Attachment and Identity in the Postpartum Period: Stability and Change." *Nursing Research,* 35(2) (1986), pp. 68-71.

Washington, A. E. et al. "The Economic Cost of Pelvic Inflammatory Disease." *JAMA,* 255 (1986), pp. 1735-1738.

Westheimer, O. "Why Don't I Feel Amorous? Facts about Postpartum Sex." *Mother's Manual* reprint, January/February 1980.

Westoff, C. F. and Jones, E. F. "Contraception and Sterilization in the United States, 1965-1975." *Family Planning Perspective,* 9 (1977), p. 153.

Williams, G. D. and Williams, A. M. "Sexual Behavior and the Menstrual Cycle." In *Behavior and the Menstrual Cycle,* Friedman, R. C., ed. New York: Marcel Dekker, 1982.

Wolfensberger, W. "Holocaust II?" *Journal of Learning Disabilities,* 17(7) (1984), pp. 439, 440.

——. "Miscellaneous Abortion News." Training Institute Publication Series, Syracuse University, 5 (2) (1985), p. 20.

World Health Organization, Task Force on Psychosocial Research in Family Planning. "A Cross-cultural Study of Menstruation: Implications for Contraceptive Development." *Studies in Family Planning,* 12 (1981), pp. 3-16.

Worley, R. J. "Age, Estrogen and Bone Density." *Clinical Obstetrics and Gynecology* 24 (1981), pp. 203-218.

Wynn, V. "Vitamins and Contraceptive Use." *Lancet,* 1 (1975) p. 561.

Youngs, D. D. and Reame, N. "Psychosomatic Aspects of Menstrual Dysfunction." *Clinical Obstetrics and Gynecology,* 26 (1983), pp. 774-784.

Zalar, M. K. "Sexual Counseling for Pregnant Couples." *MCN,* May/June 1976, pp. 176-181.

Zatuchni, G. I. "New Perspectives for Contraception." In *The Safety of Fertility of Control,* Keith L. G., ed. New York: Springer, 1980.

Useful Addresses

Health Concerns

American Medical Association
535 N. Dearborn St.
Chicago, IL 60610

American Public Health Association
1015 Eighteenth St., N.W.
Washington, DC 20036

National Health Information
Clearinghouse
P.O. Box 1133
Washington, DC 20013
Toll-free number: 800-366-4797
703-522-2590 in Virginia

Consumer Information Center
Pueblo, CO 81009

Food and Drug Administration (FDA)
Office for Consumer Communications
5600 Fishers Lane
Room 15B-32 (HFE-88)
Rockville, MD 20857

Food and Nutrition Information Center
National Agricultural Library Building
Room 304
Beltsville, MD 20705

Cancer Information Clearinghouse
National Cancer Institute
805 Fifteenth St. N.W.
Room 500
Washington, DC 20005

Cancer Hotline
(Cancer Information Center)
800-638-6694
In Maryland 800-492-6600

Office of Cancer Communications
Public Inquiries Section
9000 Rockville Pike
Building 31, Room 10A18
Bethesda, MD 20205

Breast Cancer Program Coordinating
Branch
National Cancer Institute, NIH
Department of Health and Human
Services
7910 Woodmont Ave., Room 8C09
Bethesda, MD 20205

American Diabetes Association
600 Fifth Ave.
New York, NY 10020

President's Council on Physical Fitness and
Sports
7th and D Streets, S.W.
Washington, DC 20202

American Heart Association
7320 Greenville Ave.
Dallas, TX 75231

American Foundation for Maternal and
Fetal Health
30 Beekman Place
New York, NY 10022

Reproductive Health and Family Planning

National Clearinghouse for Family
Planning Information
P.O. Box 2225
Rockville, MD 20852

Couple to Couple League
(Natural Family Planning: Sympto-
Thermal Method)
P.O. Box 111184
Cincinnati, OH 45211-1184

United Infertility Association Organization
P.O. Box 23
Scarsdale, NY 10583
Hotline: (914)723-1687

311

Dr. Thomas Hilgers
Natural Family Planning Research and
Education (Ovulation Method)
Pope Paul VI Institute for the Study of
Human Reproduction
6901 Mercy Road, Suite 200
Omaha, NE 68106

American Fertility Foundation
1608 13th Avenue South, Suite 101
Birmingham, AL 35256

American College of Nurse Midwives
1012 14th St., N.W.
Washington, DC 20036

Nurse's Association of the American
College of Obstetricians and Gynecologists
Suite 200
600 Maryland Ave., S.W.
Washington, DC 20024-2589

Center for Disease Control
(Sexually Transmitted Diseases Division)
Building 1, Room 3051
1600 Clifton Rd., N.E.
Atlanta, GA 30303

Herpes Resource Center
Box 100
Palo Alto, CA 94302

March of Dimes—National Foundation
P.O. Box 2000
White Plains, NY 10602

Childbirth and Breastfeeding

International Childbirth Education
Association (ICEA)
P.O. Box 20048
Minneapolis, MN 55420

National Association of Parents and
Professionals for Safe Alternatives in
Childbirth (NAPSAC)
P.O. Box 267
Marble Hill, MO 63764

International Lactation Consultant
Association
P.O. Box 4031
University of Virginia Station
Charlottesville, VA 22903

The Lactation Institute and
Breastfeeding Clinic
16161 Ventura Blvd., Suite 223
Encino, CA 91436

La Leche League International
9616 Minneapolis Ave.
Franklin Park, IL 60131

Maternity Center Association
48 E. 92nd St.
New York, NY 10028

Prolife Organizations

Women Exploited by Abortion (WEBA)
P.O. Box 267
Schoolcraft, MI 49087

American Life League
P.O. Box 1350
Stafford, VA 22554

Christian Action Council
422 C. St., N.E.
Washington, DC 20002

Pro-Life Education Alliance
P.O. Box 125
Fayetteville, AR 72701

Life Cycle Books
2205 Danforth Ave.
Toronto, Ontario, M4C 1K4

National Right To Life Educational Trust
Fund
419 7th St., N.W., Suite 402
Washington, DC 20004

Lutherans for Life
P.O. Box 37
Libertyville, IN 60048

Americans Against Abortion
Lindale, TX 75771

Support for Mothers at Home

Mothers at Home
P.O. Box 2208
Merrifield, VA 22116

Home Life
P.O. Box 16202
Clayton, MO 63105

Index

Cavnar, Rebecca, 219
Celibacy, 19, 150
Chambers, Oswald, 23
Chastity, 19
Chaunu, Pierre, 155
Childbirth, childbearing, 66, 98,
  101, 102, 132, 135, 139, 145,
  146, 155, 165 (Chapter 11
  passim), 195, 196, 197, 208,
  254
*Christians in the Wake of the
  Sexual Revolution* (Randy C.
  Alcorn), 71
Church, the, 33, 40, 61, 64, 65,
  128, 129, 146, 149, 150, 194,
  197, 201, 229, 233, 240
Coleridge, Samuel Taylor, 264
Comfort, Alec, 51
Common Sense Christian Living
  (Edith Schaeffer), 105
Communication, 24, 45, 46, 47,
  48, 49, 53, 54, 58, 73, 80, 90,
  91, 94, 97, 106, 109, 111, 119,
  159, 168, 170, 172, 185, 186,
  198, 238, 243, 246, 250, 251
Conception, xii, 20, 60, 79, 132,
  146, 148, 149, 150, 151, 158,
  159, 160, 161, 162, 164, 181,
  196
Contraceptives, 133, 150, 151,
  152, 153, 154, 164, 168
Contraceptive Technology, 164
Cooper, Dr. Kenneth, 205
Counseling, 29, 63, 88, 170, 178,
  219, 222, 249, 259, 60
Country of the Pointed Firs, The
  (Sarah Orne Jewett), 144
Creation, Creator, xii, 13, 14, 15,
  16, 17, 18, 23, 24, 30, 32, 36,
  37, 42, 46, 53, 54, 59, 60, 76,
  80, 81, 88, 90, 93, 96, 113,
  116, 118, 128, 141, 145, 147,
  149, 164, 165, 173, 174, 192,
  203, 204, 236, 241, 243, 244,
  253, 259, 260, 261, 266, 272,
  273
Cyclical nature, xii, 46, 53, 58,

101, 131 (Chapter 9 passim),
  152, 153, 159, 160, 161, 162,
  163, 164, 166, 199

David, 27, 49, 64, 115, 238, 240
Death, 18, 26, 196, 204, 232,
  247, 269, 271, 272
Depression, 29, 86, 176, 197,
  199, 200, 207, 246
Deutsch, Ronald M., 35
Divorce, 21, 25, 26, 260, 270,
  271
Donahue, Phil, 21
Dorcas, 201
Dr. Ruth, 21
Dysmenorrhea, 139

Earth and Altar (Eugene H.
  Peterson), 165
Emotions, emotional wounds,
  emotional health, 29, 46, 54,
  58, 61, 77, 78, 82, 87, 102,
  105, 111, 112, 115, 116, 118,
  128, 163, 166, 170, 171, 179,
  180, 181, 182, 184, 186, 187,
  188, 198, 199, 204, 219, 227,
  239, 244, 251, 252, 255, 258,
  259, 260, 261, 272
Eros, 33
Ethics, 21, 39
Eve, 13, 15, 17, 23, 24, 30, 85
Exercise, 73, 115, 129, 171, 183,
  187, 197, 200, 203, 205, 206,
  207, 208, 209, 210, 211, 218,
  220, 221, 230, 232, 233, 254,
  255, 263

Faith, 28, 37, 39, 131, 149, 167,
  193, 204, 233, 241, 246, 260
Faithfulness, 93, 180, 195, 241
Family, the, 19, 20, 42, 54, 128,
  147, 155, 156, 159, 167, 195,
  196, 197, 203, 241, 269, 271,
  272, 273
Family planning, 151, 158, 159,
  160, 161, 164, 179

Key to Feminine Response, The
(Ronald M. Deutsch), 35
Keyes, Dick, 42

L'Abri Fellowship, 42
Lactation, 52, 101, 132, 138,
166, 168, 174, 179, 186, 187,
216, 218
Lazarus, 234
Leach Road Church, 194
Lewis, C. S., 15, 191
Lost Princess, The (George
MacDonald), 229
Love, 16, 18, 20, 21, 23
(Chapter 2 passim), 40, 41, 48,
49, 50, 54, 57, 64, 68, 74, 80,
81, 88, 90, 93, 94, 102, 105,
107, 109, 110, 111, 119, 120,
128, 145, 147, 148, 149, 150,
165, 168, 172, 173, 174, 176,
177, 180, 182, 187, 189, 191,
193, 194, 195, 199, 200, 201,
203, 218, 219, 227, 232, 233,
234, 235, 237, 241, 242, 244,
246, 253, 259, 260, 261, 262,
266, 267, 269
Lovemaking, xi, 20, 22, 25, 26,
31, 32, 46, 47, 51, 52, 54, 57,
58, 59, 60, 61, 62, 63, 64, 65,
66, 67, 68, 71, 72, 73, 74, 75,
76, 77, 78, 79, 80, 83, 84, 85,
88, 89, 90, 91, 95, 97, 99, 100,
101, 102, 103, 104, 105, 106,
107, 108, 109, 110, 111, 112,
116, 117, 120, 131, 136, 143,
144, 151, 153, 159, 160, 161,
164, 168, 170, 171, 172, 173,
175, 176, 177, 178, 179, 181,
182, 183, 184, 185, 186, 187,
188, 196, 198, 208, 209, 222,
223, 225, 226, 227, 242, 243,
244, 245, 250, 251, 252, 253,
254, 258, 259, 260, 261, 262,
263, 266
Love songs, love language, love-
talk, 64, 89, 96, 100, 103, 106,
109, 243

Luteinizing hormone (LH), 133,
134, 137, 152

MacDonald, George, 191, 229,
232
Male, male/female, 13, 17, 24,
39, 52, 75, 116, 132
Marriage, 14, 16, 18, 20, 21, 24,
26, 30, 32, 33, 40, 42, 45, 46,
48, 50, 54, 55, 57, 58, 62, 64,
67, 69, 73, 74, 81, 84, 85, 86,
88, 90, 99, 100, 101, 102, 105,
110, 117, 119, 145, 147, 150,
152, 155, 165, 167, 168, 171,
173, 175, 177, 195, 196, 198,
241, 250, 251, 252, 253, 254,
255, 258, 259, 260, 263, 265,
266, 267, 269, 271, 272
Mary of Bethany, 194, 234, 235
Masculinity, 66, 81, 132
Massage, 108, 117, 118, 119-126,
176, 253, 255, 263
Masters (William) and Johnson
(Virginia), 60, 75, 79
Media, the, xi, 15, 266
Menarche, 137
Menopause, 131, 132, 135, 137,
161, 191, 195, 196, 197, 198,
199, 200, 221
Menorrhagia, 137
Menstruation, menstruality, 52,
66, 102, 131, 132, 135, 136,
137, 138, 139, 140, 141, 142,
143, 144, 151, 152, 153, 159,
160, 161, 162, 163, 164, 179,
188, 196, 198, 199, 200, 208,
216, 227
Mid-life, mid-life crisis, 192, 195,
196
Miles, Herbert, 76, 77
Ministry See *Service*
Miscarriage, 168, 182
Mittelschmerz, 134
Morality/immorality, 19, 32, 39,
258
Morning-after pill, 151
Moses, 13, 15, 24, 145